The Anabaptists and
Thomas Müntzer

The Anabaptists and Thomas Müntzer

Translated and edited by

James M. Stayer
Queen's University

Werner O. Packull
Renison College

KENDALL/HUNT PUBLISHING COMPANY KⱧH
Dubuque, Iowa, USA • Toronto, Ontario, Canada

Special Acknowledgments

"The Left Wing of the Reformation" from *Studies on the Reformation* by Roland H. Bainton, copyright © 1963 by Roland H. Bainton. Reprinted by permission of Beacon Press.

"Der Weg der Täufer in die Absonderung" translated as "The Path of the Anabaptists into Separation" by Martin Haas, from *Umstrittenes Täufertum*, Hans-Jürgen Goertz, Editor, copyright 1975 by Vandenhoeck & Ruprecht, D–3400 Göttingen. Reprinted by permission of Vandenhoeck & Ruprecht.

"Theologie und Revolution bei Thomas Müntzer" translated as "Theology and Revolution in Thomas Müntzer" by Thomas Nipperdey, from *Reformation, Revolution, Utopie*, copyright 1975. Reprinted by permission of Vandenhoeck & Ruprecht; also from *Archiv für Reformationsgeschichte*, copyright 1963. Reprinted by permission of Gütersloher Verlagshaus Gerd Mohn.

"Die Herkunft des oberösterreichischen Täufertums," translated as "The Origin of Upper Austrian Anabaptism" by Grete Mecenseffy from *Archiv für Reformationsgeschichte*, copyright 1956. Reprinted by permission of Gütersloher Verlagshaus Gerd Mohn.

"The Anabaptist Vision" by Harold S. Bender. Reprinted by permission from *The Recovery of the Anabaptist Vision*, Guy F. Hershberger, Editor, copyright 1957 by Herald Press, Scottdale, Pa. 15683.

"The Doctrine of the Two Worlds" by Robert Friedmann. Reprinted by permission from *The Recovery of the Anabaptist Vision*, Guy F. Hershberger, Editor, copyright 1957 by Herald Press, Scottdale, Pa. 15683.

"Anabaptism and Ascetic Holiness" by Kenneth R. Davis. Reprinted by permission from *Anabaptism and Asceticism*, by Kenneth R. Davis, copyright 1974 by Herald Press, Scottdale, Pa. 15683.

"Revolutionnaire Hervorming" translated as "Revolutionary Reformation" by Karel Vos, *De Gids*, Meulenhoff-Bruna, B.V., 1920.

"Het Anabaptisme in Nederland" translated as "Anabaptism in the Netherlands" by W.J. Kühler, *De Gids*, Meulenhoff-Bruna, B.V., 1921.

"Thomas Müntzer in der Forschung der Gegenwart" translated as "Thomas Müntzer in the Research of the Present" by Max Steinmetz, copyright 1975, Zeitschrift für Geschichtswissenschaft. Reprinted by permission of the author; VEB Deutscher Verlag der Wissenschaften, Berlin GDR.

"Die Stellung der Täuferbewegung im Spannungsbogen der deutschen frühbürgerlichen Revolution" translated as "The Position of Anabaptism on the Continuum of the Early Bourgeois Revolution in Germany" by Gerhard Zschäbitz from *Die frühbürgerliche Revolution in Deutschland*, Gerhard Brendler, Editor, copyright 1961. Reprinted by permission of Akademie-Verlag GmbH, Berlin GDR.

"Anabaptism and the Reformation: Another Look" by Hans J. Hillerbrand. Reprinted with permission from *Church History* 29 (December 1960): 404–423. © 1960, The American Society of Church History.

"Anabaptism: A Social History, 1525–1618" by Claus-Peter Clasen, copyright © 1972 by Cornell University. Used by permission of the publisher, Cornell University Press.

"Bauernkrieg und Täufertum in Franken" translated as "Peasants' War and Anabaptism in Franconia" by Gottfried Seebass, copyright 1974. Reprinted by permission from *Zeitschrift für Kirchengeschichte*.

The following were reprinted by permission of the *Mennonite Quarterly Review*: "The Zwickau Prophets, Thomas Müntzer and the Anabaptists" by Harold S. Bender; "The Turning Point in the Zwinglian Reformation" by John H. Yoder; "Was There a Turning Point in the Zwinglian Reformation?" by Robert C. Walton; "The Mystic with the Hammer: Thomas Müntzer's Theological Basis for Revolution" by Hans-Jürgen Goertz.

For specific references see the Bibliography.

284.3
An11m

B   402235   01

81042729

Contents

Preface

The primary purpose of this small anthology is to acquaint the sophisticated student with the development of Anabaptist studies in the last thirty-five to forty years. Accordingly the Anabaptists precede Thomas Müntzer in the title, and the smaller sampling of Müntzer scholarship has the function of clarifying Müntzer's partial and equivocal role in the background of Anabaptism. Perhaps we could say that Thomas Müntzer was the "godfather" of Anabaptism in South and Central Germany, Austria and Moravia.

Naturally scholarship dating variously from the forties, fifties, sixties and seventies cannot simply be compared on an equal level. Few historians subscribe just now to the notion of the "definitive (hence timeless) history," which inspired Harold Bender and his associates at the beginning of these four decades of Anabaptist historiography. The historical and theological essays and statements collected here are, in one sense, milestones along the road travelled by a generation of interpreters of the Reformation radicals. The introduction sketches the manner in which radical Reformation scholarship may be said to have "progressed" as historians and theologians affirmed, negated, refined and redefined the conclusions of their predecessors. Many readers will, no doubt, be skeptical about whether the deeply held religious and political beliefs of our writers can be smoothed over (or ground down) in such a way as to converge upon an historical consensus. They may see the discord of irreconcilable value systems where we see the progress of scholarship. So each reader can choose to regard these selections, with their different times of authorship and different theological and political perspectives, either as "milestones" or as the granite outcroppings of unerodable principle.

An anthology is very much a cooperative enterprise, assembling the work of various authors, editors, translators, publishers and journals. The main editorial responsibility for this project rested with James M. Stayer. He translated the articles by Vos, Kühler and Steinmetz. The translations of the articles by Zschäbitz, Haas, Nipperdey, Mecenseffy, and Seebass were a joint effort with Werner O. Packull. The editors would like to acknowledge the assistance of the office staff at the Department of History, Queen's University, and at Renison College, University of Waterloo. The editors also wish to express their gratitude for encouragement, suggestions and permissions received from Professor Hans J. Hillerbrand, Professor Roland H. Bainton, Professor Grete Mecenseffy, Professor Thomas Nipperdey, Professor Claus-Peter Clasen, Professor Gottfried Seebass, Professor Kenneth R. Davis, Dr. Hans-Jürgen Goertz, Dr. Martin Haas, Professor Max Steinmetz, the editor of the *Mennonite Quarterly Review*, Professor John S. Oyer, Gütersloher Verlagshaus Gerd Mohn, Vandenhoeck & Ruprecht, Verlag W. Kohlhammer, Cornell University Press, Herald Press, Beacon Press, *Church History*, Akademie-Verlag GmbH, DDR, VEB Deutscher Verlag der Wissenschaften, DDR, *De Gids*, Meulenhoff-Bruna, BV.

James M. Stayer
Queen's University, Kingston

Werner O. Packull
Renison College, University of Waterloo

Introduction

James M. Stayer

Thomas Müntzer was the one major religious leader and thinker of the German Reformation who associated himself with the demands and the military activities of the rebels in the German Peasants' War of 1525. This choice, for which he paid with his life, earned him the condemnation of Martin Luther, against whom he had previously directed a bitter polemic in defense of his theology. For centuries afterward Müntzer's biography was used as an object lesson by Protestant church historians, who repeated the view of Luther and Melanchthon that the inner corruption of false teaching leads naturally to the external wickedness of rebellion. When in the atmosphere of 1789 and 1848 the revolutionary democrats and socialists of Germany rediscovered the Peasants' War as an authentically German revolution with genuine mass support (and the only one there had ever been!), naturally they rediscovered Thomas Müntzer as well. Thus Friedrich Engels began the Marxist tradition that made of Müntzer the hero of a "People's Reformation," thought to be the religious expression of an "Early Bourgeois Revolution in Germany."

In the year of revolution, 1525, and in the five years thereafter, there arose a number of groups which based their membership upon the principle that only confessing adults could receive a valid baptism. Emerging on the extreme wing of the Reformed tradition (which was externally, although perhaps not theologically, more radical than Luther with its anticlericalism, iconoclasm and puritanism), these Anabaptists became a persecuted oppositional movement almost everywhere. One major exception was Münster, 1534–1535, where they created a kingdom which they hoped would foreshadow, and be rescued by, the Second Coming of Christ, but which was destroyed by a Catholic-Lutheran military alliance and subsequently defamed by a similar alliance of Catholic and Lutheran historians. The other was Moravia, where aristocrats with a tradition of religious diversity encouraged the development of their lands by communities of Anabaptist refugees. Protestant persecution of Anabaptists was from the beginning less uniform and rigorous than that of Catholic authorities. Protestant divines drew connections from Müntzer to Münster and from Münster to all Anabaptists, whom they described as latent Münsterites. But, as the Anabaptists appeared ever less a "clear and present danger," Protestant magistrates first closed their ears to learned arguments for their execution, and then in the 1570s William of Orange in the United Netherlands set a precedent for their legal toleration. Because of the toleration and patronage extended them, as well as their own perseverence under persecution, the sixteenth-century Anabaptists have survived in the Amish-Mennonite and Hutterite confessions of the present day. Their historians have preserved the bitter-sweet traditions of their century of persecution and compared their fathers' heroic witness for Christ with that of the pre-Constantinian Christians. Especially in the English-speaking countries, where religious nonconformity has a broader historical base, the Anabaptists of the Reformation have been championed as the forerunners of religious pluralism. But to rehabilitate the Anabaptists means to condemn the Reformers. Protestants who have treasured their Reformation heritage, especially those in the Lutheran tradition, have continued to insist upon the rightness of their fathers' judgments: that Anabaptists offered an inferior brand of Christianity and at least initially presented a threat to the political and social order.

Hence, the historical literature about the leaders and groups in the sixteenth-century Reformation which failed to seek or find political legitimacy is a thicket of polemic. The "losers" of history have, at least recently, provoked more passionate prose than the winners. In fact, it almost seems indecent to assume a dispassionate stance toward Thomas Müntzer, who best calls up "the smothered undercurrent of medieval pain and injustice" (Gordon Rupp), and the Anabaptists, whose most characteristic literary expression is the martyrology.

Was Thomas Müntzer a fanatical prophet of extermination, or was he a brilliant revolutionary strategist and theoretician, who failed only because he was centuries ahead of his time? Were the Anabaptists "Pharisees" with an "officious and melancholy zeal, crazily discussing truths which they ill understand and judging the piety of others by external signs" (Jean Rilliet, biographer of Zwingli)? Did there not lurk behind their moralistic facade the violence, the polygamy and the charlatanism of Münster? Or were these maligned and martyred Anabaptists the true idealists of the Reformation, who maintained the Reformers' original vision? "May it not be said that the decision of Luther and Zwingli to surrender their original vision was the tragic turning point of the Reformation?" (Harold Bender) Did the violent Thomas Müntzer have any link with the nonresistant Anabaptists? Was Anabaptism something the first leaders in Zurich had "sucked out of Müntzer" (Heinrich Bullinger)? Or was the connection of Müntzer with Münster only a flimsy pretext for the persecuting zeal of Protestant theologians? From another point of view, was it not an insult to the leader of the glorious "People's Reformation" to reduce his elevated revolutionary consciousness to the narrow sectarianism of the Anabaptists?

These questions have naturally emerged from the engagement of historians committed to Marxism, the official Reformation, or Protestant non-conformity. Yet it is now unusual to find Marxists, Lutherans, Reformed or Mennonites occupying the extreme positions they suggest. All have been weighed down in their polemical flights by less partisan professional scholars (both within and outside their own ranks) who seek to distinguish historical writing from religious and political controversy. These persons have asked some new questions that cut athwart the old ones. Did not medieval traditions of Christianity weigh more heavily with Müntzer and the Anabaptists than conceptions of revolution or religious pluralism which they could hardly have been expected to understand? As intellectual innovators were they perhaps not more conservative, rather than more radical, than Luther? If Anabaptist groups had marked differences each from each, was it useful to distinguish "normative" Anabaptist characteristics at all, or was this but an illegitimate transferrence into historical writing of the mutual excommunications of the sixteenth-century sects? Perhaps some Anabaptists were peaceful, some violent, some closely linked to Müntzer, others not, some more, others less heavily indebted to the theology of the major Reformers. Was it possible to conceive the break between Anabaptists and Reformers as the outcome of different religious objectives, rather than the result of someone remaining loyal to, and someone else betraying, the same religious objectives? Were the Anabaptists committed from the start to the numerical insignificance of sectarianism, or was this a consequence of their historical circumstances? Were Anabaptism and the Peasants' War perhaps both incidents in the great religious and social upheaval of the early German Reformation? To the extent that these new questions have inserted themselves into the discussion perhaps the dilemma of this historical area—that research "progresses" only by mobilizing the partisanship of the committed—has proven to be illusory. This ebbing of polemic has its cost: when we focus on Thomas Müntzer or one of the several Anabaptist leaders we are no longer dealing with a monster or a hero—just a man.

Although we have tried in planning this anthology to introduce the most important voices in the twentieth-century historiography of Müntzer and Anabaptism, we have had to give priority to choosing selections which best and most concisely epitomize the state of the discussion. In our short bibliography we mention some important works which do not appear here. We hope that this little book will communicate some of our own fascination with the historical writing and historical sources on Müntzer and Anabaptism and stimulate new contributions to the continuing debate.

* * *

The first four selections can be grouped as general characterizations of Anabaptism, even though the last by C.P. Clasen stresses the plurality of the movement. The writings of Harold S. Bender and Robert Friedmann illustrate different facets of the view of Anabaptism developed by conservative Mennonites in the decades surrounding the Second World War. Gerhard Zschäbitz was a prominent historian of the German Democratic Republic who avowedly worked within a Marxist-Leninist framework, albeit with a marked personal independence. Clasen disclaims any theological interest or ideological commitment related to his subject, which he treats according to methods of quantitative social history. However his conclusions contain some pointed rejoinders to the positions represented by Bender, Friedmann and Zschäbitz.

Bender's "Anabaptist Vision" is the classical statement of the view of Anabaptism which dominated academic writing on the subject until very recently. It says that the Anabaptists, not the more prominent Reformers, originated the principles of freedom of conscience and separation of church and state which have shaped the North American religious scene. Bender viewed Anabaptism as a powerful movement dedicated to carrying through without compromise the Reformers' rejection of human traditions and their appeal to Scripture. That Luther and Zwingli had reneged on their biblical principles to maintain a mass church like that of the Middle Ages and to secure the support of governments was "the tragic turning point of the Reformation." Because the Anabaptists remained true to these original principles of the Reformers they were persecuted ruthlessly by Catholic and Protestant alike. The substantive beliefs which they derived from the Bible were discipleship, the gathered church and nonresistance. Discipleship, which was the most important for Bender, was the dedication of individuals to follow the teachings and example of Christ in outwardly holy lives. The gathered church was the conception of a church based on voluntary membership of those who had committed themselves to holy living and discipleship. This view of the church was, of course, not compatible with infant baptism, by which all members of a political territory were received at birth into the form of Christianity to which it adhered. Nonresistance meant the refusal to engage in war and personal self-defence or to participate in the coercive acts of government. This "Biblical pacifism," as Bender termed it, was of special importance at a time when the Mennonites as one of the historic American peace churches had risked their authority over younger members by an unpopular prohibition of military service in World War II. Since various Anabaptist groups in the sixteenth century had been connected with unconventional sexual behavior, a "spiritualism" which denied the importance of an organized and visible church, and revolutionary violence, each of Bender's three principles served as a welcome device to distinguish "evangelical and constructive Anabaptism" from ab- berant groups.

Friedmann's "Doctrine of the Two Worlds" was another attempt to get at the kernel of Anabaptist thought. It contained different stresses from, and some latent tensions with, Bender's "Anabaptist Vision." In suggesting that the Anabaptists were inspired by an implicit Synoptic theology which emphasized Christian community rather than individual salvation, as did the one- sided Paulinism of the Reformers, Friedmann minimized the individual holiness which was so important to Bender and cast doubt on the Anabaptist claim to be authentically Protestant. Most of all, however, he underlined the dualism of the two worlds, which he claimed the Anabaptists derived directly from the teachings of Christ as portrayed in the Synoptic Gospels. Christians were called out of "this world" to become citizens of the heavenly Kingdom. The corollary of the gathered church was a "disparagement and even fear of the world . . . as the realm of the prince of darkness," which led to a hostility to worldly culture and to expectations of martyrdom. Without intending it, Friedmann had pointed to certain shadowy sides of Anabaptism which embarass modern Mennonites concerned with social outreach and devising a "politics of Jesus."

Zschäbitz believed that Anabaptism was a muted and intellectually impoverished contin- uation of the oppositional thought of the rebels in the Peasants' War of 1525. Thus, while finding in Anabaptism a diversity of groups and teachings, he assigned it a unified social significance. It was an "ideology of the poor" which kept alive the revolutionary potentialities of the Peasants' War until the Münsterite upheaval of ten years later. He distinguished between a majority of Anabaptists who shunned the world and a chiliastic minority who waited with bated breath for its destruction. Together these groups constituted the minority of the rebels of 1525 who refused to come to terms with the victory of reactionary feudalism. Only gradually after 1535 did Ana- baptism assume true "sectarian" form, when as the result of a change in its social composition it became thoroughly integrated into the larger society, although continuing to preserve traditional peculiarities whose original, oppositional significance the membership had long forgotten.

Clasen's non-theological, quantitative and social approach to Anabaptism questioned many of the previous interpretations. In the first place, he showed that as an alternative to seeking theological distinctions between "true" and "false" Anabaptists, the twenty historical Anabaptist groups, particularly the six major ones, could be subjected to systematic study. He pointed out that, in fact, Protestant and Catholic governments did have distinguishable approaches to per- secuting Anabaptists, and implied that the historical survival of Anabaptism may have had a great deal to do with the quantifiably demonstrable reluctance of Protestant governments to execute people for heresy. Our excerpts from Clasen's text illustrate his confidence in the sub- stantial completeness of the data which he quantified. Hence he declared, against the traditional Mennonite view, that Anabaptism was numerically insignificant and, against the Marxist view, that there was no connection between Anabaptism and the Peasants' War. Both assertions, at least in the form Clasen made them, have been regarded as excessively assured, and not only by Mennonites and Marxists.

* * *

The selections by Bainton, Hillerbrand and Davis are focused on the relationship of Anabaptism and the Reformation, an issue that recurs in one form or another in most discussions of Anabaptism.

Roland H. Bainton's "The Left Wing of the Reformation" implies the view of Anabaptism as a progressive, modernizing phenomenon somewhat "ahead of its time." His belief that Anglo-Saxon Protestant dissenters made a basic contribution to Western libertarianism lends substance to his definition of the Reformation's left wing as the groups which moved the greatest distance from the Roman Catholic right on the separation of church and state and the rejection of the civil arm in matters of religion. As he notes, these groups were also most removed from Catholicism in their thorough dismantling of church hierarchy and demystification of the sacraments. However, the major characteristic of Bainton's "left wing" was an emphasis on morality in religion, an "inner-worldly asceticism," which other commentators would view as more Catholic than Protestant and more medieval than modern.

Hans J. Hillerbrand expresses a very Lutheran view of Anabaptism and the Reformation. He found it necessary to take "another look" at the proposition of Bender and others that the Anabaptists carried Reformation principles to their proper and consistent conclusion. Rather, a comparison of their views with Luther's on justification and related issues such as free will, predestination and original sin demonstrates that the Anabaptists were possessed by a different religious spirit than the Reformers. Their stress upon external personal morality, which Bender had characterized as discipleship, missed Luther's conception of the profundity of sin and contained echoes of medieval Catholic anthropocentrism. Thus, although their implementation of the priesthood of all believers and their biblicism went beyond the Reformers, on justification, "the article on which the church stands or falls," Anabaptist teaching was on a lower niveau than that of the Reformation. When Hillerbrand summarized his essay for a German readership he said, pointedly: "in their efforts to correct the Reformation's teaching on justification, the Anabaptists often landed in a crass Pelagianism."

Kenneth R. Davis treated very much the same data as Hillerbrand and Bender, choosing holiness or discipleship as the center of Anabaptist teaching. He continued to use Bender's category of Evangelical Anabaptism as a device for eliminating antinomian, spiritualist and revolutionary Anabaptists from his purview, but he agreed with Hillerbrand, as against Bender, that these Evangelical Anabaptists were continuers of medieval traditions more than they were radical Reformers. From Davis's evangelical Baptist perspective the conception of Anabaptism as a laicized asceticism was not at all pejorative. Conversion, baptism as a vow of holy conduct, brotherly discipline to enforce holy conduct, and commitment to a separated community were all at the same time genuinely ascetic and genuinely evangelical. Indeed the Anabaptists continued the moderate anti-intellectualism of the monastic theology, thus expressing their biblicism through an ascetic hermeneutic which gave ethical and practical support to their pursuit of holiness.

The consensus of Hillerbrand and Davis might suggest that, rather than being the "left wing" of the Reformation, the Anabaptists were its "right wing." Marxist interpreters and others would object, however, that such an individualized and one-sidedly theological view of Anabaptism fails to do justice to its radical social content.

* * *

The origins of Anabaptism are, like its connection with the Reformation, a key to the interpretation of the movement. Lutheran critics of Anabaptism have viewed it as an outgrowth of the opposition to Luther's leadership of the Reformation, which first appeared in 1522 among Saxon "fanatics" such as Andreas Carlstadt, the Zwickau Prophets and Thomas Müntzer. More recently there has been wide acceptance of the Mennonite view that Anabaptism originated among the followers of Conrad Grebel in Zurich, who first actually performed adult baptisms in 1525. Those who stress the Zurich origin of Anabaptism note that Thomas Müntzer had little direct influence on the Swiss Anabaptists. Recent criticism of an exclusively Swiss theory of Anabaptist origins has suggested that the Swiss Brethren have been overemphasized because they fit so well with the pacifism, biblicism and separate community life which characterized later centuries of Mennonite history. This anthology is organized so as to underscore the separate origin and character of the three main branches of Anabaptism, without denying that there were some connections between them. The connection between Thomas Müntzer and the Anabaptists, which will be discussed in the last section, is important only for the branch of Anabaptism located in South and Central Germany and Austria. The other two major branches of Anabaptism, whose origins are under examination here, are the Swiss Brethren, who were not only Swiss but Swabian and Alsatian as well, and the Anabaptism of the Low Countries and Northern Germany, which is often labeled "Melchiorite," after Melchior Hoffman, its most important early leader.

The three writings on the origins of the Swiss Brethren analyze the causes and process of the break between Anabaptism and the Swiss Reformed branch of Protestantism.

John Yoder's Mennonite view of the "turning point of the Zwinglian Reformation" emphasizes that the future Swiss Anabaptists were early and committed followers of Zwingli. Only when Zwingli faltered in what both he and they regarded as obedience to the Word of God (in the matter of replacing the mass with a Protestant communion service) did Conrad Grebel and his friends reject Zwingli's leadership. Yoder says that in December 1523 Zwingli chose to yield to the authority of the Zurich Council on a matter of religious principle, in order to preserve the religious unity of the community. The stress he placed from then on upon religious unity made persecution a matter of religious duty for him and his followers. Yoder is here validating a sectarian accusation which goes back to the sixteenth century: that the major Reformers made a good beginning at restoring the gospel but then fell into sin and failed to complete their reform.

Examining the same events as Yoder, Robert Walton interprets them differently. First he points to the significant gains which Zwingli made in the direction of abolishing the mass, thus denying that he surrendered his principles. More important, Walton describes the traditional commitment to religious consensus and corporate unity which had permeated the Swiss cities in the centuries before the Reformation and which had consistently guided Zwingli in his previous career. If Zwingli from the start saw the church as a united community, rather than as a "suffering, separate remnant," then there was no "turning point in the Zwinglian Reformation"; it was rather the Anabaptists who turned away from Zwingli. But Walton does assume, along with Yoder, that the first Swiss Anabaptists viewed the church as a "suffering, separate remnant." On that point Martin Haas attacks the previous consensus.

It had been previously argued that Mennonite historians overemphasized the Swiss origins of Anabaptism because of the particular compatibility of Swiss Anabaptism with their later denominational principles. Haas suggests that, even in the historical writing on the origins of Swiss Anabaptism, a similarly one-sided selection process has been at work. He shows that in the first statements of the Grebel group in Zurich some of the characteristic teachings and stresses of the later Swiss Brethren had not yet emerged. The principle of separation from "the world," which involved avoidance of opposing religious services and civic obligations and was made tangible by the prohibition against swearing oaths and against holding of public office, only gradually developed in the first two years of Swiss Anabaptism: hence Haas's title, "The Path of the Anabaptists into Separation." To begin with, if Haas is correct, the Anabaptists were beneficiaries of, and participants in, the radical anticlericalism of the early Reformation. This anticlericalism involved resistance to tithes, the opposition of rural subjects to a church structure which was an instrument of the authority of urban governments, and, consequently, an overlapping with the limited Swiss version of the peasant war of 1525. In this atmosphere of crumbling religious and civil authority persons like Grebel and Wilhelm Reublin were sanguine that their radically laicized version of the Reformation might replace the program of Zwingli as the dominant version of Reformed Christianity. Only as this mass anticlericalism failed to prevail against the resistance of the government did the early Anabaptists reconcile themselves to the fate of being a "suffering, separate remnant." Then they went to work at purging the "impure" from among their former mass following, a process completed at the time of the Schleitheim Articles of February 1527. Such a view of Anabaptist origins has remarkable similarities to that of Zschäbitz, although it is not confined within the rather mechanical Marxist categories of class and ideology.

Karel Vos and W.J. Kühler, analyzing the origins of the Dutch and North German Anabaptism which produced both the Münster Kingdom and Menno Simons, had to acknowledge the presence of revolution and social motivation in this branch of the movement. Their disagreement was over the significance of these factors.

Vos began the exchange by a wide-ranging assault on the traditional Dutch Mennonite interpretation, which claimed that the Mennonite movement began not with the Münster Kingdom but with Conrad Grebel in Zurich. Vos acknowledged no connection between Swiss and Dutch Anabaptist origins. Himself a liberal Mennonite whose writing betrays a marked distaste for apocalyptic enthusiasm, he found the source of Dutch Anabaptism in religious fanaticism, apocalyptic fright and the misery of the lower classes. Before the fanatical Jan Matthijs proclaimed the coming of the end of the world and attracted to himself the "hysterical swill of the slums" by promising them a new world in which all their desires would be fulfilled and all their grudges settled, there had been no significant Anabaptist movement in the Netherlands. Virtually all source evidence, says Vos, depicts a movement of excess, violence and social upheaval; the peaceful dissenters were but isolated individuals. After the fall of the Münster Kingdom, which was the beacon of Dutch Anabaptism and the command-post for numerous insurrections in the Netherlands, the movement virtually collapsed. Most of its followers returned to obedience to the Habsburg government and the Roman Church. The exceptions were two small minorities, an embittered band which gave up religion for terrorism, and a group which continued to await the apocalypse. It was to this latter group that Menno Simons became the religious shepherd. The failure to admit that Dutch Anabaptism was a "revolutionary Reformation" was but the result of "Mennonite prudishness."

Kühler responded by accusing Vos of dressing modern revolutionaries in sixteenth-century costumes in his portrayal of Anabaptism. Virtually the only point on which he agreed with Vos was that Melchiorite Anabaptism had no significant connection with the movement which had begun in Zurich. He thought that the movement had been numerically significant and peaceful from its beginning in 1530. He tried to demonstrate from sixteenth-century sources that Dutch Anabaptism had primarily religious goals, and that there was no particular evidence that it was "the Protestantism of the poor." Münster was an aberration in Dutch Anabaptism, said Kühler, and there was ample evidence, some of it from Münsterite sources, that there had been peaceful Anabaptists before and during the Münster Kingdom, as well as after its collapse. In most of his objections to Vos Kühler could point to solid evidence, glossed over by his opponent. However, as he himself recognized, the decisive issue was whether or not the Münsterite revolution had dominated early Dutch Anabaptism. Arguing from the confusion and failures of Münster's operations in the Netherlands, he inferred a silent opposition and a "silent majority" of peaceful Anabaptists before Menno began his career. Like all arguments from silence, this one was equivocal and unsatisfactory, one suspects even for Kühler himself. Kühler's fate was to be attacked from both sides, by the conservative Mennonite John Horsch, who objected to any connection of Münsterite and Mennonite history, and by the Dutch socialist A.F. Mellink, whose thorough work with the sources accumulated massive positive evidence for the character of Dutch Anabaptism as a "revolutionary Reformation."

* * *

Too often discussion of the connection between Thomas Müntzer and the Anabaptists has been carried on either by persons like Karl Holl, who made a serious study of Müntzer but not of the Anabaptists, or Harold Bender, who understood the Swiss Brethren but not Müntzer. In our anthology we propose to precede the discussion of Müntzer and the Anabaptists by three essays which illustrate the range of contemporary interpretation of Müntzer himself.

The first essay by Thomas Nipperdey, a West German intellectual historian, is in many respects a modern synthesis of the traditional German Lutheran standpoint on Müntzer. This is particularly the case with his thinly supported assertion that Müntzer was a wayward disciple of Luther, his constant use of Luther's theology as a normative frame of reference and his stress on Müntzer's subjectivism, which goes back to Melanchthon, despite the modernizing terminology. Also very traditional, and a departure from some twentieth-century Lutheran interpretation of Müntzer (for instance, that of Karl Holl), was Nipperdey's insistence that Müntzer's theology was intrinsically linked to his role in the Peasants' War. Müntzer's goal was to establish an external Christian order through the action of visible saints. This "massively objective" goal of the second generation of the Reformation had replaced for Müntzer Luther's concern about the peace of the individual man with God. Due to an internal logic Müntzer's extreme subjectivism had reversed itself into a crass externalism.

Hans-Jürgen Goertz is a Mennonite who has departed from the usual Mennonite practice of accepting the Lutheran view of Müntzer without critical examination. Writing in the current of scholarship which seeks medieval intellectual antecedents for the Reformation, Goertz stresses that Müntzer inherited the intellectual framework of late medieval German mysticism. From this substantially independent point of departure Müntzer did, of course, address himself to the issues of faith and biblical authority which Luther made so topical in the first years of the Reformation. Furthermore, a great deal of apocalyptic content was incorporated into Müntzer's mystical framework. Goertz's major point is to insist that Müntzer's commitment to overcoming creaturely wickedness by revolutionary action in the social world was patterned on a democratic mysticism which prescribed extirpation of the creaturely in the soul of the individual believer as his only possible way of salvation. The result of Goertz's interpretation is to give more recognition to Müntzer as a substantial theologian with his own pattern of Reformation, but at the same time to characterize his revolutionary outlook as anti-naturalistic and backward-looking. As was to be expected, Marxist historians have not taken kindly to such an equivocal rehabilitation of Müntzer.

Max Steinmetz, the dean of early modern historians in the German Democratic Republic, has moved far from Engels' Marxist classic, which placed Müntzer intellectually close to atheism and praised him as a great revolutionary organizer. It is clear to the reader of Steinmetz's essay that Müntzer, as he says, "always remained a theologian in his revolutionary role and was shipwrecked upon theology." His theological outlook led him to demand too much of his followers and to set revolutionary goals which were not historically attainable. Steinmetz's Müntzer was a Christian intellectual activist with a program developed independently of Luther, not only from medieval mysticism, but from revolutionary Taborite sectarianism and from humanism, from which Müntzer extracted the democratic potentialities and rejected all aristocratic snobbery. He relied on the direct progressive revelation of the Holy Spirit rather than the words of the Bible, achieving a universal theism which transcended the limits of Christianity. He opposed to Luther's passive justification by faith a salvation which demanded the cooperation of man's active will; he opposed Luther's passive obedience to any government whatever with a democratic and revolutionary insistence that government was only legitimate if it served the people and won their active cooperation. One senses in Steinmetz's work a considerable effort at a realistic assessment of Müntzer, which goes beyond admission of his failures to hinting at his psychological eccentricities, and a similar struggle to repress the progressive anachronism which has blemished Marxist historical writing. Nevertheless, his Müntzer, the great democratic educator, belongs rather in the eighteenth than the sixteenth century.

* * *

At the present time the question about the connection between Müntzer and Anabaptism is focused primarily upon Müntzer's connection with the Southern and Central German Anabaptist groups led by Hans Hut, Hans Denck and Melchior Rinck, each of whom had a demonstrable or highly probable link with Thomas Müntzer. Traditional Protestant accounts of Anabaptism, both Lutheran and Reformed, attempted to depict *all* Anabaptists, Swiss Brethren, Münsterite and Mennonite, as successors of Müntzer. The response of traditional Mennonite historians was that *all* Anabaptists were successors of the peaceful, biblicist group around Conrad Grebel in Zurich. The following selections show how the discussion about Müntzer and the Anabaptists moved away from this rather sterile confrontation and eventually provided evidence in support of the separate origins and character of the major branches of Anabaptism.

Harold Bender's essay was formulated in opposition to an old Protestant historical tradition which conceived of Anabaptism as beginning in Saxony with the Zwickau Prophets and Thomas Müntzer, spreading from there to Zurich and then dispersing from Zurich to South and Central Germany, Moravia and the Netherlands; hence his attack on what he regarded as an attempt to defame Anabaptism by connecting it with fanatics and rebels. Bender's arguments were directed primarily against those sixteenth-century writers who presented the Zurich movement of 1525 as derived from the Saxon movement of a few years earlier. Although he unjustly minimized the contacts between the Saxons and the early Swiss Brethren, particularly their use of the writings of Andreas Carlstadt, Bender's main point has been accepted. No responsible historian any longer regards Thomas Müntzer as the first Anabaptist and very few would contend that he had a significant formative influence upon the Swiss Brethren. However, the point that Bender established has a much more limited bearing than he imagined, because of his uncritical acceptance of the idea that all Anabaptist movements were either founded by the Swiss Brethren or at least of a similar character with them. His statement that "rebaptism is necessarily practiced only in connection with a separated brotherhood of believers" illustrates how narrowly his view of Anabaptism as a whole was shaped by what contemporary historians would regard as one of two competing tendencies in Swiss Brethren origins.

At the close of his article Bender acknowledged in an aside that some authentic followers of Müntzer, such as Hans Hut, were converted to peaceful Anabaptism. In a response to Bender the Austrian church historian Grete Mecenseffy pointed out that there was a great deal of evidence that Austrian Anabaptism originated from the travels of Hut, and none that it was connected with Switzerland. She accepted Bender's view that Hut had been converted to a peaceful standpoint from Müntzer's revolutionary one, but at the same time she demonstrated that Hut's Anabaptism, unlike that of the Swiss Brethren, was imbued with a mysticism of suffering very similar to that which Goertz has described as the central teaching of Thomas Müntzer.

Evidence like Mecenseffy's made it possible for Gottfried Seebass to arrive at a more radical affirmation of Müntzer's paternity of Hut's South German Anabaptist movement, and conversely at a radical denial that this movement and Swiss Anabaptism had the same origin and similar characters. Not only Müntzer's mysticism, but his apocalyptic revolution as well, was continued by Hut. In a final statement Müntzer had explained the defeat of the peasants as God's rejection of their selfish greed. Hut inferred that Müntzer had been one of the apocalyptic messengers foretold in Revelation 11. According to Seebass, Hut's adherence to Anabaptism was not a conversion to pacifism but an identification of the rebaptized as the 144,000 apocalyptic elect who would, together with the Turks, punish the wicked at the end of the world in 1528. Moreover, Seebass, in direct opposition to Clasen and with criticism of his methodology, demonstrated a strong appeal of Hut's Anabaptism to the veterans of the Franconian Peasants' War. Seebass showed that if Anabaptism was not "Müntzer's legacy," nevertheless Müntzer's legacy was in Anabaptism.

* * *

Certainly the course of recent non-Marxist research has gone far to substantiate Marxist hypotheses of the socially revolutionary content and background of Anabaptism. On the other hand, it has become ever clearer that Müntzer and the Anabaptists were religious men of the sixteenth century, who, particularly in their deepest social revolutionary commitment, cannot be treated as twentieth-century revolutionaries in sixteenth-century costume. Feudalism, capitalism and demoracy were neither their motives nor the "underlying realities" of their age. Thomas Müntzer did not cause either Peasants' War or Anabaptism nor did the Peasants' War cause Anabaptism. All were swept up in a great wave of religious and social revolution committed to the "restitution of Christendom." By 1525 this mass awakening seemed to have destroyed the authority of priests and at the same time began to challenge the traditional prerogatives of rulers.

When, as many times before and after in history, the traditional authorities recovered their will, mustered their resources and suppressed their enemies, apocalypticism, separatism or some combination of the two were the only recourse of the revolutionaries who could not or would not turn back. Some of these revolutionaries had a nonviolent commitment from the start; and the historical circumstances which dictated that only the separatists would survive gave an increasingly peaceful cast to the revolutionary remnant. The fact that Northwest Germany and the Low Countries had not experienced the revolution of 1525 left them vulnerable to a more limited and warped repetition ten years later, which did much to defame Anabaptist groups which elsewhere had already become confirmed in a life of peaceful separatism. For four and a half centuries thereafter this separate people, seeking the frontiers of Russia, North and South America, has preserved the echo of a revolution far removed from modern social cleavages and materialisms. And, although he was not "the founder of Anabaptism," Thomas Müntzer was the grandest figure of that long-gone, most un-Marxist revolution.

I

The Significance of Sixteenth-Century Anabaptism

The Anabaptist Vision

Harold S. Bender

"Judged by the reception it met at the hands of those in power, both in Church and State, equally in Roman Catholic and in Protestant countries, the Anabaptist movement was one of the most tragic in the history of Christianity; but, judged by the principles, which were put into play by the men who bore this reproachful nickname, it must be pronounced one of the most momentous and significant undertakings in man's eventful religious struggle after the truth. It gathered up the gains of earlier movements, it is the spiritual soil out of which all non-conformist sects have sprung, and it is the first plain announcement in modern history of a programme for a new type of Christian society which the modern world, especially in America and England, has been slowly realizing—an absolutely free and independent religious society, and a State in which every man counts as a man, and has his share in shaping both Church and State."

These words of Rufus M. Jones constitute one of the best characterizations of Anabaptism and its contribution to our modern Christian culture to be found in the English language. They were brave words when they were written thirty-five years ago, but they have been abundantly verified by a generation of Anabaptist research since that time. There can be no question but that the great principles of freedom of conscience, separation of church and state, and voluntarism in religion, so basic in American Protestantism, and so essential to democracy, ultimately are derived from the Anabaptists of the Reformation period, who for the first time clearly enunciated them, and challenged the Christian world to follow them in practice. The line of descent through the centuries since that time may not always be clear, and may have passed through other intermediate movements and groups, but the debt to original Anabaptism is unquestioned.

. . . .

The dreadful severity of the persecution of the Anabaptist movement in the years 1527–1560 not only in Switzerland, South Germany, and Thuringia, but in all the Austrian lands as well as in the Low Countries, testifies to the power of the movement and the desperate haste with which Catholic, Lutheran, and Zwinglian authorities alike strove to throttle it before it should be too late. The notorious decree issued in 1529 by the Diet of Spires (the same Diet which protested the restriction of evangelical liberties) summarily passed the sentence of death upon all Anabaptists, ordering that "every Anabaptist and rebaptized person of either sex should be put to death by fire, sword, or some other way." Repeatedly in subsequent sessions of the imperial diet this decree was reinvoked and intensified; and as late as 1551 the Diet of Augsburg issued a decree ordering the judges and jurors who had scruples against pronouncing the death sentence on Anabaptists be removed from office and punished by heavy fines and imprisonment.

The authorities had great difficulty in executing their program of suppression, for they soon discovered that the Anabaptists feared neither torture nor death, and gladly sealed their faith with their blood. In fact the joyful testimony of the Anabaptist martyrs was a great stimulus to new recruits, for it stirred the imagination of the populace as nothing else could have done.

Finding therefore that the customary method of individual trials and sentences was proving totally inadequate to stem the tide, the authorities resorted to the desperate expedient of sending out through the land companies of armed executioners and mounted soldiers to hunt down the Anabaptists and kill them on the spot singly or *en masse* without trial or sentence. The most atrocious application of this policy was made in Swabia where the original four hundred special police of 1528 sent against the Anabaptists proved too small a force and had to be increased to one thousand. An imperial provost-marshal, Berthold Aichele, served as chief administrator of this bloody program in Swabia and other regions until he finally broke down in terror and dismay, and after an execution at Brixen lifted his hands to heaven and swore a solemn oath never again to put to death an Anabaptist, which vow he kept. The Count of Alzey in the Palatinate, after three hundred and fifty Anabaptists had been executed there, was heard to exclaim, "What shall I do, the more I kill, the greater becomes their number!"

. . . .

Before defining the Anabaptist vision, it is essential to state clearly who is meant by the term "Anabaptist," since the name has come to be used in modern historiography to cover a wide variety of Reformation groups, sometimes thought of as the whole "left wing of the Reformation" (Roland Bainton), or "the Bolsheviks of the Reformation" (Preserved Smith). Although the definitive history of Anabaptism has not yet been written, we know enough today to draw a clear line of demarcation between original evangelical and constructive Anabaptism on the one hand, which was born in the bosom of Zwinglianism in Zurich, Switzerland, in 1525, and established in the Low Countries in 1533, and the various mystical, spiritualistic, revolutionary, or even antinomian related and unrelated groups on the other hand, which came and went like the flowers of the field in those days of the great renovation. The former, Anabaptism proper, maintained an unbroken course in Switzerland, South Germany, Austria, and Holland throughout the sixteenth century, and has continued until the present day in the Mennonite movement, now almost 500,000 baptized members strong in Europe and America. There is no longer any excuse for permitting our understanding of the distinct character of this genuine Anabaptism to be obscured by Thomas Müntzer and the Peasants War, the Münsterites, or any other aberration of Protestantism in the sixteenth century.

. . . .

However, there is another line of interpretation, now almost a hundred years old, which is being increasingly accepted and which is probably destined to dominate the field. It is the one which holds that Anabaptism is the culmination of the Reformation, the fulfillment of the original vision of Luther and Zwingli, and thus makes it a consistent evangelical Protestantism seeking to recreate without compromise the original New Testament church, the vision of Christ and the Apostles. . . .

The evidence in support of this interpretation is overwhelming, and can be taken from the statements of the contemporary opponents of the Anabaptists as well as from the Anabaptists themselves. Conrad Grebel, the founder of the Swiss Brethren movement, states clearly this point of view in his letter to Thomas Müntzer of 1524, in words written on behalf of the entire group which constitute in effect the original Anabaptist pronunciamento:

> Just as our forebears [the Roman Catholic Papal Church] fell away from the true God and the knowledge of Jesus Christ and of the right faith in him, and from the one true, common divine word, from the divine institutions, from Christian love and life, and lived without God's law and gospel in human, useless, un-Christian customs and ceremonies, and expected to attain salvation therein, yet fell far short of it, as the evangelical preachers [Luther, Zwingli, etc.] have declared, and to some extent are still declaring; so today, too, every man wants to be saved by superficial faith, without fruits of faith, without the baptism of test and probation, without love and hope, without right Christian practices, and wants to persist in all the old fashion of personal vices, and in the common ritualistic and anti-Christian customs of baptism and of the Lord's Supper, in disrespect for the divine word and in respect for the word of the pope and of the anti-papal preachers, which yet is not equal to the divine word nor in harmony with it. In respecting persons and in manifold seduction there is grosser and more pernicious error now than ever has been since the beginning of the world. In the same error we, too, lingered as long as we heard and read only the evangelical preachers who are to blame for all this, in punishment for our sins. But after we took the Scriptures in hand, too, and consulted it on many points, we have been instructed somewhat and have discovered the great and hurtful error of the shepherds, of ours too, namely that we do not daily beseech God earnestly with constant groanings to be brought out of this destruction of all godly life and out of human abominations, and to attain to true faith and divine instruction.

A similar statement was made in 1538, after fourteen years of persecution, by an Anabaptist leader who spoke on behalf of his group in the great colloquy at Berne with the leaders of the Reformed Church:

> While yet in the national church, we obtained much instruction from the writings of Luther, Zwingli, and others, concerning the mass and other papal ceremonies, that they are vain. Yet we recognized a great lack as regards repentance, conversion, and the true Christian life. Upon these things my mind was bent. I waited and hoped for a year or two, since the minister had much to say of amendment of life, of giving to the poor, loving one another, and abstaining from evil. But I could not close my eyes to the fact that the doctrine which was preached and which was based on the Word of God, was not carried out. No beginning was made toward true Christian living, and there was no unison in the teaching concerning the things that were necessary. And although the mass and the images were finally abolished, true repentance and Christian love were not in evidence. Changes were made only as concerned external things. This gave me occasion to inquire further into these matters. Then God sent His messengers, Conrad Grebel and others, with whom I conferred about the fundamental teachings of the apostles and the Christian life and practice. I found them men who had surrendered themselves to the doctrine of Christ by "Bussfertigkeit" [repentance evidenced by fruits]. With their assistance we established a congregation in which repentance was in evidence by newness of life in Christ.

It is evident from these statements that the Anabaptists were concerned most of all about "a true Christian life," that is, a life patterned after the teaching and example of Christ. The reformers, they believed, whatever their profession may have been, did not secure among the people true repentance, regeneration, and Christian living as a result of their preaching. The Reformation emphasis on faith was good but inadequate, for without newness of life, they held, faith is hypocritical.

. . . .

The Anabaptists . . . retained the original vision of Luther and Zwingli, enlarged it, gave it body and form, and set out to achieve it in actual experience. They proceeded to organize a church composed solely of earnest Christians, and actually found the people for it. They did not believe in any case that the size of the response should determine whether or not the truth of God should be applied, and they refused to compromise. They preferred to make a radical break with the fifteen hundred years of history and culture if necessary rather than to break with the New Testament.

May it not be said that the decision of Luther and Zwingli to surrender their original vision was the tragic turning point of the Reformation? Professor Karl Mueller, one of the keenest and fairest interpreters of the Reformation, evidently thinks so, for he says, "The agressive, conquering power, which Lutheranism manifested in its first period was lost everywhere at the moment when the governments took matters in hand and established the Lutheran Creed," that is to say, when Luther's mass church concept was put into practice. Luther in his later years expressed disappointment at the final outcome of the Reformation, stating that the people had become more and more indifferent toward religion and the moral outlook was more deplorable than ever. His last years were embittered by the consciousness of partial failure, and his expressions of dejection are well known. Contrast this sense of defeat at the end of Luther's outwardly successful career with the sense of victory in the hearts of the Anabaptist martyrs who laid down their lives in what the world would call defeat, conscious of having kept faith with their vision to the end.

Having defined genuine Anabaptism in its Reformation setting, we are ready to examine its central teachings. The Anabaptist vision included three major points of emphasis; first, a new conception of the essence of Christianity as discipleship; second, a new conception of the church as a brotherhood; and third, a new ethic of love and non-resistance. We turn now to an exposition of these points.

First and fundamental in the Anabaptist vision was the conception of the essence of Christianity as discipleship. It was a concept which meant the transformation of the entire way of life of the individual believer and of society so that it should be fashioned after the teachings and example of Christ. The Anabaptists could not understand a Christianity which made regeneration, holiness, and love primarily a matter of intellect, of doctrinal belief, or of subjective "experience," rather than one of the transformation of life. They demanded an outward expression of the inner experience. Repentance must be "evidenced" by newness of behaviour. "In evidence" is the keynote which rings through the testimonies and challenges of the early Swiss Brethren when they are called to give an account of themselves. The whole life was to be brought literally under the Lordship of Christ in a covenant of discipleship, a covenant which the Anabaptist writers delighted to emphasize. The focus of the Christian life was to be not so much the inward experience of the grace of God, as it was for Luther, but the outward application of that grace to all human conduct and the consequent Christianization of all human relationships. The true test of the Christian, they held, is discipleship. The great word of the Anabaptists was not "faith" as it was with the reformers, but "following" (*Nachfolge Christi*). And baptism, the greatest of the Christian symbols, was accordingly to be for them the "covenant of a good conscience toward God" (I Peter 3:21),—the pledge of a complete commitment to obey Christ, and not primarily the symbol of a past experience. The Anabaptists had faith, indeed, but they used it to produce a life. Theology was for them a means, not an end.

That the Anabaptists not only proclaimed the ideal of full Christian discipleship but achieved, in the eyes of their contemporaries and even of their opponents, a measurably higher level of performance than the average, is fully witnessed by the sources. The early Swiss and South German reformers were keenly aware of this achievement and its attractive power. Zwingli knew it best of all, but Bullinger, Capito, Vadian, and many others confirm his judgment that the Anabaptist Brethren were unusually sincere, devoted, and effective Christians. However, since the Brethren refused to accept the state church system which the reformers were building, and in addition made "radical" demands which might have changed the entire social order, the leaders of the Reformation were completely baffled in their understanding of the movement, and professed to believe that the Anabaptists were hypocrites of the darkest dye. Bullinger, for instance calls them "devilish enemies and destroyers of the Church of God." Nevertheless they had to admit the apparent superiority of their life. In Zwingli's last book against the Swiss Brethren (1527), for instance, the following is found:

> If you investigate their life and conduct, it seems at first contact irreproachable, pious, unassuming, attractive, yea, above this world. Even those who are inclined to be critical will say that their lives are excellent.

Bullinger, himself, who wrote bitter diatribes against them, was compelled to admit of the early Swiss Brethren that

> Those who unite with them will by their ministers be received into their church by rebaptism and repentance and newness of life. They henceforth lead their lives under a semblance of a quite spiritual conduct. They denounce covetousness, pride, profanity, the lewd conversation and immorality of the world, drinking and gluttony. In short, their hypocrisy is great and manifold.

Bullinger's lament (1531) that "the people are running after them as though they were the living saints" has been reported earlier. Vadian, the reformer of St. Gall, testified, that "none were more favorably inclined toward Anabaptism and more easily entangled with it than those who were of pious and honorable disposition." Capito, the reformer of Strassburg, wrote in 1527 concerning the Swiss Brethren:

> I frankly confess that in most [Anabaptists] there is in evidence piety and consecration and indeed a zeal which is beyond any suspicion of insincerity. For what earthly advantage could they hope to win by enduring exile, torture, and unspeakable punishment of the flesh. I testify before God that I cannot say that on account of a lack of wisdom they are somewhat indifferent toward earthly things, but rather from divine motives.

The preachers of the Canton of Berne admitted in a letter to the Council of Berne in 1532 that

The Anabaptists have the semblance of outward piety to a far greater degree than we and all the churches which unitedly with us confess Christ, and they avoid offensive sins which are very common among us.

Walter Klarer, the Reformed chronicler of Appenzell, Switzerland wrote:

Most of the Anabaptists are people who at first had been the best with us in promulgating the word of God.

And the Roman Catholic theologian, Franz Agricola, in his book of 1582, *Against the Terrible Errors of the Anabaptists*, says:

Among the existing heretical sects there is none which in appearance leads a more modest or pious life than the Anabaptist. As concerns their outward public life they are irreproachable. No lying, deception, swearing, strife, harsh language, no intemperate eating and drinking, no outward personal display, is found among them, but humility, patience, uprightness, neatness, honesty, temperance, straightforwardness, in such measure that one would suppose that they have the Holy Spirit of God.

A mandate against the Swiss Brethren published in 1585 by the Council of Berne states that offensive sins and vices were common among the preachers and the membership of the Reformed Church, adding, "And this is the greatest reason that many pious, God-fearing people who seek Christ from their heart are offended and forsake our church [to unite with the Brethren]."

One of the finest contemporary characterizations of the Anabaptists is that given in 1531 by Sebastian Franck, an objective and sympathetic witness, though an opponent of the Anabaptists, who wrote as follows:

The Anabaptists . . . soon gained a large following, . . . drawing many sincere souls who had a zeal for God, for they taught nothing but love, faith, and the cross. They showed themselves humble, patient under much suffering; they break bread with one another as an evidence of unity and love. They helped each other faithfully, and called each other brothers. . . . They died as martyrs, patiently and humbly enduring all persecution.

A further confirmation of the above evaluation of the achievement of the Anabaptists is found in the fact that in many places those who lived a consistent Christian life were in danger of falling under the suspicion of being guilty of Anabaptist heresy. Caspar Schwenckfeld, for instance, declared, "I am being maligned, by both preachers and others, with the charge of being an Anabaptist, even as all others who lead a true, pious Christian life are now almost everywhere given this name." Bullinger himself complained that

. . . there are those who in reality are not Anabaptists but have a pronounced averseness to the sensuality and frivolity of the world and therefore reprove sin and vice and are consequently called or misnamed Anabaptists by petulant persons.

The great collection of Anabaptist source materials, commonly called the *Täufer Akten*, now in its third volume, contains a number of specific illustrations of this. In 1562 a certain Caspar Zacher of Waiblingen in Württemberg was accused of being an Anabaptist, but the court record reports that since he was an envious man who could not get along with others, and who often started quarrels, as well as being guilty of swearing and cursing and carrying a weapon, he was not considered to be an Anabaptist. On the other hand, in 1570 a certain Hans Jäger of Vöhringen in Württemberg was brought before the court on suspicion of being an Anabaptist primarily because he did not curse but lived an irreproachable life.

As a second major element in the Anabaptist vision, a new concept of the church was created by the central principle of newness of life and applied Christianity. Voluntary church membership based upon true conversion and involving a commitment to holy living and discipleship was the absolutely essential heart of this concept. This vision stands in sharp contrast to the church concept of the reformers who retained the medieval idea of a mass church with membership of the entire population from birth to the grave compulsory by law and force.

It is from the standpoint of this new conception of the church that the Anabaptist opposition to infant baptism must be interpreted. Infant baptism was not the cause of their disavowal of the state church; it was only a symbol of the cause. How could infants give a commitment based upon a knowledge of what true Christianity means? They might conceivably passively experience the grace of God (though Anabaptists would question this), but they could not respond in pledging their lives to Christ. Such infant baptism would not only be meaningless, but would in fact become a serious obstacle to a true understanding of the nature of Christianity and membership in the church. Only adult baptism could signify an intelligent life commitment.

An inevitable corollary of the concept of the church as a body of committed and practicing Christians pledged to the highest standard of New Testament living was the insistence on the separation of the church from the world, that is non-conformity of the Christian to the worldly way of life. The world would not tolerate the practice of true Christian principles in society, and the church could not tolerate the practice of worldly ways among its membership. Hence, the only way out was separation (*"Absonderung"*), the gathering of true Christians into their own Christian society where Christ's way could and would be practised. On this principle of separation Menno Simons says:

> All the evangelical scriptures teach us that the church of Christ was and is, in doctrine, life, and worship, a people separated from the world.

In the great debate of 1528 [really 1532-eds.] at Zofingen, spokesmen of the Swiss Brethren said,

> The true church is separated from the world and is conformed to the nature of Christ. If a church is yet at one with the world we cannot recognize it as a true church.

In a sense, this principle of non-conformity to the world is merely a negative expression of the positive requirement of discipleship, but it goes further in the sense that it represents a judgment on the contemporary social order, which the Anabaptists called "the world," as non-Christian, and sets up a line of demarcation between the Christian community and worldly society.

A logical outcome of the concept of nonconformity to the world was the concept of the suffering church. Conflict with the world was inevitable for those who endeavored to live an earnest Christian life. The Anabaptists expected opposition; they took literally the words of Jesus when he said, "In the world ye shall have tribulation," but they also took literally his words of encouragement, "But be ye of good cheer, I have overcome the world." . . . Perhaps it was persecution that made the Anabaptists so acutely aware of the conflict between the church and the world, but this persecution was due to the fact that they refused to accept what they considered the sub-Christian way of life practiced in European Christendom. They could have avoided the persecution had they but conformed, or they could have suspended the practice of their faith to a more convenient time and sailed under false colors as did David Joris, but they chose with dauntless courage and simple honesty to live their faith, to defy the existing world order, and to suffer the consequences.

Basic to the Anabaptist vision of the church was the insistence on the practice of true brotherhood and love among the members of the church. This principle was understood to mean not merely the expression of pious sentiments, but the actual practice of sharing possessions to meet the needs of others in the spirit of true mutual aid. Hans Leopold, a Swiss Brethren martyr of 1528, said of the Brethren:

> If they know of any one who is in need, whether or not he is a member of their church, they believe it their duty, out of love to God, to render help and aid.

Heinrich Seiler, a Swiss Brethren martyr of 1535, said:

> I do not believe it wrong that a Christian has property of his own, but yet he is nothing more than a steward.

An early Hutterian book states that one of the questions addressed by the Swiss Brethren to applicants for baptism was: "Whether they would consecrate themselves with all their temporal possessions to the service of God and His people." A Protestant of Strassburg, visitor at a Swiss Brethren baptismal service in that city in 1557, reports that a question addressed to all applicants for baptism was: "Whether they, if necessity required it, would devote all their possessions to the service of the brotherhood, and would not fail any member that is in need, if they were able to render aid." Heinrich Bullinger, the bitter enemy of the Brethren, states:

> They teach that every Christian is under duty before God from motives of love, to use, if need be, all his possessions to supply the necessities of life to any of the brethren who are in need.

This principle of full brotherhood and stewardship was actually practiced, and not merely speculatively considered. In its absolute form of Christian communism, with the complete repudiation of private property, it became the way of life of the Hutterian Brotherhood in 1528 and has remained so to this day, for the Hutterites held that private property is the greatest enemy of Christian love. One of the inspiring stories of the sixteenth and seventeenth centuries is the successful practice of the full communal way of life by this group.

The third great element in the Anabaptist vision was the ethic of love and non-resistance as applied to all human relationships. The Brethren understood this to mean complete abandonment of all warfare, strife, and violence, and of the taking of human life. Conrad Grebel, the Swiss, said in 1524:

> True Christians use neither worldly sword nor engage in war, since among them taking human life has ceased entirely, for we are no longer under the Old Covenant. . . . The Gospel and those who accept it are not to be protected with the sword, neither should they thus protect themselves.

Pilgram Marpeck, the South German leader, in 1544, speaking of Matthew 5, said:

> All bodily, worldly, carnal, earthly fighting, conflicts, and wars are annulled and abolished among them through such law . . . which law of love Christ . . . himself observed and thereby gave his followers a pattern to follow after.

Peter Riedemann, the Hutterian leader, wrote in 1545:

> Christ, the Prince of Peace, has established His Kingdom, that is, His Church, and has purchased it by His blood. In this kingdom all worldly warfare has ended. Therefore a Christian has no part in war nor does he wield the sword to execute vengeance.

Menno Simons, of Holland, wrote in 1550:

> The regenerated do not go to war, nor engage in strife. . . . They are the children of peace who have beaten their swords into plowshares and their spears into prunning hooks, and know of no war . . . Spears and swords of iron we leave to those who, alas, consider human blood and swine's blood of well-nigh equal value.

In this principle of non-resistance, or Biblical pacifism, which was thoroughly believed and resolutely practiced by all the original Anabaptist Brethren and their descendants throughout Europe from the beginning until the last century, the Anabaptists were again creative leaders, far ahead of their times, in this antedating the Quakers by over a century and a quarter. It should also be remembered that they held this principle in a day when both Catholic and Protestant churches not only endorsed war as an instrument of state policy, but employed it in religious conflicts. It is true, of course, that occasional earlier prophets, like Peter Chelcicky, had advocated similar views, but they left no continuing practice of the principle behind them.

As we review the vision of the Anabaptists, it becomes clear that there are two foci in this vision. The first focus relates to the essential nature of Christianity. Is Christianity primarily a matter of the reception of divine grace through a sacramental-sacerdotal institution (Roman Catholicism), is it chiefly enjoyment of the inner experience of the grace of God through faith in Christ (Lutheranism), or is it most of all the transformation of life through discipleship (Anabaptism)? The Anabaptists were neither institutionalists, mystics, nor pietists, for they laid the weight of their emphasis upon following Christ in life. To them it was unthinkable for one truly to be a Christian without creating a new life on divine principles both for himself and for all men who commit themselves to the Christian way.

The second focus relates to the church. For the Anabaptist, the church was neither an institution (Catholicism), nor the instrument of God for the proclamation of the divine Word

(Lutheranism), nor a resource group for individual piety (Pietism). It was a brotherhood of love in which the fullness of the Christian life ideal was expressed.

The Anabaptist vision may be further clarified by comparison of the social ethics of the four main Christian groups of the Reformation period, Catholic, Calvinist, Lutheran, and Anabaptist. Catholic and Calvinist alike were optimistic about the world, agreeing that the world can be redeemed; they held that the entire social order can be brought under the sovereignty of God and Christianized, although they used different means to attain this goal. Lutheran and Anabaptist were pessimistic about the world, denying the possibility of Christianizing the entire social order; but the consequent attitudes of these two groups toward the social order were diametrically opposed. Lutheranism said that since the Christian must live in a world order that remains sinful, he must make a compromise with it. As a citizen he cannot avoid participation in the evil of the world, for instance in making war, and for this his only recourse is to seek forgiveness by the grace of God; only within his personal private experience can the Christian truly Christianize his life. The Anabaptist rejected this view completely. Since for him no compromise dare be made with evil, the Christian may in no circumstance participate in any conduct in the existing social order which is contrary to the spirit and teaching of Christ and the apostolic practice. He must consequently withdraw from the worldly system and create a Christian social order within the fellowship of the church brotherhood. Extension of this Christian order by the conversion of individuals and their transfer out of the world into the church is the only way by which progress can be made in Christianizing the social order.

However, the Anabaptist was realistic. Down the long perspective of the future he saw little chance that the mass of humankind would enter such a brotherhood with its high ideals. Hence he anticipated a long and grievous conflict between the church and the world. Neither did he anticipate the time when the church would rule the world; the church would always be a suffering church. He agreed with the words of Jesus when he said that those who would be his disciples must deny themselves, take up their cross daily and follow him, and that there would be few who would enter the strait gate and travel the narrow way of life. If this prospect should seem too discouraging, the Anabaptist would reply that the life within the Christian brotherhood is satisfyingly full of love and joy.

The Anabaptist vision was not a detailed blueprint for the reconstruction of human society, but the Brethren did believe that Jesus intended that the Kingdom of God should be set in the midst of earth, here and now, and this they proposed to do forthwith. We shall not believe, they said, that the Sermon on the Mount or any other vision that He had is only a heavenly vision meant but to keep His followers in tension until the last great day, but we shall practice what He taught, believing that where He walked we can by His grace follow in His steps.

The Doctrine of the Two Worlds

Robert Friedmann

It has often been asked whether one may properly speak of an Anabaptist theology as such or whether the Anabaptists simply aimed to follow the footsteps of the Master in a simple and unsophisticated manner without theological speculation or foundation. As to the basic doctrines of Christianity, it is certain that they were orthodox, teaching nothing foreign to the Apostles' Creed. Since the center of their concern lay elsewhere, however, they have often been described as theologically naive. A deeper search, however, makes one wonder whether such a judgment is tenable. A movement of such strength is unthinkable without a definite theological foundation, without specific ideas concerning man's relationship to the divine and the meaning of earthly life. Even if these foundations were not expressed in a systematic way, one must assume that they were implied in all the doings and witnessing of the Anabaptists. The rediscovery of these presuppositions is a challenge to present-day research.

. . . .

It is certainly true that in the New Testament a theology in the more formal sense of the word is most explicit in the writings of Paul; but that does not mean that the teachings of Christ Himself as recorded in the Synoptic Gospels are lacking in theological foundations. It has been only in recent decades that we have come to recognize this "implied" theology of the Synoptics, so long by-passed and overlooked, as exactly the one which became so central for the Anabaptists in the sixteenth century. The teachings of Paul are essentially not different from those of Christ, but the emphasis and the categories applied are different, or at least could be so interpreted. In any case it is possible to speak of a Pauline tradition, elaborated later by Augustine, and of a Synoptic tradition, preserved in the main by those groups which Ludwig Keller once called old evangelical brotherhoods.

As we now study this Synoptic tradition or emphasis, we find that central for it is the teaching of the two kingdoms, together with the message of what the kingdom of God actually means and implies. I think it is justified to call these doctrines a genuine theology in the proper sense of the word, even though its forms of expression are different from the above-mentioned more sophisticated Pauline-Augustinian tradition. It is proposed to call this teaching "kingdom theology." In a certain sense it is a continuation of the teachings of the Old Testament prophets, in the main of Isaiah, where this basic dualism of the two realms already appears. Most important in this connection is the idea that the "other kingdom" is not merely something transcendental, something of another aeon, or something to be experienced only after death, but a reality to be expected and experienced in this life, even though in a sort of metahistorical situation.

As a matter of fact, the kingdom theology (as we see it, the very center of Christ's message and witnessing) is to be distinguished from a theology whose primary concern is personal salvation (the Protestant interpretation of Paulinism). These two theologies are complementary to each other and of equal importance. The Reformers knew this fact very well. In fact their outlook on history was decidedly kingdom-oriented, but they had their reasons for underemphasizing this two-facet content of the New Testament theology. The Pietists a century and a half later revived the kingdom idea, but being themselves the offspring of traditional Protestantism, they interpreted it in a non-Synoptic way. The real representatives of the Synoptic kingdom theology have always been the old evangelical brotherhoods, but none were more outspokenly kingdom-oriented, hence none more true to the spirit of the Master Himself, than the Anabaptists.

In the Pauline teaching the idea of original sin has a central position, making personal salvation and justification by faith a most urgent matter, while the kingdom comes to occupy apparently a secondary position. In the teaching of Jesus, on the other hand, the sense of urgency seems to be associated predominantly with the kingdom, which, of course, includes the certainty of personal salvation. To be sure, Jesus taught by means of parables and pictures rather than by way of concepts and theories, and parables allow no easy translation into a system. And yet, the doctrine of the two worlds—the kingdom of God which is to come here and now, and the kingdom of darkness which rules over all those who do not see the light—this doctrine represents definitely a very specific outlook or theology. As will be shown below, it has its own characteristic (1) value system; (2) view of history; and (3) social ethic. In short, it implies a real theology although of a character rather different from that of the Pauline tradition as interpreted by Augustine and the Reformers.

While Paul by no means taught only a theology of justification by faith *alone* (as the Reformers, in particular Luther, have done), he gave enough attention to it to make possible the development of a one-sided theology at the hands of the Reformers, running something like this: The law has come to an end; all men have inherited original sin; Christ died for us; and thus the individual can and will be saved (i.e., justified before God) if only he puts all his confidence and faith in the atoning quality of Christ's supreme sacrifice. The essential element here is faith, not works, however the latter may be interpreted. This one-sided emphasis in a fully developed Protestantism, which tended to ignore both the remainder of Paul's teaching and the Gospels as well, produced a theological system which assumed an extremely individualistic outlook. The individual, a sinner through and through who cannot do good, craves for salvation and eventually finds it by believing. The neighbor, the brother, important though he is, is in no way constitutive to this outlook on salvation. Love, we learn, is the fruit of faith, but such love adds nothing essential to the drama of completely unearned and even undeserved redemption, else it would assume the quality of works. No specific social implications could be deduced, and both Lutheranism and Calvinism became exceedingly individualistic in their teachings, while civilization at large went on independently and autonomously.

Kingdom theology is essentially of a different kind. The outlook is dualistic as throughout the New Testament. Yet while Paul preferredly contraposes *spirit* and *flesh,* categories suggesting above all a conflict in the personal and private sphere, kingdom theology distinguishes two other concepts in polarity. These concepts are *the world* (being ruled by "the prince of this world," i.e., Satan), and *the other world,* the kingdom, which is God's world. Two possibilities are here to be contemplated: either that these two realms are coexistent, although on different levels, and the kingdom of God is already present in or among those who have been born again or who are united in the name of the Master ("where two or three are together in my name . . ."); or the kingdom of God is to come, in fact its coming is imminent, and one ought to prepare himself for this imminent coming by purification and a new life. The latter idea was present already in the teaching of the Essenes, of John the Baptist, and of some Ebionites. This second interpretation of the kingdom idea we may call eschatological, while the first has no special systematic name, yet is more closely associated with the idea of rebirth and conversion. These two views, the kingdom present in every reborn Christian (or present where two or three are assembled in the Master's name), and the kingdom as the new order to be expected at any moment and for which proper preparation is needed, are intermixed in Anabaptist thought just as they are in the original source of that teaching, the Gospels. But the eschatological hope was subdued and never dominated the thinking of the Anabaptists, just as in the Gospel the implied eschatology was never to outdo the positive teachings concerning the kingdom as the newly revealed other-reality which is within the reach of everyone who earnestly longs and desires to enter the same.

As suggested earlier, the kingdom theory implies first a new set of values. Certainly, the Sermon on the Mount is the best illustration: love, forgiveness, self-surrender, hating not even one's own persecutors, these values are so radically different that they seem paradoxical and unrealizable to an unregenerate mind. Certainly they go far beyond mere ethics. Rather they imply a different dimension, the world of the pure Spirit, in contrast with all secular this-worldly valuations. In fact, these new values are unobtainable except through rebirth and a radical change of mind, concepts not too much at home in orthodox Protestantism, the religion of the many. Historically, this has produced within Christendom what the sociologists of religion like to call sectarianism, meaning that the disciples, the *Nachfolger,* the citizens of the kingdom, intentionally separate themselves from the "world," in order to share as little as possible in the affairs of the natural realm and of its citizens. They are highly suspicious of the values of this world, including even that which is usually called "culture," and they sense in it the working of destructive, non-divine forces in the background. All cathartic or puritanical tendencies have their roots in this new value system.

In the second place, kingdom theology has its own specific outlook on history, a fact much forgotten today but very much alive even in the age of the Reformation. The two realms, the kingdom of God and the kingdom of darkness, are engaged in a perennial struggle, a world drama, in which each person must choose and take his side. In the end the kingdom of God will triumph over the powers of darkness. This is the eschatological expectation. Hence the sectarian feels a high sense of responsibility in this cosmic-historic process, and therefore accepts suffering and martyrdom without flinching. Only by witnessing to the kingdom of Light can the latter ever become full reality. That this outlook, although prominent in the New Testament, especially in the Gospels, recedes with the Reformers' interpretation of Paul hardly needs further elaboration.

Thirdly, the kingdom theology includes also a social ethic, different, to be sure, from what usually goes by that name. A lack of "social ethics," or at least of what may better be called a concern for the social order of this world, was often observed in the teaching of the New Testament. The absence of any doctrine of "natural law" was observed at an early date in church history, but it was soon supplied from Stoic philosophy to promote a more adjustable foundation of church life. Thus far, however, very little attention has been given to the genuine social ethic of the Gospel message of the kingdom of God, most likely because it does not fit too well into the ways of the world at large and into the social exigencies of civilization. We mean here the brotherhood idea, the idea of the *Gemeinde,* the *ecclesia* in its first meaning, the idea of the *koinonia,* a closely knit fellowship of believers and disciples, not in the form of conventicles as in later Pietism, but in the form of the Brotherhoods as we know them in the early church, and in all old evangelical brotherhoods including the Anabaptists. All individualism and individualistic concern for personal salvation is ruled out. No one can enter the kingdom except together with his brother. The old saying that "there is no salvation outside the church" does not exactly express the underlying idea of this brotherhood ideal: actually that doctrine belongs to a different frame of reference. And yet, it simply is so that the kingdom of God means from its very beginning a togetherness, else it is no kingdom. The mere aggregation of saved souls, as in Pietism, does not constitute the kingdom; it remains just an aggregation, nothing else. The horizontal man-to-man relationship belongs to the kingdom just as much as does the vertical God-man relationship. In fact, the belief prevails that one cannot come to God (that is, attain salvation) except as one comes to Him together with one's brother. The brethren, the body of believers, constitutes the realm; hence brotherly love, *agape*, is more than mere ethics. It is one of the basic qualifications of the kingdom in the here and now.

Kingdom theology is hostile to *Kultur,* man's autonomous creation and setting of values. Actually *Kultur* or civilization is a Graeco-Roman and a Renaissance concept, not a Christian one; hence the apparent coolness of the Anabaptists toward human achievement and cultural advancement. Since the latter does not belong to the system of values embodied in the kingdom theology they meet it with suspicion, fearful lest it contain elements of destruction, elements of despondency and nonsalvation, in short, that it miss the essentials of Christ's message and world outlook. The Middle Ages, being steeped in the philosophy of history of the two realms, knew more about this tension between man-made civilization and God's kingdom than has any time since the fifteenth century.

The kingdom theology is concerned with the concrete, the life in the here and the now, although in a dimension other than the material. By no means does it teach that the kingdom is found in heaven only, and attainable only after death. This is a post-New Testament interpretation. Kingdom theology does not mean merely a glorious expectation of life after death to be reached by the pious and the ascetic; it means a radical turn in life itself, the breaking in of a new dimension into the physical existence of man. Due to its new system of values, so highly challenging to anything known to "natural" man, the group life of the disciples has always been misunderstood and disliked, in fact persecuted by the world. Hence a "theology of martyrdom" developed among the Brethren, an understanding that the citizens of the kingdom of God will necessarily meet suffering in this world. This suffering, however, is of a redemptive character and represents a necessary element in the building of God's kingdom. It was this way in the early centuries A.D., and all through history. The Anabaptists in particular accepted the idea of the suffering church in an almost matter-of-fact fashion, and every member of this group understood it without much explanation. In fact, we often discover even a kind of longing for martyrdom, a desire to be allowed to testify for the new spiritual world through suffering and supreme sacrifice.

This martyr-mindedness is usually mellowed by a restrained eschatological outlook: God will soon change the world altogether. Wait but a little while, and yours will be the triumph. Save for a few exceptions, such as that of Melchior Hofmann, the Anabaptists did not calculate the end of the world, being mindful of the words of Christ that no one knows the day, not even the Son, but the Father alone. Nevertheless, they frequently speak of "these last and dangerous times," and of the "last fury of the beast." Here they use a figure from the Book of Revelation which is otherwise little used and quoted. Beyond this, however, eschatological expectations were seldom talked about. After all, is not the kingdom realized even now through the brotherhood of the reborn? Thus, although the kingdom theology always has an eschatological slant, implying a philosophy of history, it nevertheless does not lead to unbalanced expectations such as chiliasm, adventism, millennialism, and the like.

The question may be raised whether or not the Anabaptist sources actually support this thesis of their kingdom theology. This kingdom theology was never systematically formulated by the Anabaptists; implicitly, however, it is very much there. Even as Jesus spoke mainly in parables, thus revealing His theological ideas but indirectly, so it is also with the Anabaptists. Very clear, even radical is their dualism concerning the two realms. Their disparagement and even fear of the world goes beyond that opposition which we would find in Paul's derogation of the flesh. While the latter leads to asceticism and celibacy, the Anabaptist dualism is of a rather different kind, requiring complete separation from the world as the realm of the prince of darkness. The Anabaptists, however, were not Puritans. The mere practice of purity of morals would mean little to them even though the idea of a "church without spot and wrinkle" is quite common with the Anabaptists. The Puritans certainly had one element of the kingdom theology, the strictness of discipline; but they lacked certain other elements, due to their Calvinistic outlook.

The terms most often used by Anabaptists are *Nachfolge* (discipleship) and *Gehorsam* (obedience); that is, the acceptance of Christ's leadership and that spirit which permeates His teachings. In short, their way of thinking and of evaluation is that of the kingdom theology, even though an explicit theology of this kind might not be so easily demonstrable. They felt absolutely certain that they were citizens of that other (spiritual) world here and now, and accepted the values, the outlook on history and the social consequences which follow with this position as a matter of course.

. . . .

The Position of Anabaptism on the Continuum of the Early Bourgeois Revolution in Germany

Gerhard Zschäbitz

The Marxist science of history has recognized in the class struggle of the so-called Reformation period an interconnected sequence of events, and has after careful analysis defined them as an early bourgeois revolution. No revolution has ever exhausted itself in single isolated acts or occurrences. Progressive social revolutions in turn represent processes which challenge historians to circumscribe and periodize them within the framework of the objective course of history. The revolutionary situation without which a revolution is impossible, and which grows out of an all-encompassing national crisis involving both exploiter and exploited, has to be staked out chronologically.

The theses put forth here attribute an extensive span to the early German bourgeois revolution. It ran from 1476 through an ascending phase of class struggles to a high point between 1517 and 1525. A descending period ends in 1535. According to this comprehensive view, there come to the fore indications of historical regularities and phasal development. These patterns, which lend themselves to analysis, are inherent in the complex of class struggles which we know as the early bourgeois revolution.

We assign the opening phase to the year 1476. At this time the first peasants' conspiracy of a mass character took place. Its extremely radical programme emerges in the penitential sermons of Hans Böhm of Niklashausen. In that same year the *Reformation Sigismundi* first appeared in print, after having previously circulated in seventeen manuscripts in the years succeeding 1438. Thus a reform plan which stimulated revolutionary thinking and forced numerous spontaneous conceptions into a determined direction became accessible to the broad masses. The *Bundschuh* conspiracies prior to 1517 already anticipated in their tendencies the alliances of the Great Peasants' War. In them peasants and urban plebeians united for revolutionary struggle, even though their efforts were as a whole inadequate. The demands of their programme were not limited to the interests of the peasants but took partial account of the circumstances of the city's poor and lower middle classes. They overcame, therefore, to a certain degree the limitation of medieval conceptions concerned with estates and regions. The early bourgeois revolution cannot be considered ended with the destruction of the peasants' army of South and Central Germany in the summer of 1525. The revolutionary situation was not yet eliminated. To be sure, the phase following the Peasants' War has been negligently treated with respect to the examination of its class struggles. Naturally, unless one takes into account the defense of the Anabaptist kingdom of Münster against princes and Empire, this phase does not exhibit such high drama as the Peasant's War. However, questions about the behaviour of the mass of the people in the face of the nearly complete victory of the princes should be of general historical interest.

After the Peasants' War revolutionary impulses continued to be lively among the masses—in changed form, to be sure, and adapted to the new situation of the terrible defeat. The embitterment of the masses appears to have been fed by the war-levies and fines that followed, by the continuing persecution, and the demand for reparation payments, which the monasteries raised into the mid-thirties and beyond. This resentment was also fed, no doubt, by the unqualified condemnation of the uprising by representatives of Lutheranism, from whom, at the beginning of the open struggle, the peasants had expected at least moral support, totally misjudging the class ties which made such support impossible. Especially this last point should not be ignored with respect to the religious-theological ferment of the masses in the waning Middle Ages. In so far as they learned more or less clearly to perceive the objective antagonism between themselves and the bourgeois Reformation they declined to support it. For many people, however, the content of their consciousness was rechannelled into the forms of a new heresy.

Vague hopes about a subsequent revision of the outcome of the uprising were maintained beyond 1525 through the Peasants' War in the Alps and the activity of Michael Gaismaier in Venetian and Swiss territory. Various conspiracies and putsch plans in South and Central Germany which occurred as late as 1528 must be seen as the aftermath of the revolutionary struggles. They remained isolated and without practical significance. Even though attractive radical activities were not entirely lacking, the active fighting spirit of the Peasants' War period as a whole could not persist. The military superiority of the victors was too great and the exhaustion of the masses too general.

The ideology of Anabaptism expresses the temper of the masses after the high point of the early bourgeois revolution. In spite of its extreme fragmentation and broad variation in argumentation as well as practical activity, Anabaptism shows coherent characteristics. Bourgeois historians exert a lot of effort to derive the origin of Anabaptism from purely religious motives, so as to disengage it from its social rootedness. They do not want to acknowledge that religious thinking is not an independent human attribute, but is in the last analysis the product of social conditioning in its broadest sense. No one will deny the extraordinary historical potency of religious ideology, particularly during the period of the Reformation. However, the receptivity of distinct sections of the populace for particularly nuanced teachings, the metamorphosis and further evolution of these teachings, as well as their reciprocal effect on the social base, can only be explained in terms of the contemporary class struggle, including, of course, a full consideration of the tradition of consciousness. In that bourgeois historians, led by their subjective perspectives, deny the historical restrictedness of all religious thinking, they make themselves, consciously or unconsciously, apologists for a dangerous political conservatism.

Until recently the Anabaptist movement has been treated with hostility by historians with confessional ties. In the wake of the prevailing tendency among Christian groups to play down doctrinal differences so as to form a united front against Marxism-Leninism, there is a disposition to give more favourable treatment to the early Anabaptists, to whom today's Mennonites appeal emphatically as their forefathers. In order to preserve a certain outward unanimity everything revolutionary is eliminated from a movement which was originally a spontaneous, although immature, expression of broad popular opposition. The radical wing was arbitrarily trimmed down in order to "prove" that the Anabaptist movement was loyal and peacefully disposed towards the existing authority structure from the very start. Radical or revolutionary manifestations were and are dismissed out of hand as not part of Anabaptism. A dogmatic probing rummages about among the interflowing, fermenting and groping behaviour that sprang forth out of a broad popular movement. Such scholarship classifies, rejects and selects what is "useful" according to external, often accidental rites and forms in an unscientific—one is tempted to say calculating—manner.

Likewise, the question of the regional origin of Anabaptism plays a not unimportant role. The characteristic Mennonite historical scholarship singled out Switzerland and South Germany, areas less affected by radicalism. From here the movement supposedly spread to the North and the East in purely religious form.

This simplifying point of view, derived from a history of ideas approach, distorts the historical facts. In Anabaptist teachings were concentrated the objective protests of all those who were disappointed by the practical outcome of the bourgeois Reformation and the result of the Peasants' War. Anabaptist teachings were not the only answer. Many persons resigned themselves and fled back to the bosom of the Old Church. After the Peasants' War Lutheranism could no longer rely upon the masses as its shock troops. Other people resentfully came to terms with the new conditions. Not a few, however, strove for new forms of communal thought and life and became a receptive sounding-board for teachings which were objectively in total contradiction to the ideology of the official church. The gradually developing, loosely organised Anabaptist movement consisted of crystalising cells, at first in the cities, spreading later to the countryside. Anabaptism, with its teachings, regulations for behaviour, opinions and standards of judgement, gave a sense of direction to the defeated anti-feudal opposition. To a certain extent, it formed the vanguard of the defeated anti-feudal opposition.

Through the study of court records it becomes evident that sympathies for Anabaptist teachings were very wide-spread, but this did not necessarily mean permanent membership in an Anabaptist congregation. The latter remained during the early period fluid creations without firmly outlined and solidified dogmas. Very often they stood and fell with personal ties to teachers or preachers, who exerted themselves to strengthen, spread and unify the fluctuating ideas. With respect to social origins, we encounter plebeians and representatives of the pre-proletariat, artisans of certain crafts, peasants, but also now and again representatives of the educated classes, all struggling for a new, organising ideology.

Ideological building blocks were provided from the repertoire of ideas of pre-Reformation heresies, which did not disappear as an undercurrent even during the turbulent high point of the Lutheran Reformation in 1520 and 1521. The teachings of the People's Reformation offered Anabaptism further stimulus. In several groups the influences of Zwingli and Carlstadt are identifiable. Arguments and even widely used slogans of the Peasants' War confront us. Even the teachings of Thomas Müntzer blend here and there with Anabaptist thinking, although they usually appear distorted and robbed of their political content. Anabaptism cannot, however, be directly or immediately connected with Thomas Müntzer's career.

The fundamental socio-political concerns of Anabaptist teaching were no longer in harmony with those of the period of the Peasants' War. Thomas Müntzer moved the masses to personal struggle for new social relations in harmony with God's will. A majority of Anabaptists in contrast endeavoured to ignore the "world," against which they believed that they could no longer openly struggle after the great defeat. The state as a product of evil was to be made superfluous through the conversion of all people to the true Christian life. Others fastened very temporal hopes on the immediate intervention of God for which they waited. They prepared themselves as "elect" for the day of the Lord within most exclusive communities. Not infrequently they sought to ascertain the point of time for the divine transformation from biblical and apocalyptical prophecies. Actual events were interpreted as signs of the return of Christ.

Undoubtedly this chiliastic type remained numerically a minority. Its social effectiveness, however, was considerably greater than that of the advocates of a passive self-sanctification. It offered a short term goal for popular longings and activated their revolutionary potential. However, the rejection of all socio-political structures (including ecclesiastical ones) which had been organised and dominated by the various governments is equally characteristic of the pervasive "peaceful" branch. That is the connecting, common, fundamental concern of all groups of Anabaptists.

Delayed baptism, the symbol of the movement, becomes, in spite of subjective Biblicist argumentation, an objective expression of resistance to church organisations linked to the government, by denying them the right to educate the people. This baptism is to be carried out within a community which has developed upon a voluntary foundation, into which the believer enters with full conciousness at the age of understanding, and whose disciplinary authority he acknowledges. The eucharist loses its magical character and becomes a memorial meal or a symbol of the believers' unitedness with Christ and one another. The governmentally-approved channels of priestly mediatorship are eliminated. The literal compliance with the words of the Bible amounts to more than a different intellectual interpretation. Within it there is incorporated the enmity against all representatives of official learning, who are addressed as scribes and enemies of God. As in the chiliasm of the Hussites, and even earlier, the direct illumination of the common man by God, who proclaims his will in dreams and miracles, now confronts arrogant erudition. The tendency to be in so far as possible independent of outside society plays an important role in the numerous attempts to approximate the example of apostolic communism through extensive mutual aid among the brothers and sisters. Over against the embryonic capitalistic structures early Anabaptism remained uncomprehending and defensive, since they brought nothing good to the simple people. Thus Anabaptist teachings had a conservative bent and oriented the believers toward simple manufacture with a touch of consumer communism. The rejection of the oath and of military service, the refusal of public offices, forms of expression later handed on as empty shells without content, originated from an objective opposition to the ruling authorities. Against the coercion of consciousness by the ruling class and its ideologues the Anabaptists asserted their own modes of behaviour and sought to justify them by an appeal to the Bible without human additions.

Admittedly, the relatively concrete intellectual high point attained in the course of open struggle could not be regained. Some groups placed their hopes on the Turks, who were addressed as God's instruments, and whose work of destruction they were willing to complete upon the command of God, in order to live united in a new kingdom with Christ. Chiliastic hopes, which were probably also widespread in Münster, led at times to changes in forms of matrimony; for, according to apocalyptical prediction, 144,000 believers were the prerequisite for the dawn of the divine judgement.

The latent enmity of early Anabaptism to the ruling powers, which to be sure manifested itself in very different modes, can be demonstrated from countless specific examples. How quickly the widespread pacifist standpoint could change into a fighting one under the influence of an admixture of chiliasm, is shown by the development in the Netherlands. Here the peaceful orientation of Melchior Hoffman was replaced within the shortest time by the religious militancy of Jan Matthijs. In the city of Münster the Netherlanders were also the most agile group, which pulled the others along with them. They made an essential contribution to the fact that the Anabaptist community could maintain itself for a year and a half under the most difficult circumstances. Anabaptist relief armies attempted to bring aid to the beleaguered city.

. . . .

These socio-religious ideologies which we summarise as "Anabaptist," originated at about the same time in the areas influenced by the Lutheran and Zwinglian Reformations. They amounted to a "similar answer" in an approximately analogous socio-political situation, even though—that must be emphasised again and again—in extraordinarily differentiated forms. The form of Anabaptism depended largely on the accident of which traditions of consciousness happened to be present. These ideologies were particularly widespread in the areas of the Europe of that period which were economically most developed, and in which the process of social differentiation had created a numerically strong class of plebeians and a large pre-proletariat.

. . . .

We just cannot use the term "Anabaptism" in a narrow sectarian sense. In it the spearhead of the anti-feudal opposition took concrete form after the Peasants' War. Its ideology was adapted to the diffuse and contradictory level of comprehension of the broad masses. While among several groups the tone of withdrawal from the world, the rejection of active struggle, dominated, others received impulses from old chiliastic and extreme spiritualistic traditions. Thus the Anabaptist movement constituted itself as a religio-social current with differentiated emphasis of the religious and social elements. Early Anabaptism became the collective reservoir of the manifold oppositional, radical and revolutionary responses to the revolution that had failed. These responses blended and jostled with each other for a definitive form. Thus Anabaptism produced an ideology of the poor, in which the traditions of the Peasants' War had a clear aftereffect and which contained latent within it the potential for another uprising.

The class struggles under the banner of Anabaptism have to be co-ordinated as a solid constituent within the continuum of the early bourgeois revolution, for whose fading phase there existed parallels in earlier popular movements as well as in the subsequent bourgeois revolutions.

After Münster, Anabaptism lost its revolutionary character even though the fall of the city did not signify a razor-sharp caesura. For one thing, the pressure of the authorities increased extraordinarily. Even more important was a change in social structure within the movement, which developed gradually, and through which the radical tendencies were pushed back. The ideological leadership passed to the lower middle classes. The embarassing plebeian elements appear to have been pushed aside by them. The asceticism that was preached, the rejection of public offices, etc., may have aided the economic rise of certain groups, who began, therewith, to stamp the character of the movement. Under the influence of Menno Simons and other preachers Anabaptism transformed itself into a genuine sect. It became reactionary, lost its socially disruptive force and subordinated itself in the following period, step by step, to political authority. There remained ritualistic traditions, originally historically determined products of the revolutionary situation, now no longer understood by the adherents. However, we recognise from the period of fading class struggles of the early bourgeois revolution, that already in bygone eras the masses, the real shapers of history, did not surrender to defeat without a struggle. Within the sphere of conceptions which was open to them, they continued the search for a new way out. Repulsed by the ideologies of the ruling class, they proved quite capable of forming their own conceptions, under whose banner they strove to continue the struggle.

Anabaptism: A Social History

Claus-Peter Clasen

THE MAJOR GROUPS

In all, twenty Anabaptist groups can be distinguished in our area. Only six of them, however, played roles of major importance: the Swiss Brethren, the followers of Hans Hut, the group that formed around Pilgram Marbeck, the Thuringian Anabaptists, the group that formed around Georg Schnabel, and the Hutterites. These six major groups held certain basic beliefs in common. They emphasized separation from the world and a life of discipleship. They believed that through the baptism of believers and the strict practice of excommunication it was possible to establish a congregation of pure Christians. They introduced a lay ministry. And they demanded the limitation of secular government to secular matters. But there were equally fundamental differences between these groups as well.

The Swiss Brethren distinguished themselves by their uncompromising stand in political matters: they scrupulously denied that a Christian might hold government office, swear an oath, sue in court, or fight in war. Unlike the Hutterites, who also took this position, they allowed themselves to own personal property. Emanating from Zurich, the Swiss Brethren dominated the Anabaptist movement in Switzerland and the valley of the upper Rhine, and spread to Swabia and Hesse. In Swabia, however, they encountered Anabaptist groups influenced by Hut, and did not get farther east than Augsburg. There were no Swiss congregations in Franconia, Thuringia, or Bavaria, but Swiss settlements existed in Moravia right up to the Thirty Years' War.

The second influential group originated with the Franconian bookseller Hans Hut, who had been deeply impressed by Müntzer's theology. Müntzer's view that the path to salvation led through bitter spiritual suffering lived on in Hut's Gospel of All Creatures. Possibly Hans Denck may also have influenced Hut's baptismal theology. Both regarded questions of government, oaths, and the use of weapons as externals of secondary importance. What distinguished Hut from other Anabaptist leaders was his fiery preaching on eschatological matters; he proclaimed that the Last Day would come in 1528. In spite of his special views, Hut looked on the Anabaptists in Switzerland as his fellow believers. Originating in northern Franconia near the Thuringian border, Hut's type of Anabaptism spread through Franconia during 1526–27, and through Bavaria, lower and upper Austria, Salzburg, and the Tirol in 1527. It reached into Swabia, but did not advance farther west than Esslingen. There were no Huttian congregations in the Rhine valley or Switzerland.

Pilgram Marbeck, the central figure in the third major group, rejected the rigid legalism of the Swiss Brethren. Love and faith, and not the letter of the Scripture, should guide the believer. Marbeck's friend Leupold Scharnschlager criticized the Swiss Brethren for constantly ordering the believers: "Wear not this"; "Wear not that." Nor could Marbeck's followers accept the Hutterite preaching that only those who shared their property would find the Savior. Though Marbeck and his followers agreed with Hut in placing love above laws and rules, they did not preach Hut's Gospel of All Creatures or Hut's explosive eschatology. They were distinguished from the Schnabel group in Hesse by their Christology: though Marbeck taught that one could not separate the humanity and deity of Christ, he clearly emphasized the humanity. Marbeck and his followers referred to themselves as the "Christ-believing allies and participants in the sadness which is Christ." Others simply called them Pilgramites. Owing to Marbeck's wanderings his followers can be discovered at Strasbourg and the Kinzig and Leber valleys in the 1530s and 1540s, possibly at Esslingen in 1544, at Graubünden and Augsburg from the 1540s to the 1560s, and again in the Leber valley in the 1560s and 1590s. In Moravia, Marbeck groups may already have existed in the 1530s and 1540s, and definitely existed in the second half of the sixteenth century. One group is mentioned at Austerlitz as late as 1617.

The fourth group, the Thuringian Anabaptists, were decisively set apart from other Anabaptist groups by the lingering influence of Thomas Müntzer. Hans Römer, the first Anabaptist leader in Thuringia, even made preparations for a new uprising, and some of Römer's followers still used Müntzer's liturgical writings. Müntzer's ideas also persisted among nonrevolutionary Anabaptists in Thuringia. Two believers in the area of Mühlhausen actually maintained that Müntzer had brought them to their faith; another embraced Müntzer's views on infant baptism, Christ's atonement, and inspiration. The leader Jakob Storger publicly declared that Müntzer had been one of the prophets predicted in the Revelation. Thuringian Anabaptism was also influenced by leaders from Franconia and Salzburg, by a disciple of Wolfgang Brandhuber in upper Austria, by Andreas Karlstadt, and possibly by the Zwickau prophets as well. The Anabaptists in the areas of Mühlhausen, Frankenhausen, and the Harz Mountains were extremely bitter, condemning infant baptism as a bath for dogs and pigs. Some used Karlstadt's interpretation of the Lord's Supper; others spoke of the hands of the priest as the flesh and blood under the elements. Some brethren cut bread into wine for the Lord's Supper. Others held a special view of the Trinity. In the area of Eisenach some brethren had a strong spiritualistic tendency, repudiated the resurrection of the body, spoke of marriage as an eternal spiritual estate, and held that drinking from the cup meant the shedding of one's blood. Outside of their theological views, the Thuringian Anabaptists were distinguished by social and political radicalism, which was more common in their group than in any other. In western Thuringia we find communistic tendencies in the environs of Zella St. Blasii in 1527 and Eisenach in 1537. The Anabaptists in Thuringia, then, cannot be classified as Swiss Brethren or followers of Hut or Marbeck, but must be considered a group in themselves. Thuringian Anabaptism appeared only in the area of Erfurt, Mühlhausen, Eisenach, Sangerhausen, and the Harz Mountains.

The fifth group, which formed around Georg Schnabel in Hesse, differed from the Swiss Brethren in that it recognized as Christian government, military service, and the swearing of oaths. It did not share the political radicalism of the Thuringian Anabaptists. The group held to Melchior Hofmann's doctrine of incarnation and believed that there was no forgiveness of sins against the Holy Ghost. In 1538 they also thought that the end of the world was near, though they did not preach Hut's eschatology, nor for that matter his Gospel of All Creatures. Two leaders of this group, Lienhart Fälber and Peter Tesch, had come from the duchy of Jülich, where Hofmann's doctrines had been preached. Tesch was strongly influenced by Hofmann, and may have introduced Schnabel to Hofmann's views on incarnation and perhaps also to his eschatological orientation. In any case Schnabel employed expressions that are characteristic of Hofmann. It is not clear, however, where Schnabel acquired his political views. The Schnabel group appeared only in Hesse, and only during the 1530s; we find Swiss Brethren in the same area during the second half of the sixteenth century.

The Hutterites, the sixth group, effected a profound social revolution by establishing communities in which all property was held in common and the family practically abolished, in spite of marriage. They were far less democratic than the other Anabaptist groups, establishing an authoritarian hierarchy. Though their communities were situated in Moravia, the Hutterites were active in a larger area than any other group. They roused powerful movements in the Tirol, Swabia, and Hesse, and also sent missionaries into the Rhine valley, Bavaria, and Switzerland. Only Franconia and Thuringia remained largely untouched by their influence.

During the second half of the sixteenth century, the Hutterites, the Swiss Brethren, and to a smaller extent Marbeck's followers were the only important groups in Germany, Switzerland, and Austria. Hut's followers, the Thuringian Anabaptists, and Schnabel's followers had disappeared. In Hesse the Schnabel group collapsed owing to the defection of its leaders; in Thuringia, Franconia, and Bavaria, Anabaptism was simply suppressed by the governments.

. . . .

THE ANABAPTISTS AND THE PEASANTS UPRISING

If the Anabaptists did not cause the [peasants] uprising [of 1524–1525], it is possible that the ideas and the spirit of the rebellious peasants lived on in the Anabaptist movement. Anabaptism is often regarded as a continuation of the Peasants' War. Indeed, in many areas where the peasants had risen in 1525, Anabaptism found numerous adherents in the next ten years: Zurich; Bern; Basel; St. Gallen; and Tirol; upper Austria; the bishoprics of Salzburg, Würzburg, Bamberg, and Speyer; Württemberg; Alsace, the Palatinate; the border areas of Hesse, Saxony, Hersfeld, and Fulda; and in Thuringia the areas of Erfurt, Mühlhausen, and Frankenhausen. The geographical evidence is not entirely satisfying, however. Upper Swabia and parts of Franconia, such as the areas of Rothenburg and Mergentheim, had been centers of the uprising in 1525, but during the following years very few Anabaptists appeared there. Conversely, there had been no uprising in 1525 in Bavaria, lower Austria, and the central districts of Hesse, yet within a few years Anabaptism had gained a wide following in these areas. Could it not have been mere coincidence, then, that the peasant uprising and the spread of Anabaptism occurred in some of the same places? Since both the uprising and the Anabaptist movement affected large areas of Switzerland, the Tirol and south and central Germany, it was inevitable that there would be some overlapping of the regions involved. Perhaps more to the point, during the first ten years Anabaptism was largely centered in cities, that had not been involved in the uprising. The geographical evidence, then, at best suggests a certain connection between the peasant uprising and Anabaptism; in no way can it be considered proof.

Thirty-two Anabaptists are known to have taken part in the peasant uprising, some evidence indicates five more. We may be certain, however, that there were more than 37 Anabaptists who had been involved in the uprising. In Franconia, eastern Hesse, and Thuringia alone, 24 ex-rebels were converted to Anabaptism, three of them, Hans Hut, Melchior Rinck, and Hans Römer, were to play an important role in the movement. Even so, there is no evidence that rebels became Anabaptists in great numbers.

Why should peasants who had participated in the uprising have been attracted by Anabaptism? The demands of the peasants and the doctrines of the Anabaptists had almost nothing in common. The peasants were motivated not by an abstract religious principle, such as putting into practice the Sermon on the Mount, but by a desire for social and economic change. Although the Twelve Articles contained references to the Scriptures, they did not derive from the Scriptures; the social doctrines of the Anabaptists, on the other hand, derived directly from the literal interpretation of the New Testament. To be sure, both the peasants and the Anabaptists stipulated that pastors be elected by the congregation. But whereas the peasants demanded rights and power, the Anabaptists rejected the notion of rights and power altogether. If the peasants hated individual princes and officials, they never for a moment thought of rejecting, as the Anabaptists did, all governments, courts of law, capital punishment, weapons, and oaths. Political power in itself was not unchristian to the peasants' way of thinking; it had only fallen into the wrong hands. For their part, the Anabaptists did not care who held power or whether that power was justly or unjustly wielded. Government was unchristian not because the burdens it imposed on the peasants were too heavy, but because it was an expression of force—in short, because it was government. If the peasants had seized power in 1525 and put into effect each of the Twelve Articles, the Anabaptists would still have cursed their government as unchristian.

The peasants and the Anabaptists worked on quite different principles, then, and pursued quite different social aims. . . .

Recent Marxist historians have maintained that the peasants joined the Anabaptists because they were disillusioned after their terrible defeat in 1525. . . .

While in some areas the peasants' anger against the government may have contributed to the advance of Anabaptism, there is no evidence to support the Marxist theory that after their defeat the peasants were plunged into hopeless despair and therefore found the Anabaptist doctrine of withdrawal from the world attractive. On the contrary, most peasants stayed squarely in the world. For example, the peasants in the territory of Speyer, who had fiercely fought their rulers in 1525, continued to quarrel bitterly with the Chapter during the following ten years. In the village of Bauerbach the peasants unilaterally rejected the Chapter's rights, refused to pay taxes, held back dues in kind, cut down a forest in order to finance the suits they brought against the government, pestered the government official until he entered a monastery, and violated the mandates by engaging in archery. During these same years, and in spite of government persecution, Lutheranism advanced rapidly in the villages of Speyer. This fact invalidates further the Marxist theory that after Luther's betrayal in 1525 the peasants were no longer interested in Lutheranism. From the late 1520s onward, Anabaptism also began to appear in the area, and particularly at Bauerbach. The mentality of the Anabaptists contrasted strongly with the restless mood of most peasants. Instead of insisting on their rights, they gathered in small groups to read the New Testament and pray. When threatened by persecution some set out under the cover of night for Moravia; arrested, they let themselves be executed without resistance. Of course, the terrible defeat and slaughter of the peasants in 1525 might have shaken some so badly that they sought comfort in excessive piety. These people may indeed have been receptive to the Anabaptist message of withdrawal. They were exceptions, however, for most peasants were by no means so sensitive.

Thus the evidence—geographic, numerical, ideological, and psychological—does not show a link between the peasant uprising and the Anabaptist movement.

. . . .

PERSECUTION

Whereas all Catholic and Protestant governments concurred in the policy of suppressing Anabaptism, their methods varied. First, in many Catholic territories, especially Bavaria and the Tirol, the death penalty remained the standard punishment for steadfast Anabaptists up to the Thirty Years' War. In the Protestant territories and cities, ordinary Anabaptists who refused to recant were usually expelled, and leaders imprisoned. Lutheran Saxony and the Zwinglian cities of Switzerland, which executed Anabaptists, were exceptions. Second, the legal charges used against Anabaptists by different governments were not quite the same. Catholic governments charged Anabaptists with heresy and rebellion; Luther's Saxony similarly charged them with blasphemy and rebellion. The Swiss cities, however, sentenced them to death for violating the civil laws.

Third, the legal proceedings were different. Courts of summary jurisdiction were used only by Catholic authorities, such as those in Austria, Salzburg, Bavaria, and the Swabian League in 1527 and 1528. Mass executions of a dozen or more Anabaptists were perpetrated only by Catholic governments. And only Catholic governments ever executed Anabaptists who had recanted. By contrast, the Protestant governments typically used all the persuasive powers at their command to win the sectarians back to the established church. At no time did any Protestant government pass the sentence of death on an Anabaptist who had abandoned his views. Finally, the difference between Protestant and Catholic policy toward the Anabaptists is borne out by the numerical evidence: 84 percent of all executions were perpetrated in Catholic territories, and only 16 percent in territories and cities that were Protestant or had Protestant leanings.

The severe methods used by the Catholic governments undoubtedly produced more successful results than the milder measures of the Protestant governments. In Catholic Austria, Salzburg, and Bavaria, Anabaptism was practically eliminated in 1527 and 1528. In the Tirol the mass executions achieved their aim by the middle of the sixteenth century. In Protestant Württemberg, Hesse, and the Palatinate, by contrast, Anabaptism flourished up to the Thirty Years' War.

In the long run, however, the refusal of most Protestant governments to put Anabaptists to death was much more significant than the success of the Catholic governments' harsher policy, for the German Protestants had unknowingly taken a decisive step toward religious toleration. It is unrealistic to expect the bloody intolerance of the late Middle Ages to have given way overnight to the universal religious toleration of nineteenth-century Germany: indeed, the evolution of religious toleration took centuries. But the step from executing heretics to letting them live was an essential one, even if the death sentence was replaced by expulsion. After all, the great dividing line is that between life and death: it was during the sixteenth century that most Protestant governments in the Empire chose life for the heretic. By focusing only on the views of the Reformers and disregarding the actual policy of the governments and the statistical evidence, most twentieth-century historians who have dealt with the subject, such as Ernst Troeltsch, Joseph Lecler, and Henry Kamen, have failed to grasp the role of the Reformation in the development of religious toleration.

. . . .

NUMERICAL STRENGTH

Let us assume that in the course of almost a hundred years, from 1525 to 1618, Anabaptism did indeed attract about thirty thousand persons in our area—an average of three thousand persons every ten years, or three hundred every year. Considering that we are now dealing with an enormous area, comprising south and central Germany, Switzerland, and Austria, an area that in the sixteenth century was inhabited by millions of people, three thousand new Anabaptists every ten years is really a modest figure. The sixteen hundred Anabaptists known to us in the Tirol from 1526 to 1550 constituted only 0.4 percent of the total population of 375,000. In the duchy of Württemberg, which had 400,000 to 450,000 inhabitants, the Church Council of 1570 listed 129 Anabaptists, or a mere 0.03 percent of the population.

To be sure, at certain times the sect was concentrated in certain areas. But even at Augsburg only about 1.2 percent of the population became Anabaptists between 1526 and 1528, and Augsburg had the largest Anabaptist congregation in the Empire! From 1527 to 1530 the Anabaptists at Esslingen constituted between 1 and 2 percent of the population. Only in a few villages did a larger proportion of the people accept Anabaptism: at Urbach in Württemberg as many as 9 percent of the villagers seem to have been involved with the sect between 1590 and 1609.

The number of towns and villages affected by Anabaptism might give a better indication of the strength of the movement. From 1525 to 1618 Anabaptists appeared in at least 1,821 towns and villages—an enormous number indeed. In the duchy of Württemberg, for example, Anabaptists were to be found in one-fourth to one-fifth of all communities. In most of these 1,821 communities, however, the sect appeared for only a very short time. In 78 communities Anabaptists appeared for a span of ten years; in only fourteen communities, for twenty years; and in exceedingly few communities for thirty or more years. At Augsburg, Anabaptism existed almost without interruption from 1526 to 1573, but Augsburg was an exception. In not a single community did Anabaptists appear for more than fifty years.

The number of believers in an individual community was also very modest. In only five towns and villages in Switzerland, Germany, and Austria did more than a hundred persons become Anabaptists between 1525 and 1618; in another 36, 31 to 100 persons became Anabaptists. These 41 towns and villages were in fact nuclei of the movement, which radiated out into the surrounding area. However, the communities with more than thirty Anabaptists constituted only 2.2 percent of all towns and villages affected, and in the course of the sixteenth century, the number of communities with large Anabaptist congregations declined. In 5.8 percent of all communities affected, ten to thirty persons joined the sect; in 9.2 percent, five to nine persons; and in 67 percent, fewer than five persons. In other words, in 76 percent of all towns and villages affected by Anabaptism, fewer than ten persons accepted the new doctrines in the course of almost a century! Anabaptism may have spread to a very large number of communities, but for the most part it appealed to an extremely small number of persons in a given community.

Why should Anabaptism have taken this particular form of expansion? Some leaders, such as Hans Hut, deliberately set out to spread their doctrines in as many villages as possible. Frequently government persecution prevented the leaders from staying in a place for a longer period of time and establishing larger congregations. Above all, the peculiar nature of the Anabaptist message—its strange political doctrines and excessive religious and moral demands—seem to have appealed to only a few. A leader was more likely to find one follower in a great number of communities than many followers in only one. Government persecution and the limited appeal of Anabaptism also explain why Anabaptism was able to maintain itself in most towns and villages for a short time only.

This evidence raises the question whether Anabaptism may realistically be described as a Radical Reformation—"a tremendous movement at the core of Christendom," which according to George H. Williams had the same impact on modern European society as the Magisterial Reformation, the Counter Reformation, Renaissance Humanism, and Nationalism. The term Reformation would certainly imply that large numbers of people were involved, as happened in numerous towns that adopted the Lutheran or Zwinglian Reformation. For example, at Schwäbisch Hall and Reutlingen, the massed burghers literally drove the town council into adopting the Lutheran reform, and at Ulm and Esslingen an overwhelming number of burghers voted in referendums for the new belief. But nowhere, with the possible exception of the Tirol, did large numbers of people flock to the Anabaptists. In all other areas where Anabaptist leaders preached, most towns and villages were never affected by the sect at all. And of the towns and villages that were affected, 76 percent had no more than ten Anabaptists in the course of three or four generations. The Spiritualists and Evangelical Rationalists, who are said to have formed the other two major divisions of the Radical Reformation, had even fewer followers. From a quantitative point of view, then, the Anabaptist movement was so insignificant that it is misleading to use the term Reformation at all. Anabaptism was no more than a small separatist movement.

. . . .

CONCLUSION

The Anabaptists had no discernible impact on the political, economic, or social institutions of their age. It was a fantasy to hope that love could take the place of law and government. The Anabaptist doctrine that government must not interfere in religious affairs was not adopted by any government of the period. It is also questionable whether the Anabaptists really influenced the modern notion of separation of church and state, which developed in the Anglo-Saxon countries during the seventeenth and eighteenth centuries. The rejection of interest on loans by all Anabaptist groups, and commerce by some, could not stave off the growing commercialisation of the sixteenth-century economy; of course, the more radical communism of the Hutterites had even less effect. Similarly, the Anabaptists had little, if any, influence on sixteenth-century culture. To be sure, some of their treatises and hymns reveal religious insight and powers of expression, but there is no evidence that these works circulated outside of Anabaptist circles. While the humanistic ideal of learning and elegance prevailed in both Catholic and Protestant Germany, higher education and aesthetic culture were angrily condemned by the brethren. Indeed, the Anabaptists in south and central Germany, Switzerland, and Austria already exhibited in the sixteenth century a cultural primitivism that has characterized some Anabaptist groups down to our own day.

We cannot deny that the Anabaptists displayed intense, genuine piety and outstanding moral vigor. The Hutterites also showed extraordinary organizational talent in creating an entirely new type of society. Yet these phenomena must be kept in proper perspective. However fascinating the Anabaptist movement was, it cannot be called more than a minor episode in the history of sixteenth-century German society.

Anabaptism and the Reformation

The Left Wing of the Reformation

Roland H. Bainton

The Protestant movement of the sixteenth century tended to fall apart, not only as a result of a process of disintegration, but also because of an initial divergence. The disintegration was due to the breakup of a number of forces momentarily allied by Luther's attack upon indulgences: the humanists, who regarded indulgences as a silly superstition; the German nationalists, who saw in the traffic an example of Roman extortion; and the common folk, who recognized in themselves the sheep to be sheared. All united around the reformer for whom indulgences were a monstrous blasphemy. But in a few years the differences in their points of view became apparent. . . .

. . . .

. . . If one speaks of a right and a left wing of the Reformation, the question at once arises as to the location of the body to which the wings are attached. If the sacraments constitute the norm, then Luther and the Anglicans in the main are on the right; with Zwingli, Calvin, and the Anabaptists on the left. If church organization be the test, then the Episcopal churches are on one side, with the Presbyterian and Congregational on the other. If doctrine is the line of demarcation, the Trinitarians and anti-Trinitarians can be divided. If the union of the church and state is the criterion, then Lutherans, Zwinglians, Calvinists, and Anglicans are all on one side, with the Anabaptists and other spiritual reformers on the left.

This last line of demarcation is primary for this discussion. The left wing is composed of those who separated church and state and rejected the civil arm in matters of religion. These groups are commonly on the left also with regard to church organization, sacraments, and creeds. An attempt will be made to describe the main notes of this more radical reformation.

Specifically, the groups I have in mind in rough chronological order are: first, the Zwickau prophets, who commenced a ferment of disintegration by introducing highly individualistic norms of authority; then, Thomas Muentzer, a weird combination of medieval mysticism, sectarianism, and social revolution; next, the Swiss Anabaptists, who, in their effort to restore especially the moral quality of primitive Christianity, ended by severing the connection of the church with the community as a whole, and particularly with the state; thereafter, the Melchiorites, who, under the pressure of persecution, turned to extravagant eschatology, as did the Muensterites to violent revolution; the Mennonites in the Netherlands, who repudiated such aberrations, and returned to the sobriety of their Swiss forerunners; the Hutterian Brethren in Moravia, who adopted religious communism; the Schwenckfelders, who, independently of other groups, sought to recapture the piety of the early church; and the Socinians, who were characterized alike by social, religious, and intellectual radicalism. The following discussion seeks to delineate the main ideas which appear and reappear in varying combinations among these groups.

I

The first note was ethical. The primary defect in the Lutheran Reformation according to the radicals was moral. The Reformation had not produced an adequate transformation of life. The Lutheran was not distinguishable from the Catholic at the point of conduct. Some of these critics laid the blame at the door of the doctrine of justification by faith with consequent disparagement of good works and of the doctrine of predestination with its severing of the nerve of moral effort. Others among the radicals perceived that these doctrines were not so much responsible, since justification, if genuine, would issue in sanctification, and a belief in predestination would stimulate the moral efforts of those who thought of themselves as the elect. The fault, according to these radicals, lay rather in the theory of the church, as including all members of the community by virtue of infant baptism rather than on the basis of inner conviction and moral fruits.

These critics were resuscitating an ancient conflict by which the church had long been tormented. Should the church be thought of primarily in terms of leaven, or of light? Should it think of itself as a body commissioned to permeate all society even at the risk of losing its own purity, or rather as a light set upon a hill to influence the world by example rather than by participation? The one concept has been characterized by Troeltsch as that of the church and the other as that of the sect. The one tends to be Augustinian and the other Pelagian. The one is commonly sacramental, the other moral. The one believes in the church catholic and the other in the church holy. In the early period Augustine represented the former and the Donatists the latter. In the fourth century, as in the sixteenth, this difference as to the composition and role of the church in society led the one group to unite church and state and to justify religious persecution, and the other to separate the two and to deny the competence of the magistrate in the sphere of religion. The very term "Anabaptist" was fastened upon persons, preferring to call themselves Baptists, by their opponents, who sought thus to identify them with the ancient Donatists, who also repeated baptism and likewise separated church and state.

II

A second note of the left wing was Christian primitivism. The church must be patterned after the primitive movement—back to Jesus, back even to Abraham. This is a note which commonly characterizes reformatory movements. . . . Such primitivism commonly marks the sect and leads its advocates into separation from any church which claims to be so guided by the spirit as to be in a position to set aside ancient practices in the light of new conditions. The Catholic, Lutheran, and Anglican churches have frankly taken this view. Zwinglianism and Calvinism have had much more of the primitive note, which explains why Anabaptism arose out of Zwinglianism and why Calvinism has had so many inner conflicts.

Primitivism admits of varying degrees and qualities. There is the chronological question of how far to go back. Luther was in favor of sloughing off the corruptions of the papacy. For him the fall of the church occurred under Boniface III in the seventh century, when supposedly the temporal power of the papacy had its rise. The Anglicans set the fall after the fourth ecumenical council. Everything previous for them could be regarded as normative. This view incidentally was the starting-point for both Newman and Kingsley. The one endeavored to show that medieval Catholicism could be discovered in germ in the first four centuries, and Kingsley, on the other hand, in *Hypatia,* tried to prove that the fourth century itself was an age of corruption and the fall must be set still further back. The Reformation sectaries found the dividing line in the age of Constantine, because at that time the union of church and state, to which they so strenuously objected, occurred. Others, still more radical, claimed that the gospel was corrupted immediately after the days of the apostles and that the Bible alone could be regarded as the true pattern.

But how much of the Bible? Only the New Testament, or the Old Testament as well? Some were New Testament literalists and endeavored to restore the gospel pattern by reviving the discipline of Matthew, chapter 18, the religious communism of Acts, the nonresistance and no-swearing of the Sermon on the Mount, as well as foot-washing and immersion. Old Testament literalists revived the polygamy and other immoralities of the patriarchs, as well as the eccentricities of the prophets. In imitation of Isaiah (20:3), who "walked naked and barefoot for a sign," some of the Amsterdam Anabaptists went naked through the streets, and one of their leaders, mindful of Isa. 6:6, took a hot coal from off the hearth and touched his lips, with the result that he could scarcely talk for a fortnight. Such aberrations, however, were not characteristic of the movement.

Literalism was not the dominant note, but the recovery of the spirit of the apostles. The restoration of primitive Christianity and the spiritual new birth were practically synonymous for the Anabaptists. The gift of the spirit which they craved had a twofold function: to produce, on the one hand, moral transformation and, on the other, to give religious knowledge. Here lay the root of the distinction between the outer and the inner word. The letter of the Scripture, said the champions of the inner word, will convince only the convinced. To understand the apostles we must be in the spirit of the apostles. Otherwise Scripture is nothing more than paper and ink. The Reformers, such as Luther, Zwingli, and Calvin, who relied on the outer word, were stigmatized as *Schriftgelehrten,* which cannot be rendered with a single term in English. The word means literally "those who are versed in scripture." It is also the translation of the biblical "scribe." Hence the woes against the scribes could be hurled against the biblical literalists, and biblical scholarship was derided as human learning.

The disciples of the inner word sometimes turned to mysticism and sometimes to communications of the spirit in dreams and visions which in turn became so bizarre and contradictory that the norm of the outer word had to be revived as a check. The problem of the inner and outer word, however, did not rend Anabaptism as much as might have been expected, because such programs as nonresistance, no-swearing, and religious communism could be justified on both grounds.

III

Another note characteristic of the left wing was a heightened sense of eschatology. This could easily be derived from the Bible. Those who pored over the Gospels and the Book of Revelation could hardly miss it. All the Reformers were steeped in the Scriptures and all were affected by a sense of the imminence of the end. Yet there were degrees. As for the second coming

Luther thought soon, Müntzer now, Calvin by-and-by. In the interim all were ready to essay greater or less social reform. The sects were more congenial to eschatology than the established churches.

. . . .

Eschatology in some rare instances passed into a program of revolution. Strictly speaking, the two are incompatible. Eschatology believes in an imminent divine event to shatter the present scheme of history and to be inaugurated without the hand of man. Revolution depends upon human instruments. But the one idea can readily pass into the other. If the Lord tarries, man becomes impatient and begins to argue that the prelude to the divine catastrophe is the putting of the sickle to the harvest by the hand of the human reaper. A similar ideological incompatibility has characterized the Marxian dialectic.

. . . .

This brings us to the note of anti-intellectualism. Even those of the left wing who had had a humanist training were indisposed to finespun theological speculations. In this respect they were in part the heirs of the *Devotio moderna* and Erasmus or of the spiritual Franciscans. Likewise the cult of the inner word centered on the recovery of the radiance of the gospel and eschewed the speculations of Nicaea. A favorite figure among the anti-intellectuals was the penitent thief who was saved without any knowledge of the substance and persons of the Godhead, paedo-baptism, consubstantiation, transubstantiation, predestination, election, reprobation, etc. The criticism of dogma as inimical to the life of the spirit passed very easily, however, into acute refutation of particular tenets and thus developed into a radical intellectualism.

. . . .

IV

The left wing was united in its demand for the separation of church and state. Government was ruled out of the sphere of religion. Heretics should not be constrained, for if they be brought into the church against their will, the result will be as if water were poured into a barrel low in wine. The rise in quantity will be offset by the dilution of the quality. Constraint cannot engender the religion of the Spirit and may rather disintegrate the moral integrity of the man who saves his life by repudiating his convictions. Executions do not establish doctrines. "To burn a man is not to prove a doctrine, but to burn a man." Moreover, the doctrines for which the burning is done are the least certain because precisely the most controverted. Let us then leave judgment to God, remembering that the wolves may be distinguished from the sheep by this mark alone, that the one rends and other is rent.

The exclusion of the magistrate from the sphere of religion, however, did not determine the extent of his right within his own domain. Here the problem was to reconcile the teaching that the "powers that be are ordained of God" (Rom. 13:1) and "resist not evil" (Matt. 5:39). Luther's solution was an initial dichotomy between a Christian society, in which no constraint is necessary, and the world from which force cannot be eliminated. Christ ruled only with a staff because he was only a shepherd of sheep, but the ruler of wolves and lions must be better armed. May a Christian, however, be a ruler of wolves and lions? Luther, at this point, demolished the dichotomy by the answer: "Yes, out of love for those who are not sufficiently advanced to relinquish force. The magistrate is ordained of God and the Christian may be a magistrate." "Resist not evil" applies only to private ethics, or in the case of the magistrate to an inner disposition.

But the radicals, at this point, were more outward than Luther. They recognized that the ruler is ordained of God, but only among non-Christians. God has a concern for justice and order even in the world, but the world and the church do not mix. The Christian must not participate in or avail himself of the aids of government. He has to be as a sheep for the slaughter.

With regard to the attitude toward society, the term "inner-worldly asceticism" applies in some measure to all Protestants. They differed in the degrees of their asceticism and of co-operation with secular institutions, but all stood with Luther in his repudiation of monasticism. The Catholic church had found a resolution for the antinomy of the church catholic and the church holy by segregating a special group to keep intact the ideal of holiness—namely, the monks. In the late Middle Ages the quality of monasticism had declined. Luther repudiated the whole institution and invested secular occupations with religious significance as divine callings. The precepts of the gospel had then to be worked out within the framework of society.

Protestants varied in the rigor of their interpretation of the gospel and in the degree to which they were prepared to attempt a realization within the framework of the world. Luther indorsed such an attempt within the domestic and political areas but was shy of the economic. Calvin gave his approval to all three but was more ascetic with regard to the program to be realized. The Anabaptists accepted the domestic area, repudiated the political, and went halfway with the economic. In all, they were as ascetic, if not more so, than Calvin. The communism of the Anabaptists draws our particular attention. It was Lutheran in its desire to avoid mendicancy and Franciscan in its determination to avoid luxury. It was practiced, in accord with Lutheranism, on a family rather than a celibate basis. Thus the Anabaptists, while simplifying their problem through withdrawal from the political sphere, were involved in the domestic and economic areas in the common Protestant difficulty of standing ready to follow Jesus in selling all and forsaking wife and child, while at the same time marrying and rearing families on a property basis.

V

The left wing of the Reformation was for long neglected by the historians of the Reformation who were dominated by confessional interests and preferred to investigate the groups to which they themselves belonged rather than to delve into the records of a lost cause. In recent years, however, the historians of Lutheranism and Calvinism have become increasingly aware that an understanding of their own movements is impossible apart from a grasp of the currents to which they were opposed. A deeper reason for seeking to understand the left wing, in my judgment, is that here we can discover one clue among others to the spiritual cleavage between Germany and the "West." In Germany in the sixteenth century Anabaptism and related movements were thoroughly suppressed and never again raised their heads, whereas in England in the seventeenth century the spiritual descendants of the left wing gained a permanent foothold and did even more than the established church to fashion the temper of England and America.

Anabaptism and the Reformation: Another Look

Hans J. Hillerbrand

It has by and large been characteristic of the current resurgence of Anabaptist studies to understand the Anabaptist movement as an integral part of the Reformation. Thus the two terms presently used to designate the framework of the radical dissent of the 16th century—Roland H. Bainton's now classic "Left Wing" and, more recently, George H. Williams' "Radical Reformation"—suggest a positive relationship with the mainstream Reformation. There is widespread consensus among scholars, particularly in America, that Anabaptism concurred with the Reformation on the major points of Protestant doctrine and dissented merely on secondary issues, such as baptism, the church, or political authority, around which centered indeed most of the theological polemics between the Anabaptists and the Reformers. The fact that many Anabaptists affirmed agreement with the Reformers in all essential doctrines could be cited as case in point. Furthermore, it will be remembered that all of the early Anabaptists had at one time been ardent followers of the Reformers, but had become dissatisfied with the slowness and seeming haphazardness of the reform of the church undertaken by their masters. Such dependence was well expressed by Conrad Grebel, who purportedly said that it had been Zwingli who "had led him into this thing."

Historically and theologically the correlate to such a view of Anabaptism is the assumption that it was among the Anabaptists that the Reformation was brought to its proper conclusion, since they undertook the return to Biblical religion with greater consistency than the Reformers, who were half-hearted compromisers without the courage to break with cultural ties and social considerations. Such was the picture which the Anabaptists drew of the Reformation. . . .

It is obvious that such an understanding of Anabaptism necessitates at once a reassessment of the Reformation at large. For no other reason than a dissatisfaction with this necessity, the question may be raised if it is altogether mandatory to see Anabaptism as the consistent completion of the Reformation. . . .

. . . [A] further inquiry into the relationship of Anabaptism and the Reformation is, therefore, perhaps not altogether beside the point. Such an inquiry will be attempted in the present paper. It will take the approach of a comparative analysis of the concept of justification held by Reformers and Anabaptists, which will be introduced with brief references to the problems of free will and original sin. Though such a shortening of the Reformatory principle may be questioned, its legitimacy for our purposes can be argued. For justification was the *articulus stantis et cadentis ecclesiae*, the article which—as Luther said—"keeps and rules all teachings of the church and raises up our conscience in God's presence." That the Anabaptist understanding of justification is distinct from that of the Reformers has indeed been suggested by some scholars, though no detailed analysis has been presented.

It is not the contention of this paper that its conclusions are uniformly applicable to all expressions of Anabaptism or that no contrary evidence could be cited. It is suggested, however, that our evidence is representative of a fairly large segment of the movement which must not be overlooked in any appraisal. Perhaps Anabaptism is far less homogeneous than recent scholarship has taken for granted. Indeed, such emphasis on the uniformity of the movement, once the revolutionaries had been relegated outside, fails to account satisfactorily for the complexity and embarrassing over-abundance of Anabaptist sources, where statements of outstanding leaders and simple fellow-travellers are painfully intermingled. Yet any appraisal of Anabaptist thought must give due recognition to this complex evidence. The wide variation of belief among Anabaptists is also brought out by the lengthy lists of Anabaptist sects which contemporary chroniclers compiled. Perhaps this was polemical overstatement, but in-group evidence of divisive tendencies within the movement is not altogether lacking. Sebastian Franck's comment is thus perhaps both a description of the actual situation and also a word of caution for all scholars—including the present writer—who so persistently attempt to fit Anabaptism into a generalized mold: "though all sects are divided among themselves, the Anabaptists are especially divided and torn apart so that I cannot write anything certain and definite about them."

Basic for the Reformatory understanding of justification is an anthropology which asserts, with radical pessimism, the bondage of the human will and the reality of original sin. Luther, in his controversy with Erasmus, affirmed man's freedom only in the *res inferiora* of life; in spiritual matters man is not free, he is passive, "a beast standing between two riders." The doctrine of justification held by the Reformers consequently repudiates the medieval system of divine and human cooperation in the act of justification which is *sola gratia Dei*. Whereas medieval Christianity had juxtaposed divine grace with man's free assent and active cooperation, Luther began with the *agnitio peccati*, the recognition of one's utter sinfulness as the will of God, and held that justification takes place *propter Christum per fidem*—the sinner is justified solely through trust in Christ's perfect obedience. Man is converted, as Paul Althaus has recently insisted, from unbelief to faith, and not merely from ethical laxity to moral earnestness or from the rejection of God's commandments to their obedience.

. . . .

On the other hand, Luther, particularly, never ceased to view the Christian life as a continuous tension and constant struggle between obeying and disobeying God, between doing the good and doing the evil. Sin both stays on and does not stay on. Thus Luther calls for a continuous fight against sin to overcome it. Man, even though justified, remains sinful: *Peccandum est*. Even the *homo renatus* is a sinner. Thus Melanchthon's *Loci* of 1521 know of a beginning, but not of an end of the process: "In the doing of the justified there is always something impure, which does not deserve the name righteousness." The graphic dualism *simul iustus et peccator* describes the Christian who is at once completely justified and completely a sinner. Perfection is to be sought only in a deeper and more profound realization of one's sinfulness. Man finally becomes perfect, Luther wrote, "and willingly gives his life for death and desires with Paul to depart so that all sin ceases and God's will is most perfectly done in him." For the Reformers the seventh chapter of Romans describes the life of the Christian. Thus the *Schmalkald Articles* in speaking about repentance affirm that it "continues among Christians until death, for it struggles with carnal sin throughout life as Paul testifies in Romans 7." The concept of *conversion* is, therefore, not so integral to the thought of the Reformers as it is to that of the Anabaptists.

We turn now to the position of the Anabaptists. Their view concerning *free will* is, in a way, self-evident, as the emphasis on following Christ as voluntary disciples presupposes the deliberate and conscious choice of man to do so. Sebastian Franck described the Anabaptist understanding succinctly when he said of them: "They hold free will as self-evident." Some of the most pronounced Anabaptist statements came from the South German Anabaptist leader Balthasar Hubmaier, who in 1527 devoted two works to the problem of free will, possibly as an Anabaptist commentary on the Erasmus-Luther controversy of two years earlier. Entitled "On Free Will" and "The Second Booklet on Free Will" these tracts set out to repudiate the "erroneous half-truth" that we cannot do anything good, God works in us the willing and doing, we have no free will. For Hubmaier "it is clear and evident what rubbish that they all have introduced into Christendom who deny the freedom of will in man." Man, who consists of body, soul, and spirit, is not totally depraved. The spirit of man has "remained utterly upright and intact." Indeed even the soul of man, which through the disobedience of Adam was maimed, has acquired again its lost freedom through the Word of God "which teaches us anew to will or not to will what is good and what is evil." The soul "has recovered its lost freedom. It can now freely and willingly be obedient to the spirit and can will and choose the good, just as though it were in paradise." Underlying Hubmaier's argument is obviously his concern that man, out of his own responsibility, freely accepts or rejects God's salvation. He illustrates his point with the example of a master who exhorts his servants to run that they may win a prize. The master would not do this, Hubmaier suggests, if he knew that his servants are incapable of running and tied in chains. Since man is exhorted by Law to do good it can be similarly said that he must be able to do it.

The South German Anabaptist Hans Denck also expressed the view that man can distinguish between good and evil and make his own free decision on what to follow. Denck's tract *Was geredt sey das die Schrifft sagt Gott thue vnd mache guts vnd böses* of 1526 pursues the same theme as Hubmaier when it says "therefore it is a fabrication when false Christians say they can do nothing but what God works in them." Among other arguments Denck cites a passage from the Old Testament where Moses is quoted to have said to the people of Israel: "the commandment, which I command you today . . . is in your mouth and heart to do it." From this statement Denck concludes that the realization of the law must be possible. Other Anabaptists, such as Peter Riedemann and Menno Simons, shared the point of view of Hubmaier and Denck. Man has the ability to choose between God and Satan. Thus free choice determines man's eternal destiny: "It is up to us and free will whether we want to accept such offered grace or not." The influence of Erasmus is noteworthy here as he had defined free will as *"vim humanae voluntatis, qua se possit homo applicare ad ea, quae perducunt ad aeternam salutem, aut ab iisdem avertere."* This is precisely what the Anabaptists stood for when they emphasized the necessity of responsible choice on the part of man. Frank Wray has aptly summarized the Anabaptist position as follows: since God is righteous he cannot be responsible for evil. Without free will there can be no real commitment to discipleship.

Turning next to the Anabaptist view of original sin we note the significant role which it played in Anabaptist doctrinal writings, though the term *original sin* itself is rarely used; it is not found in the Scriptures, one Anabaptist asserted. One observes a certain ambiguity in Anabaptist comments about original sin, particularly as regards children. It seems that there are two divergent views held by Anabaptists. Some writers assert that the newborn child is pure and unblemished, for God has created all things well. Thus one Anabaptist claims: "we have a sufficient number of clear and pure passages to prove that all the children of the world, yes, indeed all creatures, are created good and pure by God." . . . The two *Loci classici* of original sin (Gen. 8:21 and Psalm 51:5) are expressly refuted by these Anabaptists. In commenting on the Genesis passage which speaks of the fact that the imagination of man's heart is evil from his youth, one Anabaptist distinguishes, for example, between *infancy* and *youth*, and designates the latter as the time of the beginning of sin. We discern how such argumentation provided the proper ground for the Anabaptist rejection of infant baptism, which was, of course, unnecessary if the infant was "good and pure." Only subsequent, willful violation of God's commandment makes reconciliation and baptism necesary.

A second group of Anabaptists interprets these Scripture passages along traditional lines, by insisting that all human beings—even infants—have a sinful nature which they inherit from Adam. Thus Claus Felbinger writes: "no man was born of woman in the seed of man without sin, for they all share in the original sin which comes from Adam" and Menno Simons declares that "I was shapen in iniquity and in sin did my mother conceive me. I came of sinful flesh. Through Adam corrupt seed has been sown in my heart from which so much misery has sprung." These Anabaptists point out that sin originally had a two-fold consequence: physical death and spiritual damnation. The coming of Christ has brought, however, a decisive change as far as children are concerned. The curse of spiritual damnation has been removed from them though they still must die a physical death. . . .

There is agreement among all Anabaptists, however, that an evil inclination is present in adults. One statement may here stand for many: "Thus original sin is, first of all, *cor malissimum*, the evil heart which Adam had, by which he was destroyed, which was inherited by all his descendants. Out of this much godless fruit has grown and is still growing." Thus the Anabaptists concede that man is sinful and alienated from God. But this does not describe man's complete nature; we encounter a decisive difference with the Reformers, for man is not totally depraved. The "inner man" delights in God's law and knows that it is good, exclaims one Anabaptist. Man has within him a tendency for the good which Hans Denck puts into words: "I feel that there is also something within me which strongly resists my inborn naughtiness and points me to life and salvation." Man consequently brings about his spiritual damnation by his own decision, his willful and conscious sin. It is no surprise then that the Dutch scholar W. Kühler felt that the seemingly orthodox views of Menno and Dirk Philips concerning the natural sinfulness of man are nothing more than an illusion, as these Anabaptists essentially assert the good in man.

The Anabaptist view of man exemplifies a dualistic characteristic. It affirms a human will that is impaired, yet free to decide for good or evil, and juxtaposes a concept of original sin which allows them to affirm *both* the evil and good in man. It constitutes a consistent point of view of which the Anabaptist teaching on justification can be considered a proper extension.

As we come to the problem of justification we note a certain consensus between the Reformers and the Anabaptists inasmuch as the latter always insisted on their basic agreement with the Reformers on this point. Frequently such Anabaptist statements have been taken at their face value with the comment that the Anabaptists merely added an ethical emphasis to the teaching of the Reformers. Nonetheless, the most characteristic impression received from a perusal of Anabaptist testimonies and writings is an ambiguous one. Hand in hand with the affirmation of *sola fide* justification goes a pronounced condemnation of the teaching of the Reformers. The Anabaptists denounced and derided the Reformers for their failure in bringing about visible ethical consequences in the life of the Christian. "They teach contrary to Paul (Rom. 6) that one cannot be free of sin and live in righteousness" charged an Anabaptist, and another one added: "Many say, especially the Lutherans, that Christ is their righteousness and goodness, although they still live in all abomination and lasciviousness which thing is nothing else than to draw near to God with the mouth while the heart is far from him." Luther's profound but dangerous advice to Melanchthon, *pecca fortiter*, was for the Anabaptists—and also for Catholics—all the proof necessary of the ethical inadequacy of the Reformation. Thus the Anabaptists said at the conclusion of the Franckenthal Disputation of 1571 that "even if they would agree in matters of doctrine, they could never agree in matters of living," and an Anabaptist tract characterized the followers of the Reformation with the words: "they wish to obey God only with the soul and not also with the body, in order that they may escape persecution." . . .

Such Anabaptist dissent against the ethical inadequacy of the Reformation can be observed in the cradle of the movement in Zurich. Zwingli's earliest recollection about the subsequent alienation between himself and the Anabaptists was that he had been approached "that they should establish a special people and church and have Christian people therein who would live most innocently." The impression that the issue evolved around two differing views of the church is misleading. What separated Zwingli and the Zurich Anabaptists was a differing understanding of the nature of justification, from which resulted, to be sure, different views concerning the church. While Zwingli saw the Christian in the tension between "divine and human righteousness," the Anabaptists saw only the *totaliter aliter* of the converted Christian. This view led the Anabaptists to the postulate of a *believers'* church, a *visible communio sanctorum* which Zwingli, on the other hand, could not affirm. Obviously the Anabaptist view of the church is a derivative concept, as Harold S. Bender, in contrast to Fritz Heyer and Franklin H. Littell, has rightly pointed out. Not the church, but the probity of the *people* within the church, stands in the center of the controversy between the Anabaptists and the Zurich Reformer.

Like Zwingli, Luther also faced the challenge of a *rechte Kirche*. On two occasions in the early 1520's, he considered the possibility of an *ecclesiola in ecclesia*, where "those who wanted to be earnest Christians" would come together in close fellowship, but he never pursued this plan. Indeed, when in 1526 the Landgrave of Hesse proposed its realization, he outrightly rejected it. He did "not yet" have the necessary people, he said—and the radicals have ever since chided him for such devious compromise. But the Reformer's "not yet" was not so much the expression of his inconsistency, as of his understanding of the Christian who was at once both saint *and* sinner, *justus et peccator*. For Luther the Christian life had no uniquely empirical dimension. When Caspar Schwenckfeld approached him in this matter, Luther could ask if he had ever seen two Christians standing together. The Reformer's exclamation, "God save me from a church in which there are only saints," is, *cum grano salis*, much of the same character.

A positive delineation of the Anabaptist understanding of justification presents certain difficulties. To begin with, the term *justification* itself is rarely used by Anabaptist writers. This must not necessarily be construed, however, to signify a paucity of theological terminology in general, for certain *termini technici*—such as *Gelassenheit*—do occur quite frequently. The absence of any extended use of the term *justification* should rather be attributed to the fact that the Anabaptist approach to the Christian religion was such that the problem of justification did not occupy the prominent place which it did among the Reformers. . . . The emphasis is not, as among the Reformers, on the divine forgiveness of sins which would be apprehended by faith, but on man's commitment to live a holy and devout life. Luther's quest for a merciful God is different from the Anabaptist zeal for a life of obedience to God. In place of Luther's evangelical discovery that man is justified by faith in Christ's work of redemption, the Anabaptists suggested that God through Christ will forgive those who in humility and obedience imitate Christ's suffering. Man becomes aware of his sinful nature, repents of his sins, and is forgiven *through a commitment to be Christ's disciple*. It is the integral place of this additional commitment which marks the distinctive feature of the Anabaptist view. Commenting on his conversion, Menno Simons recollects "until of *my own* choice *I* declared war on the world, the flesh, and the devil, renounced all my ease, peace, glory, desire, and physical property and willingly submitted to the heavy cross of my Lord Jesus Christ that I might inherit the promised kingdom." From another Dutch Anabaptist, Dirk Philips, comes the admonition to "remember the covenant of the most high which you *voluntarily* desired and accepted." Thus justification is understood as a covenant, wherein God offers his grace through Jesus Christ and man pledges "that he would desist from sin and follow God."

. . . . . : . . . .

Man must, according to Anabaptist thought, make a voluntary response to enter into the divine covenant. The nature of this response is a decision for a life of holiness and suffering. These two characteristics, inextricably linked together, are the marks of the true Christian. Their presence makes it possible to observe if a man has truly entered into the covenant and become Christ's disciple.

There is abundant evidence that the Anabaptists considered the new life in Christ both mandatory and possible. Believer's baptism was understood as symbol of a commitment to discipleship as is expressed in words of the Zurich Anabaptist Felix Mantz who commented on the significance of baptism as follows: "We see in these words what baptism is and how it should be used, namely if one, converted through God's word, changes his mind and wants to walk henceforth in a new life." Other Anabaptists affirmed in similar terms that the Christian delights in a holy life. For the Reformers this was outright mockery; thus the *Confessio Augustano* rejected those "qui contendunt, quibusdam tantam perfectionem in hac vita contingere" and the *Formula Concordiae* similarly spoke against the view "quod homo Christianus vere per Spiritus renatus legem Dei in hac vita perfecte implere possit." . . .

The difference between the Reformers and the Anabaptists at this point arises obviously from a different conception of the nature and profundity of sin. For Luther sin was precisely such evil inclination, this *concupiscentia*, the "sublimia ista et profunda cordis peccata," even if it did not express itself in overt acts. The Anabaptists, on the other hand, were concerned with external acts and seemed to assume that outwardly good behavior was indicative of inner purity of heart. When the Anabaptists and the Reformers therefore spoke about good works, they talked in the final analysis past each other. For the Anabaptists such works consisted in definite external manifestations which could be empirically observed and enabled a more or less conclusive evaluation of the Christian profession—such as not stealing, not committing adultery, not lying, etc. For Luther, on the other hand, such external acts were *res inferiora* whose outward observance or nonobservance did not make a Christian. Reading the lengthy descriptions of the characteristics of the Christian life in Anabaptist writings one is impressed not only by the high ethical vigor, but also by the fact that most of the points covered were, for Luther, either part of general morality with no specific Christian quality or altogether unessential. To note just one example: Peter Riedemann's *Rechenschafft* notes at great length about such matters as "the making of clothes," "greeting," "the giving of the hand and embracing," "celebrating," "traders," "inn-keepers," "standing drinks," and "coming together." Luther, on the contrary, felt that "the church is hidden, the saints are hidden" and held that even the heathen could lead an outwardly moral life when he expressed the hope that most people "were good pious heathen who kept the natural law." In a penetrating analysis W. v. Loewenich has shown how Luther's understanding of God as *deus absconditus* and of faith as *argumentum rerum non apparentium* led to the postulate of the "hiddenness" of the Christian life, which, unlike differences of sex or race, cannot be perceived empirically. Here the difference between the Reformer and the Anabaptists emerges most clearly.

Harold S. Bender's famous essay on *The Anabaptist Vision* delineated the motif of disci-pleship as the essence of Anabaptism and suggested that it presupposes the Reformation concept of justification by faith alone and is merely its proper and practical extension. The question may be raised if the very concept of *discipleship* does not embody certain synergistic presuppositions. One is always impressed with the Anabaptist emphasis on man's part in his relationship with God. To be sure, for some—but by no means for all!—Anabaptists grace is prevenient and man cannot earn this free gift. But he can voluntarily respond and by living in obedient discipleship pull the lever which extracts such grace. . . .

. . . .

It should be clear from our analysis that the Anabaptist understanding of justification does not follow the pattern set by the Reformers. It breathes a different spirit as some scholars, such as W. J. Kühler, Winthrop Hudson, or George Williams, have pointed out. This must be said particularly concerning the anthropocentric tendencies in Anabaptist thought, which can hardly be overlooked.

. . . In Anabaptism as well as in Catholicism, anthropocentric tendencies upset the equi-librium of the work of God and the work of man. There, as well as here, the result was a work-righteousness which found its expression in the phrase from the *Ausbund*: "Whoever does right, is justified."

We conclude that by and large the Anabaptist position is closer to Catholicism than to the Reformation; and it comes as no surprise, then, that the Tridentine Canon on Justification is strongly reminiscent of Peter Riedemann's view as expressed in his *Rechenschafft*.

The time-worn charge of the Reformers that the radicals were "nil nisi quidani est novus monachismus" had therefore a certain validity. It was a caricature, to be sure, even as much of the polemics of the 16th century was caricature, and did not do full justice to the Anabaptist position. But instinctively—or theologically—the Reformers saw that in the Anabaptist system man was given once more an important place. Their violent reaction is understandable.

But Anabaptism was not simply a medieval sect as Ritschl suggested. Some of the most resolute repudiations of Catholicism stemmed from the ranks of the Anabaptists. The sacramental and sacerdotal character of the Catholic Church as well as the emphasis on tradition as a normative principle of Christian truth came here under severe criticism. Positively, the affirmation of the priesthood of all believers and the principle of *sola scriptura* are basic to Anabaptist thought. In fact, a case can perhaps be made that the Anabaptists, with their emphasis on the brotherhood character of the church and their extreme Biblicism, went beyond the Reformers in these areas. The influence of the Reformation upon Anabaptism was undoubtedly profound—and Holl's thesis of the dependence of the *Schwärmer* on Luther is, at least partially, justified. Anabaptism cannot be understood aside from its reformatory context. It is a child of the Reformation, though perhaps not—if the imagery is permissible—an altogether legitimate one, for as we have seen, in some crucial aspects it is indeed very close to Catholicism.

The picture of Anabaptism is thus an ambiguous one. A definite affinity with the Reformation on the one hand gives validity to the description of the movement as Radical Reformation. This is coupled, however, with a unique proximity to Catholic thought, making it impossible to see the movement exclusively as a result of the Reformation. The postulate of Anabaptism as a Christian tradition in its own right may be the answer to our problem.

Anabaptism and Ascetic Holiness

Kenneth R. Davis

HOLINESS AS THE DOMINANT PRINCIPLE OF INTERPRETATION

Holiness, ascetically conceived, functions as the single, overarching, interpretive principle which dominates the whole ecclesiastical perspective and theological formulation of Evangelical Anabaptism. . . .

The soteriology of Anabaptism also takes its uniqueness from its interaction with the dominant theme of holiness. Explicitly Anabaptism's definition of who and what is a Christian is basically and consistently conduct centered. The initial dispute between the Grebel-Manz group and Zwingli was precisely over this issue. Similarly, the Schleitheim Confession of 1527 is less a confession of faith than the statement of a minimal test of conduct, ascetic in nature, for the identifying of the true Christians. The Sattlerian ascetic, test-"standard" in the "Schleitheim Articles" includes as its principles: the repentant spirit, amendment of the external life by the abandonment of gross sins and by a positive effort toward the imitation of Christ, absolute submission to the will of God as revealed in the Scriptures and to the discipline of the brotherhood, and the sacrificial and practical practice of brotherly love. The same stress on an ascetic test for the recognition of a true Christian is found in Weninger; that is, a Christian is one who "does right." Similarly the testimony at Zurich by an unknown associate of Hottinger (cir. 1525–26) describes a Christian as one who "desists from sins and desires to experience a reformation or bettering of life and conduct."

Since, for Evangelical Anabaptism, the provision for salvation includes taking seriously both the precepts and counsels of the gospel, especially the command, "Be ye holy; for I am holy" (1 Pet. 1:16) and an accent on regeneration which enables one to do so, a conduct-oriented holiness becomes the primary norm for distinguishing the godly from the ungodly, true Christians from the non-Christians, the true church from the false church and the world. The *Satisfaction of Christ* elaborates on the point that the all-sufficiency of Christ's atonement is operationally effective only on condition of the exercise of an ascetically practical faith.

Also, a repentance-centered doctrine of conversion is central to Anabaptist soteriology, and this repentance includes a continuous will to holiness or the penitent life, a kind of mortification. Though generally subscribing to justification by faith, faith is always in conjunction with or even subsequent to repentance, and includes typically ascetic elements such as attitudes of obedience, surrender, and self-renunciation. Repeatedly the life of Christ and His atonement are given ascetic purposes: an example for the development of holiness and the actual extirpation of sin in this life. The Christian is "to make known the obedience or righteousness of His Father not only in words but also with works."

. . . .

From the earliest beginnings of the movement, Manz insisted on an ethical basis for the valid administration of believer's baptism. He required that it be administered only to those "who reform, take on new life, lay aside sins. . . ." He rests his doctrine of baptism on, first, the idea that John the Baptist was the divinely appointed forerunner to Christ, and therefore the essentially ethical nature of John's baptism indicates the necessary and prerequisite preparation for the proper receiving of the Christ.

Second, he insists that the same ethical interpretation which characterized John's baptism carries over also as the prime significance for Christian baptism, as was taught by Christ, and this the church was commanded to maintain thereafter. Manz writes:

> Also, just as John baptized only those who reformed, forsook evil works, and did good . . . so also the apostles received from Christ . . . the command . . . [to] teach . . . that forgiveness of sins in His name should be given to everyone who believing on His name should do righteous works from a changed heart . . . so they also were poured over with water externally to signify the inner cleansing and dying to sin.

Baptism is here presented as a sign or testimony of an ascetic conversion which in turn equates with the Grebel group's norms for what constitutes a true Christian. Accordingly, Manz continued further by accenting that baptism derives its primary significance from Paul's words, in Romans, chapter 6, that baptism represents a death to the old life and a rising to a new. Manz also insists that "Christ baptized no one without external evidence of readiness." Thus the Anabaptists' espousal of believer's baptism and their rejection of infant baptism was not based primarily on the problem of the relation of faith to the infant, a problem which caused many Reformers to hesitate over infant baptism, but by an ascetic interpretation of the baptism's significance which precluded infants. This is what is essentially Anabaptist and it is never Zwinglian. Zwingli correctly recognized that to accept the Anabaptists' position on baptism would lead to the acceptance of an ascetic theology.

. . . .

Not only was baptism the external witness to a strongly ethical interpretation of the nature of a true Christian, and closely tied to a necessary and previous ascetic conversion, but in several ways it went beyond an external sign and testimony to continuing significances which are also ascetic. First, Hubmaier emphasizes that baptism involves a confession of, and an initial act of, a continuously intended self-surrender or *Gelassenheit*. Hubmaier also often uses derivatives of the term *ergeben* (to yield) in relation to baptism. He asserts that baptism implies "that one has already surrendered himself [*sich schon ergeben hab*] to live according to the Word, will *and rule of Christ*." Thus the decidedly ascetic significance of living under a "rule" is tied to baptism. Second, both Beachy and Armour have elaborated on the Anabaptist concept of baptism as an initiation "pledge," or covenant, or an act of placing oneself henceforth into, and under the discipline of, the brotherhood. Hubmaier expressly states that the brotherhood's authority for discipline and admonition comes "from the baptismal vow."

. . . .

Moreover, it appears to have become general practice among the Anabaptists to maintain something of a probationary novitiate before baptism. It was an interval of testing and instruction. Verheyden gives several examples of candidates for baptism having to wait for several years because, according to Dureck Lambrecht's testimony, "One has to reform his life beforehand," that is, before being eligible for baptism.

. . . .

In summary, then, the meaning of baptism for the Anabaptists included several unique, ascetic features. It was a voluntary witness to a personal, ascetic conversion; a voluntary commitment or pledge to the penitent life and to acceptance of the rule of Christ, including placing oneself under the authority and discipline of the "keys" of the brotherhood; and a voluntary commitment to place one's possessions at the disposal of the brotherhood when need arose. It also required a prior period of probationary scrutiny and opportunity for instruction.

. . . .

Poschmann points out that there was even a Catholic view, especially in the ascetic tradition, which conceived of baptism as an act of penance, and which interpreted the vow of the "religious" as a kind of second baptism, a *conversio* to a life of ascetically defined and perpetual penance. Concerning the expression "second baptism," Pourrat comments that it

> is grounded on the entire renunciation of the world implied in the monastic profession. This renews and completes the renunciation of the devil and the world which is promised at baptism. Medieval theologians taught further that religious profession might remit all penalties due to sin.

With a remarkable parallelism of terminology, Hubmaier refers to Anabaptist baptism as a "necessary renunciation of the devil and his works." Hubmaier actually states that the vows of monks and nuns came in historically when the genuine Christian duty of baptism of believers was abolished and that baptism has a significance similar to when "youths are inducted into orders." Again, he writes, "Because we do not realize what baptism means, and what baptismal vows demand, Satan has started conventual vows." It is perhaps significant that Zwingli was also aware of the same figure and imagery with reference to baptism. He compares baptism to the "cowl" that introduces initiates into a monastic order. Moreover, Erasmus, of the imitation of Christ tradition, had previously emphasized that baptism "pledged" one to the Christian or penitent life. Thus, much concrete evidence verifies that there is a close tie between Anabaptist baptism and the vow of the religious.

Are there similar ascetic overtones in the Anabaptist understanding of the Lord's Supper? While the symbolism changes, the answer is positive since even a cursory analysis reveals the same uniquely ascetic approach as appeared in their understanding of baptism. A few examples are sufficient to substantiate this parallelism.

For Grebel, the observance of the Lord's Supper reflects primarily a continuing personal commitment to the brotherhood as the visible body of Christ. He insists that there could be no *true* observance, rather only an outward and ritualistic observance in which "love will be passed by," unless the "rule of Christ" is functioning effectively in close association with its administration. Also, the right discernment of the body of Christ, he continues, requires a willingness by the participant to live and suffer for Christ *and* for the other members of His body in the brotherhood. He adds that "if one eats who will not live the brotherly life . . . and dishonors love," he eats "unto damnation."

. . . .

Clearly, the close relationship in Anabaptist sacramental theology of the Lord's Supper to baptism, to fraternal love and discipline, and to the ascetic nature of both conversion and the separated life in the brotherhood, elevate the ascetic factors to a uniquely dominant role.

. . . .

The Anabaptist doctrine of the church also is molded around and dominated by a theology of ascetic holiness. The following is mostly a summation since considerable primary evidence has already been presented confirming this point.

First, the pervasiveness of ascetic holiness in relation to Anabaptist ecclesiology is illustrated by their understanding of what constitutes the proper basis for membership in the church. All their ecclesiology is based on the fundamental point that the church be reconstituted so as to be made up only of repentant, spiritually regenerate, and voluntarily baptized believers, who then function corporately as a holy living, disciplined brotherhood. Zwingli understood the objectives of the original Grebel-group to be the creation of a church composed exclusively of those "living piously." The church, then, is a family, a brotherhood of the reborn, and conduct is the sign which must validate the reality of the rebirth. Conduct, by which the familial relationship is demonstrated, is also consistently conceived according to traditional ascetic norms.

Second, this ascetic requirement for membership is then extended to encompass the essential character of the church's corporate image. The Anabaptists rejected, corporately as well as individually, any notion of an exclusively internal holiness, or of an invisible church, which failed to have a corresponding external, holy manifestation. They refused to recognize any congregation as a valid expression of the Christian church if its corporate conduct was widely divergent from the biblical ideal of the holiness of the mystical church. Thus, there is a sense in which the Anabaptist "brotherhood-church," as Zwingli recognized clearly, represents not only a fellowship whose goal is the perfection of its individual members but also a fellowship which must exhibit, corporately and at all times, a measure of outward perfection in reference to the conductual ethics of the gospel. The church must not be an obviously mixed society. It must not tolerate open sin. . . .

On the other hand, their brotherhood-church does not demand, or claim to have attained, absolute perfection or purity; a distinction which Zwingli overlooks in his polemics. Tares are still possible, but are so hidden as to be known only to God. There is to be no ignoring of open sin, no toleration in the church of those who willfully defy the laws and standards of Christ. Anabaptists fully recognized the existence of weak and immature Christians but even these must submit to, and reflect, the "perfection of Christ" by living under, and by being aided and sustained by, the "Rule of Christ" (Matthew 18) and the brotherhood.

The dominance of the ascetic is illustrated further not only by the Anabaptists' understanding of the nature of the church's membership and of its essentially holy character, but also by their understanding of its purpose. They emphasized the individual's need of the brotherhood-church for personal spiritual growth toward perfection and to ensure holy living; this, too, has obvious cenobitic overtones. The brotherhood was uniquely the place wherein the gifts of the Holy Spirit to each believer were operative to the common profit of all. All members shared together in a mutual, spiritual interaction for the purpose of edification and also correction. Hubmaier pressed the importance, even the necessity, of brotherly discipline and correction for both personal perseverance and growth in the faith. He saw this right to discipline as emerging from and grounded upon the individual's baptismal vow which, as was previously noted, also substantially parallels the monastic vow of initiation. Only the "ascetic" brotherhood-church was recognized as having the keys of binding and loosing, with its concomitant power of the ban, by which the holy conduct of both the individual and the church was ensured.

Their doctrine of the holy church is also inseparable from the ascetic doctrine of separation. Therefore, the brotherhood provides the necessary means for expressing at least a partial social withdrawal, and it is from this base of separation through the holy brotherhood that Anabaptists give visible witness to the body of Christ as the kingdom of God. At this point of witness through separation they activate also the social norms and virtues and the love ethic of the ascetic tradition. . . .

The brotherhood was intended also as a base for the proclamation of the gospel everywhere. That is, the Anabaptist church was a "sealed band of athletes of the Spirit," whose goal was not only to manifest the perfection of Christ, individually and corporately, but also a specialized agency for spiritual service and mission. All of [this] throughout the Middle Ages in the West was also closely associated with the ascetic tradition.

. . . .

Anabaptist eschatology is also molded by ascetic idealism. Novak has characterized it as an "eschatology of the cloister." This classification seems to be substantiated at several points. The "coming again" of Christ is generally conceived by Anabaptists in terms of the culmination of the continuous but intensifying spiritual conflict between the kingdom of God and Satan. This conflict is to reach a dominating crisis in the last stage of history. Christ's return is then understood as primarily a time of validation and vindication for the true Christians for their otherworldly loyalty, citizenship, and conduct and for bearing suffering for Christ's and righteousness' sake in this life. A new age of the reign of Christ through the establishment of a spiritual kingdom for the presently persecuted, martyred, separated, waiting, true church was thought to be at hand. The martyr and the faithful bearer of persecution for Christ's sake are the true soldiers of Christ now, spiritually fighting the powers of the darkness and waiting for the *eschaton*, the triumph by Christ at His coming.

This eschatology is radically different from Müntzer's. Rather, the Anabaptists' expectancy is proclaimed strongly as the grounds for a patient acceptance of persecution, the maintenance of holiness of life and conduct, for separation, and for mission and vigorous proselytization. It is consistently an ascetic, not militant, eschatology.

In his letter to the Anabaptists at Horb, Sattler presses the urgency of preaching and the harvesting of souls because the final sorting, "the time of threshing is nigh at hand (Luke 10)" and because the world rises up against those who testify the truth to it. He also urges diligence in persevering in assembling together to promote personal and corporate holiness "because the day of the Lord is approaching." Finally, he ends his plea by urging that they "sanctify" themselves, since the end, with its rewards for separation and for those "clothed in white," and the Shepherd are "nigh at hand." Therefore, he urges, "Flee the shadow of this world." Christians must strive to be found "unspotted from sin . . . at the coming of the Lord Jesus."

Thus, their eschatological perspective becomes predominantly a motivation to ascetic conduct, to perseverance in the spiritual struggle, to patient bearing of suffering, and to the obedient fulfillment of Christ's commands; it becomes primarily the time of the vindication of such a life—typical of the expectations and emphases in the ascetic tradition.

Finally, and perhaps most significantly, the proposition that Anabaptist theology was structured predominantly around ascetic idealism also holds true for their basic hermeneutical principles. In common with the Magisterial Reformers, the Swiss founders and the vast majority of Anabaptists adhered to the Bible as divinely inspired, *en toto*, and as the sole and final authority for Christian faith and practice. . . .

. . . .

Along with Zwingli, they held that the Scriptures were rightly understood only by the Holy Spirit's inner witness, but never, not even in the South German branch, was God's will to be discerned by some inner light independent from or totally separate from the Scriptures. The Holy Spirit must illumine and make alive, but the Scriptures function as a "regulation of the Spirit." Thus they avoid both a sheer, cold literalism and a subjective, individualistic spiritualism. But the Anabaptists maintained that the only ones who have the Holy Spirit within, and thus are able to interpret correctly, are the pious, and the pious are equated exclusively with those who exhibit the fruit of the Spirit, who lead holy lives. Again the holy life is the normative and distinctive issue, the key to the right interpretation of the Word of God.

There are at least [several] ascetically oriented facets in the development of the distinctively Anabaptist hermeneutic. The first is a limited kind of anti-intellectualism, including a simplicity of obedience without any admixture of or pollution by human inventions or philosophy. This, too, is a mood which was strongly asserted within some branches of the ascetic tradition. It is a limited advocacy of "pious ignorance"; it does not deny some usefulness to intellectual tools, though asserting the inadequacy and danger of intellectualism without piety. They were usually highly skeptical of traditional "scholastic" scholarship. Skepticism about scholarship's role and usefulness for biblical interpretation is not uniquely Anabaptist, though it is stronger among them than among the Magisterial Reformers, partly due to the early martyrdom of most of their more scholarly leaders. Rather, what makes the Anabaptist position different from the Magisterial (though similar to Erasmus) is their insistence that the one most necessary factor above and beyond academic skills is a pious faith; without that, Scripture cannot be rightly understood.

Second, their dualism related to the baptisms of water and of the Spirit, or to mortification and spiritual regeneration, rather than Luther's law and promises; this takes on hermeneutical significance. It is most clearly enunciated in an early tract, perhaps by Sattler, entitled, "How the

Scripture Is to be Discerningly Divided and Explained." Three principles of interpretation are explicitly given: simple obedience to Scripture's "clear" commands, related to the Anabaptist's anti-intellectualism; getting repentance, faith, and baptism into the biblically correct order; and then there is also a long table of typically ascetic opposites, a dualistic key to clarify the correct thrust of scriptural teaching as it relates to the penitent life, death versus life, evil-good, flesh-spirit, external-internal, and so on. Similarly, the external baptism of water, it notes, is coupled with mortification on one side, whereas on the other, the internal baptism of the Spirit is aligned with the virtues of the new life. But in this case, quoting John 3:5, both sides are made essential for entrance to the kingdom of God.

. . . .

One must conclude that the Anabaptist movement from the beginning, with only minor variations, had a common and unique hermeneutic which arose from their defense of an essentially ascetic and ethical conception of Christianity. Augsburger's conclusion from Sattler's writings that Anabaptists possessed an ascetic hermeneutic, which was not only Christological but ethical and practical, over against a soteriological hermeneutic centered on justification by faith in Luther, can now be extended justifiably to characterize all the major branches of Anabaptism. In place of the primacy of justification by faith is placed "the call to holiness, to sharing resurrection life," and to an explicit imitation of Christ.

Asceticism clearly dominates the theology, soteriology, and sacramental teachings, ecclesiology, eschatology, and even the unique principles of biblical interpretation of Evangelical Anabaptism. Such domination requires the recognition of Anabaptism as a sixteenth-century expression of an ascetic theology of holiness which in one sense is "Protestant" but nevertheless makes questionable whether the Anabaptists can be considered part of "the great Protestant family" of the Magisterial Reformation.

Theologically, Anabaptism's perspective and purpose is markedly medieval and ascetically oriented, with repentance, a discipleship of holiness, and a two-kingdom dualism functioning as pivotal issues. Institutionally, they insist on a brotherhood church which calls for a state of relative "perfection," similar to the way which that term is used of Medieval Catholic religious communities, and in contrast to Luther's *Volkskirche*. This includes the ideals of sharing and sometimes even the common life, the ethic of love in the brotherhood, and the necessary therapeutic functions of brotherly discipline. In practice also, the spirituality of the monastery is generally maintained; that is, while the threefold ideals of chastity, poverty, and obedience are biblically adjusted and laicized, they are not abandoned. Accordingly, this chapter expands and verifies, theologically, Ritschl's contention that Anabaptism represents the laicization of monastic spirituality outside the Roman Catholic organization.

However, unlike the medieval Catholic religious, the holy life for Anabaptists was more than a superior way within the larger Christian schema; it became the sole and exclusive way to salvation. But even this variation also began within the ascetic tradition itself long before the Reformation.

Anabaptism's Multiple Origins: Switzerland and the Netherlands

The Turning Point in the Zwinglian Reformation

John Howard Yoder

The most competent research into the beginnings of Anabaptism in Zurich has dated the very first clear disagreement between Ulrich Zwingli and those of his followers who were later to become the Swiss Brethren from the late afternoon of October 27, 1523. Two days of public debate in the course of Zurich's second disputation had made clear that neither the celebration of the Mass nor the use of images in worship was scripturally justified. The intention of the burgomaster to adjourn the meeting until the next afternoon, at which time the doctrine of Purgatory should be discussed, had just been announced when

> Conrad Grebel rose and thought that the priests should be given instructions, since they were all present, as to what should be done about the Mass; [the disputation] would be in vain, if something were not done about the Mass. Much had been said about the Mass, but there seemed to be no one willing to forsake this abomination before God. Furthermore there were many more abuses in the mass [*i.e.,* in addition to the claim that it has sacrificial character, which had been discussed thus far]; one should speak of them as well.
>
> *Zwingli*: My Lords [*i.e.,* the Zurich city Council] will decide how to proceed henceforth with the Mass.
>
> *Simon Stumpf*: Master Ulrich: ["Master" was Zwingli's academic title.] You have no authority to place the decision in the hands of My Lords, for the decision is already made; the Spirit of God decides. If then My Lords should adopt and decide anything against God's own decision, I shall ask Christ for His Spirit, and shall teach and act against it.
>
> *Zwingli*: That is right. I shall likewise preach and act against it if they decide otherwise. I don't place the decision in their hands. Nor shall they pass judgment on the Word of God (this applies not only to them, but to everyone). This convocation did not have the purpose of deciding for or against the Word of God, but to ascertain from Scripture whether the Mass is a sacrifice or not. Hereafter they will deliberate as to the way in which that may be done most appropriately and without disturbance.

This exchange of arguments is somehow disappointing if one expects to find in it the expression of two irreconcilable views destined to give birth to the two major religious phenomena of modern Christendom, state-church Protestantism on the one hand and the Free Church on the other. Zwingli did not ascribe any normative authority to the state; in fact he explicitly denied that "My Lords" had anything to say over against the Word of God. The one concession he did make, namely the assignment to the Council of the responsibility of appropriate and orderly execution, does not seem to have provoked any objection from Conrad Grebel. Not only did Grebel accept Zwingli's explanation as given above; he also declared himself satisfied on the following day after Zwingli had discussed the "other abuses" to which Grebel had objected in the celebration of the Mass.

It is not difficult to understand how historians have come to ascribe such fundamental importance to this segment of the October disputation. They have, rightly, fixed upon the question of the authority of the state in religious matters, and have sought for the earliest point where something was said which could be construed as expressing a disagreement on this question. This is a legitimate method in historical research, yet not the only usable one. History is interested not only in knowing when we can see the first hints of a later difficulty; it is just as important to know when the actors in the drama themselves became aware of the problem. This apparently did not happen between Zwingli and Grebel in October. They seem not to have seen the problem until nearly three months later.

If the study of church history is to have real significance for the Christian church in our day, it must attach especial importance to the analysis of those "breaking points" which have left Christians with a heritage of dividedness in faith and life. It is therefore no idle academic recreation when we seek to ascertain as exactly as possible just how and why this most significant of all "breaking points" within Protestantism came to be reached.

. . . .

Zwingli's attitude toward the question of procedure and the authority of the state may be summed up as follows: (1) The state has no right to judge on what Scripture says. (2) There can be adiaphora, morally neutral matters in which concessions to the unconvinced are in order. But the questions involved now are not adiaphora but deeply theological issues of right and wrong. (3) There can be such a thing as a necessary respect for the convictions of the "weak in faith," in application of the teaching of I Corinthians 8; but such considerations are valid only for a limited time, and no longer apply to images and the Mass after the teaching that has been done. (4) The state's authority is limited strictly to finding the most suitable means of execution for the decision made in the disputation.

On none of these points have we any sign of disagreement on the part of Grebel. In fact, his request for instructions to be given to the priests about the Mass can hardly be construed otherwise than as involving action by the Council. It thus seems clear: there were not two clearly defined camps, divided on the question of state versus biblical authority. Zwingli was no less biblicistic and no less impatient than Grebel. Grebel was no more legalistic and no less considerate for the "weak" than Zwingli.

If then the division did not occur in October 1523, how and when did it come about? The only possible explanation seems to be that either Zwingli or Grebel significantly changed his position sometime in the following months, and it is to the testing of this hypothesis that we must now turn. Grebel is inaccessible during these months, having left no known documents—another sign of his dependence on Zwingli. But the events following the disputation can be followed with some degree of clarity in so far as they reveal the positions of Zwingli and the Council.

Conrad Schmid had proposed, near the close of the disputation, that the abolition of the Mass and images should be preceded by an educational effort backed by the Council's full authority. The Council followed this suggestion and ordered the printing and distribution of an *Introduction,* which Zwingli wrote immediately, dealing with the sense in which the Law is done away with, with images and the Mass, in a popular, expository way, with no statement as to how their knowledge was to be applied except for a word against iconoclasm. Meanwhile the Council ordered everyone to hold his peace. The *Introduction* was proclaimed as the official teaching of the Council on November 17. Thus far the Council seemed to be moving forward, carefully but surely, in a way which justified the confidence placed in it to deal, not with questions of principle, but with applications.

Barely three weeks later, on December 10, new agitation against the Mass stirred the city. A number of old liturgical books were found where they had been thrown by the wayside, and the chaplains of Zwingli's own parish, the Grossmünster, refused to sing Mass any longer because of the way the common people jeered at them. This commotion, which could hardly have come to a focus as it did without Zwingli's consent, stirred the Council to renewed action. It seemed to indicate that at least one segment of the populace was ready to see the Mass abandoned. The Council requested an advisory memorandum (*Ratschlag*) from the three reforming pastors, Zwingli, Leo Jud, and Heinrich Engelhard. Apparently Zwingli and his friends had become aware of new reasons for fearing that the Council would procrastinate, for they expressed here a kind of determination which surpasses anything they had said before.

> We intend to begin said usage [the evangelical observance of the Lord's Supper] on Christmas Day, in simple conformity to the institution and practice of Christ; for we can no longer withhold from the world the right to the proper celebration [of communion]; and *even if it should not be permitted, we must offer both body and blood, bread and wine to those who so desire, or stand condemned as liars by the Word of God.* (Italics ours)

This powerful statement is significant for a number of reasons. Zwingli, failing utterly to respect the division of authority which he accepted in October, here announces his intention to go ahead on his own and sets a date for the institution of the Lord's Supper according to evangelical conviction, whether the Council so desires or not. He further shows for the first time an awareness of the possibility that the Council might construe its authority to carry through the Reformation in the reverse form of an authority to delay the putting into effect of those changes which the October disputation had decided on; in the face of this possibility Zwingli's determination does not waver. It is further remarkable that Zwingli desires this change to take place on a basis of tolerance. Those priests who desire to continue with the Mass should not be hindered; they will simply not be replaced as they get old. No one shall be forced to attend Mass or communion, or to read Mass against his will. This document states a truly revolutionary platform which, if applied by its authors, could have changed the whole course of Protestant church history.

Unfortunately, this plan was not carried through. Upon receiving this document the Council referred it to a larger commission. Zwingli and his two colleagues were members of the commission, but they were outweighed by eight councilmen and the three prelates of the Zurich church. This commission produced another document, again written by Zwingli, in which most of the same things were said as in the first, but in a radically different way.

> The previous opinion submitted by the three pastors is without a doubt the rightest of all and the most in conformity with the Word of God. Therefore nothing shall be undertaken in this matter which does not tend toward the point at which the simple pattern of the pure Word of God will be followed. Since however feelings are divided at present—many being just as foolish as we ourselves were not long ago—it will be necessary to make some concessions to the immature until they can attain the age and strength to take solid food.

Having made this plea for compromise which sounds more like Conrad Schmid's earlier language than like Zwingli's, the memorandum requests the institution of evangelical communion for those who desire it, without the abolition of the Mass. This principle of tolerance is stated more clearly than in the previous memorandum, but the compromise for which the introductory paragraph was preparing the way is not this principle, which is neither new nor a compromise, but rather the fact that the threat of the three pastors to go on on their own even if forbidden has been dropped. The second memorandum expresses the same ideals and goals as the first, but not the same determination, and at this critical point that made all the difference in the world. When on December 19 the Council rejected not only the first memorandum but in fact both of them and ruled that there should be no change at all with respect to the Mass (a third memorandum concerning images was accepted in principle) Zwingli and his colleagues no longer objected. They did not raise their voices, they did not instigate further popular commotion, they did not as they had promised offer bread and wine to those who so desired on Christmas Day of 1523, and they continued to celebrate Mass for sixteen more months.

It would thus appear that it was in the period of barely a week between the two memoranda—the first was written after the disorders of the 10th and the second before the Council session of the 19th—that the back of Zwingli's firm resolve was broken. It can hardly be mere coincidence that it was just at this date, namely in a letter dated December 18, that Conrad Grebel expressed his first clear criticism of Zwingli. In mock debating style he proclaimed the thesis he was prepared to defend:

> Whoever thinks, believes, or says that Zwingli is performing his duties as a Shepherd, thinks, believes, and speaks ungodly.

This indignation at Zwingli's present compromise has led Grebel to see as well that its seeds were already present in October, namely in the utterly unrealistic distinction between matters of principle and of application which had been accepted there. He now believes that "the Word was overthrown, trampled upon, and enslaved by its most learned heralds" in the course of the disputation, even though he himself had not seen this at the time, having accepted in good faith Zwingli's assurance that the Council would act soon. The Zurich Council was doing nothing new in taking upon itself religious authority; this it had been doing increasingly for decades, and the friends of the Reformation, Grebel among them, were quite happy that it did so in November 1522 (Zwingli's employment as pastor) and January 1523 (the first disputation). Only when the state acted *against* the Reformation could the problem of the state as such be posed. This happened between October and December, as the Council first delayed and then refused completely to take measures which were clearly necessary. Only at this point could the religious leaders be expected to clarify their own positions. Zwingli accepted the state's refusal, and thus revealed that his announced willingness to stand by his convictions come what may "or stand condemned as a liar" had only been a bluff. Grebel chose the other path, preferring Zwingli's intentions to his actions. Once this issue was clear he could see that it had already been latently present in October.

Zwingli cannot have made the decision he did without some kind of inner crisis. To take a course which he had warned, just one week earlier, would involve unfaithfulness to the Word of God, cannot have been easy for him, nor can it have been easy to live with this decision during the months that followed. It is thus not surprising that Zwingli worked out a new justification for what he had done. He refers to it clearly some three years later when asked for advice by the Bern reformers Haller and Kolb. "The Lord's Supper should not be introduced hurriedly," he counsels them, because of the danger that one part of the city will be celebrating Mass and the other the Lord's Supper. This breach of unity in the form of worship would be worse than the offense involved in having no evangelical communion at all. Thus it is better to maintain the Mass unitedly until it becomes possible, having won the unequivocal support of the state, to abolish it unitedly. Otherwise there might be uncontrollable conventicles hidden in every corner and no means of eliminating them. "This the Lord revealed to me, when the Mass was to be abolished among us [at Zurich]." This is the only point found in the course of the writer's study of the writings of Zwingli where the Reformer claims in this way to have received divine revelation bearing upon a particular problem of his strategy of reformation. Such a claim to exceptional and immediate divine sanction for his program does not usually seem necessary to Zwingli, in view of his great confidence in the clarity and efficacy of the Word of God. That he makes this unusual claim just at this point is a strong hint that he must have been aware he was making a fundamental shift in his position which he could not justify otherwise.

Up until the two memoranda of December 1523 Zwingli conceived of the Lord's Supper as something essential to the life of the Christian and of the church. His reason for its introduction, according to the first memorandum, is that the pastors no longer have the right to withhold the Lord's Supper from those who desire it. This memorandum provided for the *daily* celebration of communion. But from December 1523 on the Lord's Supper is first of all something one can get along without. It is less important than maintaining the unity of the whole people through uniform religious observance. This is the first and theologically the deepest change Zwingli had made. But another was more immediately important at the time. This argument of Zwingli's abandons tolerance as a strategy of reformation. Both December memoranda had been ready, in view of the urgency of the institution of the Lord's Supper, to accept the continued observation of the Mass, so that both forms of worship would be going on side by side. Zwingli now expressly rejects this readiness as involving the sacrifice of that unity of the entire people which must be maintained above all else, even, if need be, above true communion.

By thus seeing the basic nature of Zwingli's shift in position we have at the same time found the crux of Grebel's clash with him. To place the unity of Zurich above the faithfulness of the church is not only to abandon the church; it is also the demonization of the state, for persecution becomes a theological necessity. The suppression of dissent is for the Zwinglian Reformation from this point on not an unfortunate expedient but a matter of faith. Grebel did not reject the state as an agent of the church as long as there was some hope that it might carry through the Reformation on a basis of tolerance. Grebel's and Mantz's own proposals to Zwingli also had involved the use of the state. But when at the same time Zwingli accepted that the state should not have to carry through the Reformation immediately, and insisted that it should be intolerant for reasons of principle, Anabaptism had become a necessity even though infant baptism had as yet not become an issue.

Was There a Turning Point
of the Zwinglian Reformation?

Robert C. Walton

. . . .

This study will confine itself to a consideration of Yoder's explanation for *Zwingli's willingness to accept a further delay in the abolition of the Mass.* Yoder, who assumes that the *Täufer* were Zwingli's children, asserts that the issue which finally divided Zwingli from his progeny was the question of the magistracy's right to defer the final abrogation of the Mass. The crisis took place early in December 1523, when Zwingli stated his determination to institute a reformed communion service by Christmas regardless of the wishes of the Zurich Council, and then gave in to pressure from the government, and agreed to a continuation of the Mass for another fifteen months. According to Yoder, when Zwingli made this decision, he abandoned the church, because he placed "the unity of Zurich above the faithfulness of the church" and thus made persecution a "theological necessity." Conrad Grebel, who "did not reject the state as an agent of the church as long as there was some hope that it might carry through the Reformation on a basis of tolerance," was unable to accept the consequences of Zwingli's action. The events of December 1523, followed from the Council's original decision, which was taken at the end of the Second Disputation in October 1523, to postpone the nullification of the Mass and the removal of the images from the churches until the populace and clergy of the entire canton had been properly prepared for such a step. To do justice to Yoder's argument it is necessary to consider his reconstruction of what took place in December, and to compare his account with the sources.

Although there is no conclusive evidence to support the assumption, Yoder believes that Zwingli was behind the fresh series of demonstrations against the Mass which took place on December 10, 1523. The Council was sufficiently alarmed by the outbreak to ask the advice of Zwingli and the two other people's priests concerning the Mass and then to refer the entire question to a larger commission made up of the three priests, the Abbot of Kappel, the Provost of Embrach, the Comtur at Küssnach and eight members of the Council. The response given by the three priests left no doubt that they were determined to introduce a reformed communion service, and that this change was to be carried out "on a basis of tolerance."

Zwingli was also the author of the report presented to the Council by the commission and, although it agreed with what the people's priests had requested, it did not show the "same determination." The commissioners called for concessions to the "weak" which entailed retaining the Mass, but allowing those who wished to take part in an "evangelical communion" to do so. The Council ignored both suggestions and simply retained the Mass. Neither Zwingli nor his two colleagues raised any objections to the Council's decision. This abject surrender to the wishes of the magistracy prompted Grebel's angry letter of December 18th to Vadian and marked the turning point in the Reformation. Yoder claims that Zwingli later justified himself in a letter to Haller and Kolb at Bern which asserted that the Lord revealed to him the need to retain the Mass until it could be completely abolished. Zwingli's basic shift in policy meant the abandonment of toleration and led to "demonization" of the state, as well as a policy of persecution for the sake of religious uniformity.

. . . .

When it issued its mandate on December 19th, the Council did not ignore the report of the commission. The mandate stated that the Mass was to be retained, but, in keeping with the commission's directive as well as the request of the people's priests, agreed that no cleric should be compelled to say it. . . .

. . . .

Nevertheless it can be argued that, when the civil authority allowed some to go on saying the Mass, the government opposed the command of the Word. However this is not quite the case: those who were permitted to continue to perform the traditional service did not receive complete freedom. The government told them to say it "in the form that is closest to the will and Word of God." The Second Disputation had concluded that the Mass was not a sacrifice and that God had forbidden men to make sacrifices to him. The decision denied the doctrine of transubstantiation and also precluded the ultimate toleration of those who might wish to adhere to the traditional form and doctrine of the Eucharist. When the magistrates told the adherents of the traditional service that they must follow the form "closest to the will and Word of God," they took the same position which the conclusion of the commission's report had taken; the Bible taught that the Mass was not a sacrifice, and in fact forbade any reference to the Mass as such which emasculated it.

The Council's mandate was conceived in such a way that the outward forms of the traditional service were allowed to remain, but the doctrine which they expressed was denied. A reformed sermon was preached as part of the service, all reference to the Mass as a sacrifice removed, but, in keeping with the proposals Zwingli himself had made in the *De Canone Missae Epichiresis*, published on August 29, 1523, the external shell of the old ceremony, including the use of Latin chants and clerical vestments, was retained. This is not to say that Zwingli or the Council believed the external forms of the old ceremony should be permanently continued. During the Second Disputation Zwingli had said that they should be done away with slowly. The nature of the changes which the Council had sanctioned made their slow suppression inevitable and to a conservative the deletion of any reference to the Mass as a sacrifice amounted to its abolition.

It was probably with this in mind that Zwingli later accused the *Täufer* of causing difficulties over external matters, for after this change only the empty hulk of the old ceremony remained. What was lacking was a service which would replace the Mass, but the time was not right to introduce it. In the interim the compromise ceremony was to be held, while the program of education, sanctioned by the Council, to prepare the people of the canton for the final abolition of the Mass was implemented. The magistracy's behavior, though marked by caution, leaves no doubt of its support for Zwingli's program. The compromise imposed by the civil authorities which suppressed all reference to the Mass as a sacrifice and freed the clergy from the obligation to say Mass indicates that the magistrates sought to obey the Word of God, and did not wish to oppose the Reformation. Though he may well have wished for more, Zwingli could afford to be satisfied with the outcome of events.

Yoder has alluded to Zwingli's letter to Haller and Kolb at Bern which was written on October 11, 1527, to show that Zwingli had to justify his surrender to the state in December 1523 by claiming that his action was prompted by divine revelation. He would interpret the concern for both the full support of the Council and the cultic unity of the city which Zwingli voiced in the letter as the result of Zwingli's conversion to the idea of a state church in December 1523. Another interpretation, which is applicable to Yoder's general conception of the motives for Zwingli's behavior in the early weeks of December as well as to his explanation of Zwingli's reference to divine revelation in the letter to Haller and Kolb, is possible.

Except for a passing mention of Zwingli's tendency, which he considered unfortunate, to see the magistracy as the legitimate representative of the Zurich congregation, Yoder pays little attention to the corporate nature of the city's constitutional traditions or their influence upon Zwingli's attitude from the very beginning of the Reformation. Like the other South German and Swiss cities of the period Zurich's constitution was dominated by a corporate theory of government and society which assumed that church and state were one and recognized no distinction between the political assembly of the city, which consisted of all the citizens, and the church congregation. They were one and the same. Before the Reformation began, the magistrates had already taken on a semi-sacral character, because they were the delegated representatives of a Christian people in a society which had come to see itself as a small-scale *corpus christianum*. The corporate ideal recognized no limit to the magistrates' authority and so, at the same time the Council consolidated its control over the local assemblies (*Gemeinden*) in the Zurich countryside, it was able, in the interests of the "common good" to win far reaching authority over the affairs of the church throughout the city's domains.

Despite the control which the magistrates exercised over the church, they had never attempted to alter its doctrine or liturgy. In these matters the councillors were content to accept the authority of Rome and Rome's intermediary, the Bishop of Constance, to whose See they belonged. Zwingli was able to win the support of the government for a reform of the church's dogma and cult because, as Moeller has suggested, he identified from the first the visible church with the political assembly of the city, and naturally assumed both the place which the magistracy already occupied in the secular and religious affairs of the commonwealth and the fact that the government's support of true religion was essential. Then he convinced the town fathers that the authority of Scripture, properly interpreted by a Christian gathering, was the sole norm for the faith and practice of a Christian community. Once this had taken place the Council was independent of any outside religious authority and was able to justify the suppression of traditional religious practices in terms of its responsibility to God to provide for the well-being of the people.

There is ample evidence from Zwingli's later career that he thought of Zurich as a unified Christian community. Toward the end of life he was to say: "The Christian man is nothing else than the faithful and good citizen; and the Christian city is nothing other than the Christian church." But what of the earlier period?

Yoder refers to a letter written by Zwingli to Myconius on July 24, 1520, in order to substantiate his claim that Zwingli originally believed that the church consisted of a suffering remnant and that this belief provided the foundation for the ecclesiology of the *Täufer*. However, the terms of the letter are ambiguous. It was written at a time when Luther was threatened with excommunication and Zwingli thought that he might well suffer the same fate. Zwingli does say that those who preach Christ must suffer persecution and asserts that the church must be reborn in blood. If this were all that Zwingli said, it would certainly provide good evidence that he believed true Christians belonged to a church which was a suffering, separate remnant. In the same letter, however, Zwingli employed imagery taken from the parable of the wheat and tares to argue that, despite persecution, the advocates of reform must win time in order to bring their harvest to maturity and fruit. A little later he said that those who wished to purify the church should arm many Herculeses to carry out the filth from the stables. These passages can certainly be used to illustrate Zwingli's interest in maintaining unity within the church, i.e., the Zurich commonwealth which, as his use of the parable of the wheat and tares reveals, he conceived of as a mixed body. His aim, "the rebirth of Christ and the Gospel," is expressed in terms of a gradual transformation within the existing institution. He does not speak of a clean break from it. Zwingli and his friends were to arm Herculeses who would cleanse the stable not depart from it. The letter is a realistic appraisal of the problems which the reformers faced.

One of the clearest statements which Zwingli made concerning the place of the magistracy in the reform of the church is contained in a letter to Ambrosius Blarer, written on October 9, 1523. The letter discussed the steps which the Council had taken to deal with the problem posed by the iconoclasm of September 1523 and then considered the general progress of Christian renewal during the year.

> The senate has given four [men] from its order and just as many from the lesser order, who are called the two hundred by us, who with the three Bishops [the three people's priests] who are in the city, may examine diligently the passages of Scripture concerning the images and afterwards deliver a summa to the senate of the two hundred; this [the senate] is the highest authority among us. In the meantime those private persons who have contended in battle with the images are held in prison.

Then he added a postscript:

> I send the decree of the senate [concerning the reform of the Chapter] which, as I hope, will give an example to many free cities, just as the discussion of the Gospel which was held at the end of January. Nor should you wonder that general matters are thus dealt with here. Everything is right with us, but not even by a moment is it given to relax labor and vigils.

Zwingli's references to the "highest authority" reflect very clearly the position which the Great Council occupied in the city and presuppose the corporate structure of the city government. It is most significant too that at this time Zwingli thought the way in which the reform was being carried out with the aid of the "highest authority" should be an example to other free cities.

. . . .

After the Second Disputation Zwingli wrote a letter to Vadian on November 11, which described both the measures taken by the Council to prepare the people in the countryside for the final abolition of the Mass and the images and Zwingli's reaction to the government's treatment of the iconoclasts, in particular Lorenz Hochrütiner who had been banished. Zwingli began by thanking Vadian for the part which he had taken in the Disputation and then advised him, "Accept those things which have followed after." Then he considered Hochrütiner's treatment and explained why he thought that the Council's decision was justified. Hochrütiner had been dealt with very strictly; "why this is you yourself know." His conduct had frightened those who were as yet too attached to the traditional forms of worship to understand what he had done; to them Hochrütiner had opposed Christ. To prevent this element from turning away from the Gospel, it was necessary to make allowance for their weakness.

> But yet it has not been done contrary to reason, for you are not unaware that men are accustomed to fear such people, not because of the thing itself, but because of the glory of Christ. For there are some who would turn away from the Gospel of Christ, unless you give in to their infirmity a little.

As he had done consistently throughout his career Zwingli favored a policy of caution for the sake of the weak. His purpose was always to win them for the Gospel and thus to maintain the unity of the Christian commonwealth, which is what the corporate theory of a society which believed that right religion was essential to its well-being required.

. . . .

At this point a word about the reasons for the concern for the "weak" is necessary. The religious unity of the community was basic to the traditions of urban society and government in the sixteenth century. Concessions to the uninstructed or unconvinced were conceived of both by Zwingli and the Council as transitional measures which would allow further opportunity to secure a consensus for basic changes in the cultic practices of the community. Ultimately these measures were not aimed at achieving a reform by toleration. The object of the Council's decision to delay the abolition of the Mass was to prepare everyone for what it intended to do: to impose a service which conformed to the requirements of Scripture rather than the teachings of the old church. Once established the service would stand as an outward expression of the unity of the Christian commonwealth.

The letter to Haller and Kolb can also be interpreted in this context. Yoder is indeed correct when he says that Zwingli's letter to Haller and Kolb, who were facing serious opposition to their plan for the abolition of the Mass, was based upon Zwingli's own experience at Zurich. Even after the Mass had been replaced in 1525, the traditionalists in the city had asked to be allowed to attend Mass in one of the city's churches. Permission was not granted, but, until after the Bern Disputation of 1528 when the privilege was withdrawn, those who wished to do so were free to attend Mass outside the canton.

. . . .

Zwingli wished to help Haller and Kolb avoid a premature and partial reform which would leave the way open for a permanent concession to the traditionalists. He had just barely prevented such a thing from happening at Zurich and, at the time he wrote to Haller and Kolb, still had to accept the fact that some attended Mass beyond Zurich's territories. The key to his own success in thwarting the wishes of the conservatives was the support which he had received from the Council. He may well have felt that what had taken place was a warning from God against an untimely change which threatened to prevent the complete triumph of a service which conformed to the teachings of Scripture and would destroy the cultic unity which he felt was necessary for a healthy body politic. His own willingness to accept a compromise, which was hardly a compromise as far as the conservatives were concerned, had been clearly justified by the result. This would explain the next passage of the letter:

> The Lord revealed this advice to us when we were in the process of abrogating the Mass, and if we should not have acted in this way, the opposition would have obtained permission for them to say Mass in some recess. But once, however, [the Mass] was rejected by public authority, no one is now allowed to undertake anything of this kind.

If anything, the letter to Haller and Kolb indicates that Zwingli regretted having pushed for the abolition of the Mass before the time was right and, in order that they might avoid the danger of diversity in cultic practice, advocated that Haller and Kolb follow an even more cautious policy at Bern than he had pursued at Zurich.

. . . The magistracy did not in fact go against either God's Word or the Reformation in December 1523, and, as far as Zwingli was concerned, December 1523 was not a turning point in the Reformation. It was but another stage in the ongoing "rebirth of Christ and the Gospel," carried on, as it had been from the first, in alliance with the civil magistracy which acted as the delegated authority of a Christian people. Yoder does Zwingli less than justice when he claims that Zwingli abandoned the church to assure unity in society. As Zwingli understood the problem church and society were one; to maintain the unity of the commonwealth was to defend the church.

The Path of the Anabaptists into Separation: The Interdependence of Theology and Social Behaviour

Martin Haas

SHIFTS IN ACCENT IN ANABAPTIST WRITINGS

A comparison of the most important writings of Anabaptists in Switzerland between 1524 and 1546 suggests a considerable and striking shift in the accent of their content.

The letter to Müntzer in September 1524 by [Conrad] Grebel and his like-minded friends placed the accent on the demand to execute the Reformation fully and not to be swayed by those who were weak in faith. For *indulgence of the weak* would lead to a mixing of human wisdom and custom with God's Word, hence to deviation from the truth. Areas were enumerated in which at that time the Grebel circle regarded the Reformation as being hindered. Compared with later writings it is conspicuous that the conduct in the Christian *Gemeinde** is mentioned only briefly. It was deplored that many hyprocritically considered themselves Christian but in reality showed no *fruits of faith*. Everyone, meaning the majority, produced no works of faith but continued in his old vices and sinful ways. Thus a topic very important in later Anabaptist thinking was dispensed with by means of this short allusion. The entire remainder of the letter concentrated on explaining where the organizational structure and ritual elements of the Church threatened to remain subject to human ceremonies, in spite of the whole Reformation movement. *Baptism based on confession of faith* had not yet been introduced. The clergy clung to their *benefices* and the rents and tithes connected with them. The images had not been removed everywhere. Neither had the *ban* been introduced into the *Gemeinde* in accordance with Scripture. . . . The majority of the people permitted themselves to be misled by the *false preachers* who were mere anti-papalists, so that only a few true disciples of the Gospel remained. Nowhere was it asserted, however, that the numerical balance had to remain that way. It was obviously accepted that this reflected the momentary situation and could be changed. Especially during the first years, the Anabaptists did everything they could to get a larger following, and in the Swiss area their success was at times considerable. . . .

In the Schleitheim Confession of 1527 the accent has shifted noticeably when compared with earlier writings. Baptism was discussed in the same terms as before, with the exception that "repentance and change in conduct" connected with baptism received greater emphasis. The *ban* and the Lord's Supper continued to be upheld. Together with baptism, they became the external signs of the Christian *Gemeinde*. Also continued was the view that a true minister lived without benefices and tithes. What was new was the long passage concerned with separation. In a large variety of expressions the *Gemeinden* as children of light were instructed to have nothing to do with the dead works of darkness. They were to have nothing in common with those outside; for

*The translators decided to use the German word. The context should make it clear whether *Gemeinde* refers to the Church, a congregation, parish, the community or to the Anabaptist fellowship.

Christ and Belial could have nothing to do with one another. This division applied to all areas of life: public worship, public meetings, going to Church, drinking houses and the sphere of temporal justice, such as sureties, etc. The demand for separation was underlined in other sections in which doctrines not found in earlier writings were adopted. Among the new teachings in comparison to 1524/25 was the view that believers were not permitted to give the *oath*. By this refusal the Anabaptists placed themselves apart from the political and social community, which found its most prominent visible expression in the common swearing of the civic oath. The long discussion concerned with the oath illustrates especially that the view had gradually asserted itself that it was necessary to isolate oneself from society by this means. The postulate that a Christian could not sit in a position of *secular government*, because this would lead to a division of the Christian body, went almost as far. Later utterances of Anabaptists show that the articles laid down at Schleitheim triumphed by and large within Swiss Anabaptism. Evidence is provided by the great disputations with the Anabaptists at Zofingen (1532) and Bern (1538). The development towards separation is not only confirmed but made more precise and accentuated in the writings composed by the Anabaptists during the later period; these writings are now available in the edition prepared by Heinold Fast. . . .

These observations regarding the development towards separation raise certain questions.

On the one hand they touch the area of the history of ideas. Did differences exist between the Anabaptist movement of 1525 and its later development subsequent to the Schleitheim Confession? Is the shift in accent a sign of a different conception of the Church? Or were the later views already fundamentally present in earlier expressions but simply in incomplete form? The questions relate, on the other hand, to actual behaviour in everyday life. Was there a change in Anabaptists' behaviour to the world around them? Did the initiative for this change in behaviour pattern come from the Anabaptists themselves? Or was the opposite the case: did the Anabaptists not change at all, except in a merely external fashion imposed upon them by the world around them?

The answers which this essay seeks for the questions above will be taken not so much from Anabaptist writings as from their everyday behaviour, so as to illustrate the interdependence of theology and behaviour.

FEATURES OF THE EARLY REFORMATION PERIOD

Caution is necessary when one speaks of change or constancy in the early Reformation period. The assertion that a Reformation movement abandoned its earlier stance and adopted a different position carries just as much danger of over-simplification as the view which assumes an absolute constancy of standpoints. This applies to everyone, Luther, Zwingli and the Anabaptists. On the one hand, this over-simplification consists of the fiction that the earliest beginnings of a Reformation movement contained nothing different from what was increasingly elucidated in later confessions. Thus the assertion is made in regard to Luther's theology that it became constantly clearer, that is, that he did nothing else than elucidate his original insights step by step. Thus later denominational dogma was read back into the beginnings of the movement and made into the criterion of the original movement. Up to now this has also happened with Swiss Anabaptism. Early evidence was largely seen in the light of later results and alternative possibilities of development were ignored. . . . On the other hand, a fiction of change was achieved by reading your own denominational standpoint into the earlier expressions of the people who were to become your enemies. Hence they could be accused of having abandoned their own standpoint. This reproach was already raised by the earliest Anabaptists against Zwingli. He was said to have originally taught the same thing as the earliest Anabaptists, but through weakness he had subsequently fallen to the world. In our time [Harold] Bender and especially [J.H.] Yoder adopted this view. Since concepts of continuity and change are encumbered by denominational thinking, it is worthwhile to approach our questions from different assumptions. It appears to me that Franz Lau and Roland Bainton offer a point of departure. Lau coined the expression *Wildwuchs* (best translated as *wild profusion*) for the beginning of the Reformation movement. In this way he characterized the fact that a multiplicity of Reformation branches grew on the basis of an assumed Biblicism and the related proclamation of the Word. Their common standpoint was a biblically-oriented criticism of the Church, but the question where, to what extent, and by what means the reforms were to be carried out was at first left unanswered. As a result contending solutions came to the fore wherever the political situation made the implementation of reforms possible. Only gradually, and with the substantial aid of the secular arm, did certain uniformities become established. They became more distinctive with the emergence of confessions. It is possible with justification to go beyond Lau and describe as "wild profusion" even the early views of those Reformers who later dominated; because their teaching, too, was originally not settled and firm. . . .

What was true of the "major Reformers" may be relevant also to their followers, who, depending on their educational background, suffered particularly under the uncertainty of the wild profusion of the Reformation. This essay intends to sketch in outline how the Anabaptists found their way from wild profusion to the shaping of their own confession.

Roland Bainton described the Reformation as a momentary alliance of diverse attempts at reform and thereby pointed to the many strata of the movement. . . . It was part of the process of the main Reformation up to the point of its establishment, that these diverging strata were cast off or pressured to give up their original notions in favour of settled points of view. The Anabaptists may have been subject to the same internal development. The Schleitheim Confession is an example of how some separated themselves from competing currents within the movement.

In what follows, therefore, the development of Swiss Anabaptism toward confessionalism will be illuminated. However, it is not the intention here to reconstruct the theological argumentation which developed in debate with the Reformers. Rather it will be shown through the external behaviour of Anabaptists, individually and as a group, how diverse desires and notions were united in early Anabaptism, and how they gradually fell apart again. From this there results a sketch of how the movement broke free from its phase as a wild profusion of the Reformation, to the development of norms and patterns of behaviour which eventually led to the structure of later Anabaptism.

ANABAPTISM DURING THE PHASE OF "WILD PROFUSION"

The early years of the Reforation moved on a broad wave of *anticlericalism*, which was directed against monks as well as priests. The full measure of such emotions is only perceived when one studies the literature of popular pamphlets up to 1524, rather than the theological writings of leading Reformers. A significant part of this literature had no other aim but to awaken anticlerical emotions. The priests as a class were depicted as selfish, depraved, uneducated, greedy, and drunken, as using the existing system of church taxes for purposes of carousing. Whoever referred to priests as filthy bellies and pigs could count on widespread approval. As a contemporary remarked, no doubt rightly, the great number of uneducated laymen, and in particular the peasants, were interested primarily in the struggle against the clergy rather than in the refined theological considerations of the leading Reformers. The audience pricked up its ears and missed nothing as soon as someone thundered against the clergy. To the popular mind Luther and Zwingli were exponents of this struggle, and rightly so in the eyes of contemporaries; for did they not with some of their particular invectives join the common chorus?

But what was to take the place of the clergy and its organization? Zwingli pitted the healthy *Gemeinde* of good Christians against the badly educated and depraved hierarchy of the Church. Besides, both he and Luther preached the priesthood of all believers. What was this supposed to mean? Conclusions were drawn in the popular literature. Through the refusal of the tithe the hierarchy, which was of no use and accomplished nothing, could be deprived of its material foundation. The *Gemeinde* was the place where God's word was active. And because before God the clergy were not preferred over the laity, the right to examine the priests was granted to the *Gemeinde*. When they proved unsatisfactory and acted against the Gospel they were dismissed, their support was withdrawn and someone else was elected in their place. In this fashion the right of the *Gemeinde* to elect its ministers was confirmed. If no minister could be found, then the task could also be performed by a layman. He was fit for the task even if only moderately educated; because in the pamphlet literature the peasant had often enough been glorified as the one who with unpretentious Biblical arguments prevailed over the conceited priest, with his education which was directed toward personal profit. Particularly in a Swiss tract, entitled "Hans Knüchel," we find the demand for this type of lay-preacher. Thus notions developed that called for the total destruction of the priestly estate and an overturn of all cultural values. With the destruction of the hierarchical structure of the church external political influence on the *Gemeinde* was eliminated as well. For until then to a considerable extent the appointment and hence the supervision of priests had been under the control of monasteries or more or less feudal secular authorities who exercised the right of collation.

At least in the territory of Zurich, where the Reformation made its first impact, the impression was created that such radical conceptions of the *Gemeinde* might enjoy the sympathies of Zwingli and the government. As late as 1522 Zwingli kindled anticlerical feelings for purposes of motivating the rural population for the Reformation. Anticlericalism was the vehicle through which the people could be mobilized for the further development of the Reformation. Even the government showed a strong disposition to support the rural *Gemeinde* against the collator and the priests of the old faith wherever the Reformation could be advanced in this fashion. Important events of early Anabaptist history in Zurich are part of this context. When Witikon, a village above Zurich, elected its own minister, Wilhelm Reublin, it came into conflict with the Grossmünster chapter, which possessed the benefice. The Council cautiously tolerated the situation, with the proviso that the payment of taxes to the Grossmünster was to be continued. For the time being the Council also supported Höngg, where Simon Stumpf was active, against its collator, the Abbot of Wettingen. Thus the *Gemeinde* appeared to succeed at first in establishing its right to elect the minister.

It was soon realized that the Council's acquiescence did not by any means imply consent to a radical conception of the *Gemeinde*. When in 1523 the peasants in the nearby dependencies of Zurich refused their payments to the Grossmünster, the Council decided that nothing of substance was to be changed in the existing tax structure. It demanded the payments and threatened punishment in case the refusals were repeated. It did not tolerate any further challenges in principle to the rights of the collators. Reformed lords and governments who were disposed to further the interests of the Reformation continued to hold the right to appoint ministers. Not just any layman but only theologically-schooled individuals were eligible for appointment to religious office. Zurich did not even allow any infringement of the rights of non-resident Catholic collators, as long as they were prepared to consider the prevailing ideas of the Zurich church in their appointments. The old church organization was retained where the Reformation had established itself. It was only moderated and modified in spheres where change was regarded as having a Biblical basis.

Ultimately Zwingli, too, developed a different view of the Reformed organization of the *Gemeinde* than his anticlericalism had led many to suspect. Thus he did not leave church policy to the free judgment of the *Gemeinde*, which might change the form of worship and remove the images at its own discretion. Leadership was to be in the hands of the Council. To be sure, it was tied to the evangelical beliefs, regarded as true. How these truths would be translated into action, when Zwingli wanted to realize Reformation objectives, remained a question of political possibilities. The weighing of these possibilities he left to "my lords," reserving for himself the right to urge and to prod when necessary. This was in accord with the Erasmian model of cooperation between the political leadership and the "bishop"; because the political and ecclesiastical *Gemeinde* form a single unit. Similarly Zwingli also basically retained the ecclesiastical organization, even though he was prepared to modify it in case of severe abuse. Finally in his pamphlet "On the Office of the Minister" Zwingli justified the system of collation of benefices as Biblical, at least where the Reformed leadership had been established, by arguing that individual persons who were Christian believers could appoint ministers.

The consequences for the area of Zurich were striking: essentially the same ministers served the *Gemeinden* before and after the Reformation "turning point." The clerical estate had saved itself by moving over more or less *en bloc* into the Reformation. It took its directions from the government and the local theological center of gravity. Only about twenty percent preferred to remain in their old faith and to relinquish their posts as ministers. They found employment in areas that had remained Catholic. Only one, Simon Stumpf, sacrificed his position for the sake of radical convictions which offered no secure future. *Resistance* grew against this development. During the period of unrest the demand surfaced in numerous peasant articles that the *Gemeinde* itself should elect its minister. With this the peasants announced what conclusions they had drawn from the anticlerical campaign. They wanted to eliminate the Church as a factor of authority at least in the domain of the *Gemeinde*. At the same time they believed they were championing the general ideas of ecclesiastical reform when they also opposed the abuses of the feudal structure outside the Church.

As far as the election of ministers was concerned, other dissidents made the same demand. The *Gemeinde* that emerged from the Grebel group and eventually affirmed adult baptism likewise fought the influence of worldly powers in the Church. They turned against the right of the collator to appoint ministers and denied the government's competence to determine and impose reforms on the *Gemeinde* from above. The members of the church themselves should remove images and baptismal stones, celebrate the Lord's Supper and change the practice of baptism by an appeal to the Bible, without waiting for orders from the government. No doubt this went beyond the usual demands of the peasants. Nevertheless, wherever the Anabaptists were able to take root they turned up as allies of the peasants, and aimed to destroy the church organization dominated by temporal government. This situation prevailed during the months following the first adult baptisms of January 21, 1525, starting with Zollikon and Waldshut. In Witikon and Zollikon Reublin and Brötli acted as free ministers elected and maintained by the *Gemeinde* (Reublin from 1522 in Witikon and Brötli a little later in Zollikon) until they were driven out by governmental power. Likewise they and other leaders in Hallau, in the neighborhood of St. Gall, and in the jurisdiction of Grüningen, struggled for the rights of the parish against minister, collator and temporal government. Through this they made themselves a part of the peasant upheavals and found a willing hearing among the rural population. Under the leadership of Brötli and Reublin the *Gemeinde* in Hallau moved into action and expelled the minister, which was within its right at least in regard to the church of St. Ulrich. They also refused to make payments to the monastery of All Saints in Schaffhausen. When the government of Schaffhausen tried to intervene, the *Gemeinde* defended itself with arms. In the neighborhood of St. Gall, particularly in Tablat, the peasants also assumed the right to hear a minister of their own choosing. They sided with the Anabaptist leader Krüsi. He in turn solicited a promise of aid from the surrounding region should the bailiff use force to arrest him. To be sure, in the jurisdiction of Grüningen, a dependency of Zurich, the peasant uprising had already subsided when the Anabaptists gained a foothold in July 1525. But in Hinwil they took control of the worship service and strove for a conflict between minister and *Gemeinde*.

. . . .

It is not surprising, therefore, that the Anabaptist worship service was originally by no means separated from the world. Everyone could join it in St. Gall. Krüsi preached openly beside the church of St. George. Other preachers could be found at the lodge of the shooting society outside the city, also at the open place before the Multergate enclosed by lime trees. . . .

In Hallau, where the majority of the village belonged to the Anabaptists, Brötli probably preached in the church. At any rate adult baptism was pretty certainly practised there. The *Gemeinde* in Zollikon, too, had moved at least part of its activity into the church. There Jörg Schad baptised close to forty persons who had gathered from the whole surrounding area. The disruptions of sermons by Blaurock in Zollikon and later in Hinwil also point to the fact that the aim was to win the entire village community for the Anabaptist ideas and by no means to bring about a separation. By interrupting the minister, Blaurock likewise demonstrated his conception of the *Gemeinde*, according to which it was intolerable that a government-appointed minister alone should be listened to. In accordance with I Corinthians 14, other members were to be given a chance to speak, too.

. . . .

The case was similar with the Lord's Supper. From Grebel's letter to Müntzer it is possible to draw the conclusion that, because faith and love were to precede the communion, Grebel wanted to admit only those who were joined in brotherly love to the meal of union. Later on this notion became associated with the idea that only those who had been baptised could participate in the

Lord's Supper. However, at least one celebration of the Lord's Supper, open to everyone who desired it, is documented for Zollikon. In St. Gall the Anabaptist communion was even celebrated openly under the lime trees near the Multergate. This was no doubt intended as an invitation so that as many as possible might join.

Grebel and Hubmaier appear to have intended a dominant Anabaptist Reformation that could wrest the leadership from the Zwinglian orientation. After the failure of his efforts in Zurich Grebel stopped only briefly at Zollikon, leaving subsequent work there to his companions, while he concentrated on Schaffhausen, where he hoped to win Sebastian Hofmeister, the dominant preacher. One of Grebel's relatives, Hans von Waldkirch, was an influential councilor and later burgomaster of the city. Grebel's lengthy residence in Schaffhausen can only be interpreted as an attempt to spread the Anabaptist Reformation with the aid of the local spiritual and political leadership. Inasmuch as Grebel was not aiming at a Reformation by governmental command, he had not betrayed his conception of *Gemeinde*. In St. Gall, Vadian, another relative of Grebel and also a politically influential councilor, had remained ambivalent on the question of baptism as late as 1524. Grebel travelled to St. Gall in order to win him over, and at the same time was active in the *Gemeinde* which had formed there. Hubmaier worked towards a similar objective among the spiritual leaders. He attempted to win some of the key personalities for Anabaptism, including Oecolampadius, Hofmeister, Jud and others.

When Grebel recognized how poor his prospects were in Schaffhausen and St. Gall, he turned to work in the *Gemeinden*, where this was still feasible. He had to be satisfied with areas which were territorial dependencies, and hence with the role of opposition. In mid-summer 1525 he shifted his activity to the population in the jurisdiction of Grüningen.

The Anabaptist movement had become a many-layered complexity of expectations. Especially its conception of *Gemeinde* gained widespread sympathy, because it corresponded most closely to the expectations raised by the anticlerical campaign. The Anabaptist attacks upon the beneficed ministry were perceived to be a consistent continuation of the anticlericalism of the early Reformation period. Particularly the uneducated, who could hardly understand the nuanced theological issues of the Reformation, saw in anticlericalism the central issue of the movement. Thus the tithe and the choice of the minister became the issues around which the entire movement really crystallized. Anabaptist leaders sought support from the emotions aroused by these issues, and to a degree whipped these same emotions up, in order to win whole communities for Anabaptism. Principles that had originally been cherished by the Grebel circle disappeared in the whirlpool created by the mass movement. For anticlericalism had brought many notions together in the reservoir of Anabaptism, among them: the readiness to rebel in the struggle for the *Gemeinde* principle, the possibility of armed resistance, mass baptisms that retained only a fraction of the original emphasis on a changed disposition, the open Lord's Supper that stretched the boundaries of brotherly love very far.

IN SEARCH OF IDENTITY

During this phase of resistance Anabaptism can be called a mass movement. The actual number of those baptised is not important for this designation. We are poorly informed about the numerical strength of the *Gemeinden*. Careful and substantiated estimates suggest that more than half of the inhabitants of the village of Zollikon allied themselves with Anabaptism. A contemporary considered the proportion to have been even higher in Hallau. Estimates concerning St.

Gall fluctuate. It makes no difference whether the Anabaptists there numbered eight hundred or somewhat fewer; because it is not clear whether the peasants of the Abbey of St. Gall or even those from Appenzell were included in that figure. Over two hundred persons were present in one of the meetings.

However, the designation "mass movement" is justified by Anabaptist behaviour during this period. Even though there were documented cases in which acceptance followed only upon self-examination and confession, the general influx was of such proportions that admittance to the *Gemeinde* took place relatively easily. In St. Gall, for example, it became a mere formality. Moreover, a certain openness to compromise was apparent in the Anabaptist willingness to join the collective movement of anticlericalism. In these circumstances it was not surprising that there was a readiness among Anabaptists to abandon earlier ideas in order to accommodate the larger number. This is a mode of behaviour that openly announces the willingness to become a mass movement, and to relinquish strict control over members of the *Gemeinde*. From the point of view of sociology of religion this was not a case of separatism, much less of sectarianism.

Opposition arose against this trend. Chronologically it paralleled the development described above and created a competing ideal within the movement. The core of the group seeking a different identity for the Anabaptist church centered on Grebel, Mantz, Blaurock and members of the *Gemeinde* in Zollikon, although Grebel, too, had at times sympathized with the general mood of rebellion. In the final analysis the tendency toward separation prevailed not only through its own strength, but because the government did its share in breaking the mass movement, thus forcing Anabaptism into isolation. This process will be described below.

The position of the minister (*Vorsteher*) in the Anabaptist *Gemeinde* was defined very early. He had no benefice but was sustained by free gifts, if he needed support at all. Johan Brötli, for example, had earned his livelihood in Zollikon through the work of his own hands in order not to burden anyone. For that same reason a former priest joined the Anabaptists because he wanted to live from the labour of his own hands without other income; and the former monk Uliman learned a trade in St. Gall. Already in February 1525 in a conversation with Hofmeister, Grebel had made the general observation that the pulpit preachers and those who held benefices could never preach the real truth.

The position of the Anabaptist minister, more correctly referred to as *Vorsteher*, appeared from the beginning very limited. No monologues were permitted in the worship service, because it was reminiscent of the preachers of the old faith. This appeared to be Blaurock's point when he interrupted the official sermon in Zollikon and demanded the right to speak also. It was customary from early on that everyone who could read, read one after the other at Anabaptist gatherings. Furthermore it is conspicuous that a very large number of the *Gemeinde* at Zollikon participated in preaching and in baptising. This implied that the personal responsibility was rather dispersed and that in this *Gemeinde* there was no single dominating office of minister. The weight of the *Gemeinde* was greater than that of the minister. . . .

The dominance of the *Gemeinde* over the minister was evident in the *Gemeinde's* authority to watch over the minister's conduct and to remove him if necessary. This occurred in the case of the prominent leader, Lincki, who had been among the Anabaptist spokesmen at the Zofingen disputation of 1532. During imprisonment at Basel he swore an oath, which from the Anabaptist point of view offended against Christian conduct. From that time on he was no longer accepted as a teacher by the Anabaptists. Later this practice apparently gained more and more ground; for instance, Marpeck criticized the Swiss, especially those in Appenzell, saying that the flock was too frivolous in punishing the shepherds.

. . . .

There is no change of Swiss Anabaptist behaviour or conception as far as the organizational structure of the *Gemeinde* is concerned; its main features remained constant. Insofar as the sources permit an overview, the Swiss Anabaptist movements followed this pattern everywhere. However, this form of organization, by raising an unbridgeable barrier against the practices of the Zwinglian Reformation, became an important element in the process of *institutional* separation. During disputations with Anabaptists the Reformed ministers supported with Scriptural citations their view that the right of the collator had a Biblical foundation. Furthermore they justified the hierarchical structure of offices, which was modified rather than abolished by the Reformation, with an appeal to I Corinthians 12:28, Rom. 12:6 ff., and Eph. 4:11,13. Beyond that, the prevailing principles of hierarchical order were openly transferred from the secular to the Christian *Gemeinde* as norms to be aspired to. The Anabaptists wanted nothing to do with such a pagan assembly because they perceived this hierarchical order as unchristian.

Separation, however, has still another significance. It is not only a matter of being conscious of the gulf separating you from those who believe differently. Otherwise the expression would be applicable to the Reformed and Catholic churches as well. But for them separation never received the central confessional character that it had in Anabaptist formulations. Rather the Anabaptists coupled with it a behaviour pattern which expressed their consciousness of being the only elect Christian minority. This behaviour was conditioned by a series of historical events.

Governmental pressure forced the suppression of the peasant movements. Among other things this meant that it had become hopeless, against the will of the government, to achieve the *Gemeinde* structure that had won so many sympathizers. Accordingly the right freely to elect the minister could not be generally realized, and the hope that the tithe would be abolished proved an illusion. The weapons employed for restructuring the *Gemeinde* failed over against the military strength at the disposal of the rulers. Thus for a great number of Anabaptists and Anabaptist sympathizers the goal which had made the movement attractive proved unattainable. Eventually the Anabaptist movement offered too little for the mass of sympathizers, because Grebel and other prominent leaders decided to pay tithes and rents to the pagan world, even though they wanted to have nothing to do with the official church. Thus further support of Anabaptism—with all its risks—was no longer worthwhile for a majority of sympathizers.

For casual adherents Anabaptist *baptismal theology* was difficult to understand. The general population stood on an educational niveau which did not permit their participation in theological controversies. Anyone examining the role of the "masses" in the Reformation movement discovers soon enough that there was no spontaneity. Wherever in Switzerland the common people intervened directly before 1525, they acted upon the incitement of those with theological schooling. They could be mobilized most easily for iconoclasm, breaking fast restrictions, tithe refusal, and insulting priests and monks of the old faith. These were issues that even the poorly educated could grasp.

. . . .

Furthermore by generalizing about the entire movement from a few isolated occurrences the government had by 1527 successfully discredited the Anabaptists in the eyes of the public. Sexual excesses in St. Gall and Appenzell, Thomas Schugger's murder of his brother, and some isolated inclinations towards the removal of private property were generalized as typical. By this means the Anabaptists were branded as having broken the social taboos of their time. In various places this led no doubt to a defensive social reaction against them.

Alongside these efforts by the government to press the movement into isolation and besides the behaviour of society in general, the Anabaptists themselves took measures that proved of primary significance on their path into separation.

To these belonged first of all *the refusal to take the oath.* In the letter of the Grebel group to Müntzer nothing was as yet said about the oath, and this principle was in the beginning entirely unknown among the Anabaptists. When the first Anabaptists from Zollikon were arrested and questioned, they showed themselves entirely prepared to take an oath that in future they would no longer baptize. But the behaviour of some individuals was already different. Mantz before anyone else refused the oath. The conviction that it was wrong to swear the oath appears to have slowly spread from this point on. . . . It was promoted by Grebel, Mantz and Blaurock in their visits to the *Gemeinden*, and, the more it spread, the further the whole movement placed itself politically aloof from the rest of society. For the oath was the form that validated the entire political and judicial system. According to the traditional perception a community was unthinkable without the oath. Every refusal of the oath, including the oath of political fidelity, placed the person outside the system.

. . . .

Finally the question of *whether a Christian could be part of the governmental authority* also assumed increasing significance in the early Anabaptist *Gemeinde*. In the letter to Müntzer the Grebel group had at first only denied the government any right to intervene within the Christian community by means of decrees. It was not the government's business to determine questions concerning images, the Lord's Supper, baptism, etc. However, because of the interdependency of ecclesiastical and secular authority it was impossible to determine the precise limits of governmental influence. The statements of the Anabaptists were therefore not uniform on this subject. These expressions ranged from a statement of readiness to obey, to the comment that believers' baptism will ultimately limit governmental authority to the point that it would be "abdicated" in a very large sphere. Since it proved impossible to persuade "my lords" to relinquish their pretensions to religious authority, the radical conclusion soon followed that a Christian has no place in the government. It was believed that secular office led to a division of the *Gemeinde* and that rulers because of their secular interests did not attain the proper standard of Christian love; they tolerated compromise. This view grew out of the concrete situation in Zurich in which the Anabaptists were a minority but was also supported by theological arguments. The other Anabaptist *Gemeinden* did not at first accept it without questioning. . . .

[Examples from St. Gall and Schaffhausen] illustrate that conversion to Anabaptism and withdrawal from political office did not take place at exactly the same time. This behaviour indicates that the position of the Christian in public office was not yet rigorously clear. Only gradually did the conviction of Grebel and Mantz, that the Christian had to remain aloof from all political office and leadership, carry the day. It is not entirely certain whether the government on its side contributed somewhat to the Anabaptists' isolation by excluding them from its ranks on the occasion that the offices were filled. The sources are silent on this subject.

Changing attitudes to the question of tithes and rents also were important in the Anabaptists' path into separation. As noted earlier, wherever the Anabaptists held a large following they attempted to achieve their own kind of church structure. Rejection of the tithe was part of it. Perhaps it has to be seen as a reaction against the mingled motivations that inspired the broad influx into the movement that opposition grew up against the rejection of the tithe. It was totally in keeping with nonresistance—acceptance of suffering in the face of the world, separation from unchristian authority—when individual preachers admonished their followers, who tended toward rebellion, not to resist the world by refusing the tithe. . . . A true Christian paid the tithe, even though he did not believe the minister of the established church, and himself had no place in it. Blaurock said this with particular clarity in the jurisdiction of Grüningen which was seething with rebellion: those who refuse the tithe are not Anabaptists; whoever belongs to the Anabaptists pays the tithe. Thus the Anabaptist leaders themselves completed the break with those postulates that originally contributed to the attraction of the movement. They separated from those whose seriousness of motive was questionable.

It belonged to the characteristics of the Anabaptists that they attempted to make the church visible for their followers; visible, as it were, with *external signs of solidarity*. . . .

These signs may be accepted as the expressions of a minority which in spite of persecution wanted to remain together. At the same time these peculiar traits were to further the self-consciousness of the fellowship and brotherhood. The Bible provided the criteria for these norms. Other customs were however a clearer expression of separation. The Anabaptists no longer greeted those whom they met and who were not part of the fellowship, in order to indicate that they had nothing to do with the world. II John 10 f. provided the standard. Naturally a common lodging and common meals were no longer possible with the people of the world. Kessler found it noteworthy that the exhortations for this type of behaviour came from Conrad Grebel. The recommendation was later taken up in a literal sense by Marti Weniger and at least indirectly by the Schleitheim Confession. The Anabaptists in Solothurn, too, held to similar regulations in 1533. They did not participate in the common duties of the village population either in keeping watch or in the fire brigade. In Bern they confirmed that they would never cite one another before a secular court. In Solothurn and in Zurich members of the Anabaptist group were buried near their own dwellings rather than in the cemetery. Sattler, as well, described forms of separation when he advised the brothers concerning divorce. To be sure he did not advocate real divorce, but he left the possibility open that a brother or a sister might leave the family if the family persisted in unbelief. For one ought not to love father, mother or wife more than Christ. Numerous documents give proof that many Anabaptists followed this admonition.

Church discipline in general remained the most important means to make the fellowship self-conscious and visible for its members, and the obvious basis for separation from the world. . . .

Without doubt the eagerness with which the instruments of discipline were applied led to a quick cleansing of the group. Whoever did not repent openly before the *Gemeinde* and change his conduct was no longer accepted. Because the *Gemeinde* possessed the power of the keys, those who remained outside it and were shunned as heathens would also forfeit heaven.

Anabaptist conduct was so radically regulated that the Anabaptists were henceforth conspicuous in contrast to the surrounding world. Their earnestness and dedication distinguished them from the official church and gave them their own profile. This enhanced the internal coherence of the movement by the formation in solidarity of a new life style. However, it also accentuated the distance from the rest of society which was perceived as wicked. The quality of the Anabaptist way of life was acknowledged even by the ministers of the established churches when they complained that the Anabaptists attracted the most pious and best of all.

Anabaptist sermons were marked from very early on by thoughts of separation. To be sure we possess few summaries of sermons, but we know that Jakob Schnider selected Mathew 24, Luke 14, and John 15 as his texts. The emphasis was first of all upon manner of life: for Christians could be recognized by their fruits. This compulsion toward a positive principle of distinction was strengthened by the threat of the coming Judgement. At the same time these passages could be used to stress the chasm separating their group from the vile official church; for it was a sign of the end-time that false prophets would arise in order to mislead the people (Matthew 24:11). The Christians were hated by the world and must suffer persecution (John 15:18 ff.).

In the wake of such a tendency to separatism the behaviour toward the worship service in the official church changed. Previously, in the context of "wild profusion," worship services had been disrupted and attempts were made to win over the whole *Gemeinde*. Then came the counter movement. As early as March 1525 an Anabaptist in Zollikon had decided no longer to attend sermons because nothing had really changed in the church. The structure of the *Gemeinde* had remained about the same, because the system of benefices remained still in effect. The parsons continued to mislead the people as they had done for a long time. This conviction remained. By March 1526 the Anabaptists had clarified their position. The members of the fellowship encouraged each other not to attend the sermons of the established ministers. They feared being misled by false teachings. The circle was complete. In order to remain unshaken in their own conviction they stayed among themselves. One Anabaptist was excommunicated, placed under the ban and given over to damnation because he suggested the inclusion of the local minister in discussions among Anabaptists. The conduct of Hans Hottinger during June 1525 in Zollikon illustrates the changing attitude in relation to the official church. He no longer aimed at discussion in the Church, but called out to the *Gemeinde*: "Beware of the false prophets, go out, go out!" The determination to separation could not have been clearer. Not only Anabaptist teaching but Anabaptist conduct as well implied a critique of the established church. They refused to participate in the Lord's Supper, because all sinners were permitted to participate without any signs of repentance or remorse, and without the use of the ban. For the Anabaptists, however, open sinners could have no place at the Lord's table.

THE WEIGHT OF SEPARATION

Originally Anabaptism combined two tendencies: first, the obligation to follow Christ in conduct and, secondly, the intention to restructure the organization of the *Gemeinde* radically, that is, the clerical order and the system of church-taxes. In principle the two objectives were not mutually exclusive. However, at first the second tendency received special attention and recognition wherever the movement went beyond Zollikon. Originally the Anabaptist leaders sought not only advancement of their cause in influential circles but support for it among the masses. Especially Grebel was concerned with decisively influencing the direction of the entire Reformation and aimed either to supplant Zwingli or, later, to compete with him. The Anabaptists and the peasants, especially, found themselves in the collective reservoir of anticlericalism and refusal of the tithe.

The expected breakthrough did not materialise, because the union of the rulers and the beneficed clergy prevented it. The broad stream of sympathizers had to recognize that the desired order of the *Gemeinde* could not be achieved. Thus they no longer dared to engage themselves for the cause. These external circumstances drove the Anabaptists into a minority position.

The influential leaders developed the teaching of the movement in a parallel fashion and in accordance with their understanding of the demand to follow Christ. To it belonged factors that promoted isolation: the refusal of the oath, the denial that secular authority could be Christian. Through this trend the movement separated itself from its earlier followers, and strengthened the effect of discrimination by the government. It insisted on nonresistance and repelled all influences to the contrary. At the same time the Anabaptists were satisfied with eliminating tithes and rents merely within the structure of their own group. Over against the world they were prepared to honor these obligations.

The minority community strengthened itself by orienting its entire conduct and customs rigorously according to the Bible. The solidarity of the children of light became internally visible to the brothers and sisters and at the same time they distinguished themselves from the world which they disparaged as luke-warm and sinful. For fear of being seduced they broke off contact with outsiders or at least reduced it, insofar as there was any. Only economic dealings remained open.

Doctrines developed in conjunction with this external behaviour. This was not only illustrated in the Schleitheim Confession, which assigned great weight to separation, but also by Anabaptist statements during the disputations at Zofingen and Bern. The Christian's duty to separate from the world was the criterion for questions of right conduct, the right church, the commission of the ministers (*Vorsteher*) and the use of the ban. Separation became absolutely *the* essential trait of the Christian.

Even then, the importance of separation is not to be overestimated. The Anabaptists themselves left the possibility open that if conditions changed the barriers might fall.

Meanwhile the Anabaptists had established the conduct of their *Gemeinde* and their doctrine in such a way as to lack the possibility for such a change. Soon their *Gemeinde* structure was no longer derived from the flexible authority of the leadership, but from rigorous group pressure, which demanded the full surrender of the individual. The total integration of the individual into the fellowship led to a corresponding fulfillment of all norms. The longer this condition persisted, the more deeply rooted became the new behaviour pattern and with it the separation from the world. As long as the conditions in the "world" did not change fundamentally and society did not open itself to tolerance, the chance for a change in Anabaptist attitudes diminished more and more.

The beginning of this distinctive form of the Swiss Brethren did not go back as early as Zollikon. The life of that *Gemeinde* was too brief to permit the development of norms and doctrines of the sort we have described, although it provided important impulses. Neither did this beginning occur in Hallau or St. Gall, where Anabaptism was combined with a mass movement. It appears that the first *Gemeinde* which combined in itself all the described traits existed in the Zurich Lowland. Felix Mantz, Blaurock, Michael Sattler, Karl Brennwald, Pfistermeyer and Konrad Winkler had been active in this area. The *Gemeinde* stretched all the way to Schaffhausen and into the *Freiamt*. For this very reason it already carried the traits of a minority. This was the model that asserted itself victoriously at Schleitheim and thereafter spread in Switzerland and in South Germany.

Revolutionary Reformation

Karel Vos

Our Mennonite forefathers were extremely sensitive about the subject of Münster. Even now there are some who would prefer that the matter not be discussed. They would rather have the pleasant aspects of our history brought to light. Formerly it was no joy to hear the reproach: you really descended from the Münsterite revolutionaries with their polygamy. That reproach coming both from Catholics and Reformed was uncomfortable at the time of the persecutions, when people belonged to the Dutch Baptists who had gone through the years of upheaval. Their children and grandchildren had to hear this taunt continuously at the time of the Dutch War of Independence, when the Reformed discovered with envy that the nonresistant sheep of Christ were such excellent businessmen. In order to deny the reproach another origin was sought for. The opponents themselves suggested a linkage with Thomas Müntzer and the Peasants' War. "No," it was answered, "we stem from the Swiss Baptists who began a baptist Reformation in 1522 at Zurich under the leadership of Grebel and Mantz." That way, the movement had begun before the time of Hoffman and Matthijs and some of the brothers merely went astray. Others went further and asserted a Waldensian origin. That idea, however, was given up a long time ago as indefensible. Blaupot ten Cate suggested the hypothesis that an independent study of the Bible had given rise to a baptist movement in the Netherlands, which was accordingly independent from foreign influence. In that case it would be necessary to date its beginning after 1525, the year when Dutch Bibles first began to circulate. Then came Scheffer. He painted a picture with such pretty colors that since his time all Dutch Baptists have thought that the Münsterite stain was washed away. His exhaustive study of the Reformation in the Netherlands to 1531 established that it was entirely independent from Luther, although there were a number of Lutherans connected with it. Our Reformation exhibited a distinctive trait that was anti-Lutheran—namely, a widespread disbelief in the miracle of the mass. He labeled the proponents of this standpoint as "Sacramentarians." The Dutch Baptists were supposed to have been recruited from these circles. In order to establish the earliest possible beginning date of the movement, he tried to prove that there had been heretical views in the Netherlands even before Luther's emergence (e.g., Menno already doubted the miracle of the mass in 1516).

So as to avoid the conclusion that the Dutch Baptist movement began with Hoffman, hence after 1530, he tried to make it plausible that there had been baptist seeds in the Netherlands ever since 1525. Thus there would have been baptist circles before the chiliastic preaching that the millennium would dawn with the second coming of Christ in 1534. He postulated an intensive propaganda before fall 1533, the time that Jan Matthijs set Hoffman's followers, the Melchiorites, on a revolutionary path. Particularly in North Holland there were supposed to have been many baptist congregations with numerous followers and a great number of teachers. At Amsterdam there were supposed to have been thousands of peaceful baptists; and the number of revolutionaries who attacked the town hall in 1535 was very small. A small number were assumed to have been misled into the Münsterite uprisings. In 1536 Menno joined the baptists whose teaching has been described, and from them he received the ideas which he thereafter defended in writing.

· ·

Anyone who would undertake at this time to maintain Scheffer's essential position must first prove that the Sacramentarians made more than a sporadic appearance, that they really formed congregations and not loose circles. He must prove that before autumn 1533 there was already a significant number of baptists, that the formation of congregations was being considered, and particularly that there were many peaceful baptists, and that in the years before 1535 they had some other impulse than merely the notion that the imminent arrival of the kingdom of God would soon give rise to an entirely different society. All the knowledge that we possess of this early period we owe to archivalia concerning the suppression of the revolutionary disturbances and the closely related persecution. When Scheffer asserts, "The majority had an aversion to violence," this is said without any proof. . . .

In fact a baptist Reformation movement did begin at Zurich in 1522. But it had no direct contact with the Netherlands. Hoffman is the connecting link. The Zurichers built up a positive baptist conviction, a dogmatic whole of which the central point was baptism on confession of faith. As early as 1527 their teachers at [Schleitheim] instituted a confession which encompassed their principal points of doctrine. They spread their teaching to Strassburg but it contained no mention of a peculiar belief about the incarnation of Christ. This belief (that Christ did not receive his material body from Mary) is a distinguishing characteristic of the Dutch Melchiorites, accepted on the authority of Hoffman; taken over by Menno, it was held by later Mennonites until far into the seventeenth century. The confession of [Schleitheim] only became known in the Netherlands around 1560; and the Waterlanders who had a more liberal doctrinal position than Menno's adopted it only at a much later time. To be sure, Hans Denck had proclaimed liberal beliefs among the Swiss-South German congregations (e.g., doubts about the divinity of Christ), but such ideas were propagated in the Netherlands only after 1545 by Adam Pastor, and then only in the East. There is not a bit of proof that before the Münsterite upheavals there was present in the Netherlands even the slightest knowledge of the Swiss baptists. Moreover the Swiss were no chiliasts; in other words the belief in the imminent second coming of Christ was not in the foreground for them.

Entirely independent from them Melchior Hoffman began to make chiliastic propaganda in Germany: the millennial kingdom was to be instituted in 1534; Strassburg was to be the New Jerusalem. However when he came to Strassburg he established connections with the baptists and took over the practice of rebaptism from them. He called it the sign of Thau, which must be worn on the forehead by anyone who wanted to be received into the heavenly kingdom. Thus rebaptism is not the central tenet of a new Protestant teaching but the sign of the covenant which all covenanters must possess in order to participate in the future earthly glory. Hoffman attached so little special worth to it that in 1531 he commanded that baptism should cease for a two-year period. Such a command would have been incomprehensible if he had regarded baptism as the central point of his teaching. Hoffman gave no indication of revolutionary ideas. However, Pirenne observed correctly that a belief that promised the overthrow of the existing order, as well as the coming of a glittering wonderworld, would be extraordinarily attractive to the unpropertied classes.

He stated that the government, on observing such a movement assume a mass character, would see a threat to civil society; indeed such a teaching, so well suited to the uncomplicated thought processes and the childlike simplicity of the common people, must necessarily take on a revolutionary character.

In the Netherlands, until 1531, there were merely circles of Sacramentarians. In one of these circles of Amsterdam, Trijpmaker, who had come into contact with Hoffman in East Frisia, proclaimed the chiliastic belief and baptised a few dozen from the lesser citizenry, workers and sailors. Hoffman himself also spent a few weeks in the Netherlands. When Trijpmaker's propaganda spread beyond Amsterdam he was arrested and executed, together with eight of his coreligionists. Sicke Freerks, a tailor, who had been baptised in Emden, proclaimed the new belief in Leeuwarden and was beheaded shortly thereafter. In consequence, however, a small circle of unbaptised Melchiorites originated in the capital of Frisia. At a generous estimate there were a few hundred rebaptised persons in Amsterdam and its environs when they were intimidated by the execution of the group of nine and simultaneously Hoffman's prohibition of baptism came to be known. For two years a silent propaganda was continued among the common people to the effect that in 1534 the heavenly kingdom would dawn. The chiliastic idea flourished continuingly among the poor. They called themselves "covenanters." Men of common origin, called prophets, proclaimed that God would deliver Amsterdam to the covenanters after a three-day period of darkness. The massive propaganda for baptism began only immediately before the start of 1534, and indeed with exclusive attention to the approaching Day of the Lord. The poor and the unemployed, the wharf workers and sailors and manual laborers, many of them illiterate, who submitted to rebaptism did so pretty much spontaneously from fear of the Day of Judgment and hope for partnership in a rich life. Such an assemblage from the dregs of the population cannot be looked upon as a baptist brotherhood, as Scheffer would have us believe. How small their following was thought to be is illustrated by Assendelft's report of 22 February 1534, which estimates the number in all of North Holland at between five and six hundred. A prisoner put it more correctly at three thousand. Indeed it must be kept in mind that, according to the judicial records, a very great number of the imprisoned chiliasts were unbaptised (I suspect the overwhelming majority of those apprehended in 1534). And it was particularly women—Thiessen noticed this, too—who were attracted by the ecstasy of Anabaptism. The fanatical pronouncements came from the mouths of women.

Anabaptism turned into a mass movement and thus became revolutionary in the fall of 1533 through the emergence of the new prophet Jan Matthijs, who sent forth twelve missionaries. The view that the revolution was incited by a bitter persecution is incorrect. Until February 1534 there is scarcely any mention of persecution which likewise shows that the Melchiorite movement did not yet amount to much. Otherwise the government would surely have intervened. The fierce language of Jan Matthijs, the rumor that at Münster the bishop had been expelled and the New Jerusalem set up, the notion that the Day of Judgment was at hand, plague, famine, the rising cost of living, the appearance of three comets (in 1531, 1532 and 1533) as messengers of the imminent end of the world, all brought the small group to fever pitch. Herman, a chaplain from the Hague, preached that the poor had a right to a rich man's property. The spark in the powder keg was the appeal from Münster in February 1534 to assemble at Bergklooster and to set out for Münster: "Let whoever has a knife or a spear or a gun bring it along, and let anyone who does not have one buy it." The multitude was no longer to be restrained. The latent revolutionary became an active one. That a short letter was capable of mobilizing a *levee en masse* proves that the mood of chiliastic ecstasy was totally prepared for this. Thousands of hearts were so disposed that the ships could be manned, "in order to journey to the Promised Land," with wives and children on board, to be sure, but also properly armed with spears and guns. They hoped that their needs would be supplied once they got to Münster. The Waterlanders travelled away joyously, thinking that the towers of Westzaan were already beginning to sink.

Shortly before the beginning of the journey to Bergklooster, the government learned about it. Hasty orders were dispatched to calm the people and bring them to reason. The government concluded that some local officials had been guilty of dereliction of duty; Jan Hubrechts, bailiff of Amsterdam, was suspended. The people were warned that the government could not permit the departure. Here and there arrests began on a limited scale. A rebaptised, runaway priest was killed on the spot. By decree mercy was promised to anyone who confessed to his priest within six days. Only fifteen complied. Still the movement was regarded as so inconsequential that it was thought possible to bring the country people to reason by sending an expedition of 25 soldiers through the villages. But to calm the demented multitude proved even harder than to check the drifting ice on a swift river. Men, women and children boarded ship. At Haarlem seven ships were captured, at Amsterdam six, at Kampen twenty-seven; twelve ships got away. Near Kampen three thousand were taken prisoner, in Holland several hundred. We have further information only about those arrested in Holland. The booty in weapons was great: near Kampen, 1000 to 1500 spears, many guns, halberds, four small banners, four drums and other weapons. The government achieved such a rapid victory because the established citizenry immediately took its side. Without this assistance the government with its small military force would not have had an easy time of it. But the aid proved how frightened the propertied class was. Besides, confronting the well disciplined soldiers was only a motley crowd, badly equipped and badly led. And at Kampen they were taken by surprise. . . . Of the prosecuted [Anabaptists taken off the ships in Holland] about nine-tenths were pardoned after having declared that they were misled due to their own simplicity. They escaped with a monetary fine. The remaining ten per cent were executed, and some who showed no repentance were burned. Since there was only a very small yield from most of the confiscations and the amounts of the individual fines were small (e.g., 3 florins), it is clear that the overwhelming majority belonged to the lesser citizenry. This was more than obvious in the reports: (23 February 1534) "they are people without means or influence"; on the other hand, it was stated (25 February 1535) that the "money" is on the side of the government. Therefore we have to assume about anyone involved in these trials that he was prosecuted on account of his revolutionary behavior, unless the contrary can be shown from the documents. I have not encountered such a document. It was a large group in which naturally there were different degrees of revolutionary feeling, but in each individual there lived the expectation that in a short time the power of the government would come to an end, that God would intervene and that an entirely new order would begin. Scheffer gave birth to the legend of the "peaceful" Jacob van Campen. A reading of the documents shows, however, that he confessed to have assented to the command from Münster that everyone in the covenant should buy weapons, and that he owned a sword. He was not a peaceful but a fearful man, who when the covenanters planned an attack would change his lodging during the night in order to be on the safe side. Elsewhere anyone arrested after the ships were stopped in April 1534 belonged to those who attracted the attention of the government by their rebellious behavior during the days when the desire to journey to Münster bubbled up everywhere. Mary of Hungary [regent of the Netherlands] prosecuted them "as ill-bred people, beggars and workers, whose single goal was to plunder churches, noblemen, citizens and merchants, so as to assemble a great pile of stolen goods and then to share them among themselves as they were needed."

The regent may have exaggerated. But it is certain that they maintained a "common chest." There is some evidence that suggests a communistic tendency. It is my impression that the victims belong not in a baptist but in a chiliastic martyrology. The simple fact of their rebaptism doesn't make them into baptists who have embraced a Protestant teaching in which baptism on confession of faith is the central tenet.

All the places where according to the documents a great number of Melchiorites lived were known for revolutionary disturbances. There is no single peaceful region to point to. It is my impression that it can only be shown that individual men turned against the violent ones: Menno and the brothers, Obbe and Dirk Philips. But they were in this period ardent chiliasts—Menno and Dirk remained chiliasts to their death, although the ardor disappeared—and Obbe's preaching at 't Zandt caused religious lunacy among some of the persons he baptised. Menno's state of excitement, as late as 1537, is visible in his "On the Spiritual Resurrection." For him, too, the New Jerusalem descends from heaven.

Revolutionary Anabaptism led to all kinds of excesses. It was by no means rooted out but continued to smoulder on for at least ten years in a number of places; and the government had to continuously intervene during this period to check attacks on the social order. There was also a persecution of Davidjorites in 1539. At this point we will examine some of their opinions. The excesses led to polygamy in Münster, to sexual debauchery among the followers of David Joris and the later Family of Love, and to religious frenzy [elsewhere]. Jan Matthijs himself was subject to such frenzies; besides him, we have "God the Father and God the Son" at 't Zandt, the King of Zion at Poeldijk, and at Amsterdam, the Naked Walkers, who threw their clothes away, and the Sword Walkers, who ran through the streets, yelling "Repent! Repent!" The cry, "Slay all priests and rulers," betrays the mentality that dominated in these circles. Obbe complained that the false brothers, who were contradicted by him and Dirk, swore to kill them. And, when he left the movement around 1540, he wrote that he greatly lamented the "inexpressible spiritual presumption which broke out from the very first hour", and that the baptised immediately cried out that the unbaptised "should be rooted out"; that was "no Christian congregation but an abomination of desolation."

Meanwhile Menno was stimulated by the execution of Sicke Freerks to begin a study of the Scriptures on baptism. This brought him to conceive baptism on confession of faith as a central doctrine. But chiliasm affected him, too. In 1534 he joined the covenanters and received rebaptism. Only in January 1536 did he leave the Roman Church, after he had already written against the blasphemy of Jan of Leyden. The next year he was ordained as a baptist bishop by Obbe. But he was so fully aware that he had to work in circles that were not free from revolutionary stain, that in 1540 he could write these extenuating words: "I do not doubt but that those who have formerly transgressed a little against the Lord, when they intended to defend their faith with arms, have a merciful God." The congregation in Holstein, served by Menno for years, was formed by ex-Münsterites, namely, by the refugees from the twelve ships which escaped at Kampen and travelled to Dittmarschen. Dirk Philips was the teacher of a congregation at Danzig which was created by refugees from the Amsterdam rebellion of 1535. There is yet a further reason to judge that the number of peaceful Anabaptists was not great; no sooner was Münster fallen than the mass support shrank back into something sporadic. Thus, as soon as most Anabaptists found their chiliastic expectation mistaken, they returned to the bosom of the mother church. There remained a much reduced group who had not abandoned their hope for a heavenly kingdom, besides a number driven by a bitter spirit of vengeance who burned churches and cloisters (the followers of Batenburg and Appelman). Let us see how things stood with the remnant of the Melchiorites. Here I must begin by establishing that Kühler was in error when he accepted, on the authority of Blesdijk, that already in 1536 Obbe was no chiliast and awaited no other experience in the Kingdom of Christ than that of persecution. Actually when Obbe came to this realization, around 1540, he left the movement and warned Menno and Dirk in vain. Both of them remained chiliasts, hoping for the coming of the Lord.

. . . .

In 1539 there appeared Menno's extensive work, *Exposition of Christian Baptism.* In the same year his chief writing, *The Foundation of Christian Teaching,* went to press. It appeared in 1540. His third major work, *On the Genuine Christian Faith and its Power,* appeared shortly thereafter. With these three little books and some other smaller writings (e.g., his "Meditation on the Twenty-Fifth Psalm," also from 1539) Menno won people's hearts; his influence increased steadily. To be sure, some of the elders who had followed his leadership fell away, Pastor became a Unitarian and Frans Kuiper returned to Rome. Then in 1551 Leenaerdt Bouwens joined the group of elders. It was due to the glowing zeal of this brave ex-rhetorician, who defied mortal danger continuously as itinerant bishop, that the members of the baptist congregations became quite numerous. But it was Menno's accomplishment that anything whatever turned out all right. The chiliastic Melchiorites, whose initial rapid increase was explainable by the prevalent tense longing for social change, first came to number in the thousands not because of an innocent play of the imagination among pious convinced Protestants, but due to a revolutionary disposition portraying itself in biblical form. After their ranks were decimated by persecution and by the return of the majority to the Church of Rome, there remained splinter groups of the pious awaiting the Second Coming of Christ with exultant joyous hope. Alas, mixed among them was the hysterical swill of the slums whipped up into religious ecstasy. The Dutch Baptist brotherhood was recruited from this mixture of elements. It was Menno's accomplishment to set forth for them the foundation of Christian teaching in the form of popular instruction, and to present to them the dogmatic basis upon which a baptist faith could be built up. It was still provisionally chiliastic, but baptism on confession of faith was its central doctrinal point.

To be sure Cramer was partly right to assert that the Mennonites descended from propertied forefathers, provided that we refer to those who joined from 1540 onwards. The numerous writings which appeared after that time presuppose a reading public with substantial purchasing power. Also, certainly, between 1530 and 1540 there were a number of the well-to-do, even of the nobility, who joined. Some of these latter converts came under the influence of their chaplains. These propertied chiliasts consisted in part of idealists who joined either from religious or economic motives. Many a person would have seen something unjust in established social relationships. One or another would have been moved by the desire to strike a pose, or perhaps by a quarrel that he had with a magistrate or a priest. Superstition, too, played a role; the fear that in a short time a new world would come into existence. In this context the extraordinary magnetism exercised by fanatical preachers upon over-excited women must not be underestimated. But during the period of Münster over against a small number of the propertied there stood an overwhelming multitude that belonged to the lesser citizenry. This is evident particularly in the vocations of the teachers: some village pastors and monks, manual laborers, barbers, goldsmiths' journeymen. The last vocation is noticeable. Apparently there was such a depression that they couldn't earn anything.

For years among the Dutch Baptists there has been an effort to slide over the Münsterite period, to present the events as not so bad, to obscure them by fantasizing about a majority of the peaceful. With some individuals there is still an impulse to describe everything in the best light possible, best of all to pass over it in complete silence. The time should be past for misplaced shame about events that occurred almost four hundred years ago. It is genuine Mennonite prudery not to face up to the fact that there is a great deal of truth in the hoary Catholic reproach that we really descended from Hoffman and Münster. It is more forthright to say that a tragic mistake stands at the beginning of Dutch Baptist history: an untimely attempt to seize power which was smothered in blood and tears, but which aimed at a more satisfactory social order than was allowed by the misery of those days when hunger and pestilence ravaged the poor. The black stain of Münster and the even darker stain of Davidjorite moral contamination cannot be washed away. Fanatical idealism was mixed with an unholy lust for power. Immature minds wanted to lead. Excessive tension awakened blazing passion. But a slain Jan Matthijs is worthy of respect in comparison with a soft-living David Joris, who saved his skin at the right moment and lived luxuriously at the expense of those whom he misled. The Münsterite time period is one of adventurers. But the revolutionary disposition, disguised in a strange language, issued forth from a worldview of liberty and equality. They wanted a society with a better distribution of worldly goods. Also the period had its noble, idealistic personalities. If they erred, nevertheless they are worthy of respect.

From the darkness to the light: God brought forth a higher level of virtue from sin and from confusion he created order. From the fermenting mass there appeared a small harvest of pious souls. Menno and his co-workers had sowed the seed from which the brotherhood came forth. By the beginning of the Dutch struggle with Spain this brotherhood numbered a hundred thousand members in hundreds of congregations, living according to the grandiose ideal of a community of saints, a congregation without spot or blemish, before whose eyes the world lay in wickedness, and within which the children of God, separated from the world, might assemble in order to find their eternal salvation, the open gate to heaven.

Anabaptism in the Netherlands

W.J. Kühler

In *De Gids,* December 1920, Pastor K. Vos published an article entitled "Revolutionary Reformation." In it he tried to show that Anabaptism in the Netherlands was an almost exclusively rebellious movement. It is necessary to face up to the fact, he thinks, "that a tragic mistake stands at the beginning of Dutch Baptist history: an untimely attempt to seize power which was smothered in blood and tears." According to him, the movement, at first peaceful but sporadic, suddenly became a revolutionary mass phenomenon in the fall of 1533. The great increase in numbers came from the poorer classes who, in their chiliastic ecstasy, desired a society with a better distribution of temporal goods. However, with the fall of Münster, the new Jerusalem, most of them returned to the Roman Church; and the remainder was headed by David Joris, the man of sexual hallucinations. Around 1540, after the flight of this leader, Menno was able to win people's hearts; with him first begins the real history of the Dutch Baptists, a group recruited from a heterogeneous mixture of pious but overwrought splinter groups and the hysterical swill of the slums. That, in short, is the new picture that Pastor Vos has sketched for us.

A protest must be registered against this conception—not out of Mennonite prudery, as Vos likes to say, but for the sake of historical truth. This question, moreover, may be expected to arouse public interest, for more than the past of a small religious denomination is at issue. In the years 1530–1540 the history of those who insisted on adult baptism is more than ever interwoven with the history of the Netherlands.

A precise and objective investigation of the official documents, which are unfortunately very scanty, presents us with the following picture. The baptist movement originated in the Netherlands through the preaching of Melchior Hoffman. This movement was chiliastic, but unanimously averse to the smallest hint of resorting to force of arms. In accordance with its character it spread quietly. However, after three years it was no longer possible to restrain the fanatical longing for the Kingdom of God among a few demagogues. They wanted to hasten the coming of the Lord through arbitrary acts and preached revolution. Favored by all sorts of circumstances, some of them economic, they were successful in sweeping some of the Anabaptists along with them. A spotlight fell upon this rebellious movement which was dangerous to established society. Nevertheless it was not more than a passing deviation, of no significance for the future. The peaceful Anabaptists, on the other hand existed before Münster, during Münster, and after Münster; they gained in influence as soon as the fall of the New Jerusalem brought them relief. Naturally their ideas did not remain unaltered by all the experiences and shocks which they lived through; but Menno joined them and the future Dutch Baptists stemmed from them. I should like to clarify all this further in a concise survey.

When the Reformation swept through Europe like a storm in the beginning of the sixteenth century, it was generally believed that the end of the world was near. Luther preached and wrote that he hoped for the speedy arrival of the "dear Day of the Lord," on which Christ would cast down the Antichrist. But he disallowed all further reflections on the when and how of the Second Coming—all "pure lies" in his eyes. A born ruler of men's minds, he was successful in keeping his followers under control.

But there soon arose among the followers of the Reformation a party which went further than Luther, or Zwingli, wanted. These were the radicals, the individualists in the religious sphere. They recognized authority only in the Bible, as they themselves interpreted it, placing the commandment for a pure life in the foreground as they turned their backs on the world. From the beginning on these Anabaptists were chiliasts. When the first rebaptisms took place in Switzerland, Zurich was soon filled with prophets preaching repentance, who cried out their "Woe!" over the alarmed city on the streets and in the marketplaces.

Chiliasm manifested itself in varying degrees. Indeed, it was one of the prime characteristics of Anabaptism that it was heterogeneous in every respect. It appeared in various countries but nowhere did it form a mutually harmonious party, a firm monolithic entity. Never did the baptists recognize any confession as having binding authority. And if they regarded their lack of unity as a defect and worked for centralization the ever fiercer persecution made this almost impossible for them. Thus there was room in this comprehensive movement for the most antagonistic ideas and personalities; Hans Denck and Jan of Leyden, Obbe Philips and Jan Matthijs were all Anabaptists. Their history contained both deep moral seriousness and horrible degeneration. We have seen how in the accelerating confusion and pressure of the times again and again the impure elements would try to push to the fore. In Switzerland the rebellious doctrines of Thomas Müntzer were rejected; in South Germany Hans Denck had to draw upon all the authority of his powerful personality in order to overcome the followers of Hans Hut. The same drama repeated itself in the Netherlands, too, as various factions originated within Anabaptism.

The father of Dutch Anabaptism was Melchior Hoffman, an honorable, restless seeker who found peace only when he absorbed himself with burning enthusiasm in the glory of the Second Coming of Christ. He began as a loyal follower of Luther but soon turned away from Luther. He inclined to the teaching of Zwingli, to that of Carlstadt, but he came to a genuine meeting of minds with neither of them. Eventually at Strassburg he joined the Anabaptists but his accession was in no sense a submission to their standpoint. He received a great deal from them, but he contributed just as much. On two matters in particular did he exercise a profound influence. Firstly there was his distinctive teaching on the incarnation of Christ; secondly came his chiliasm, which, from now on more than ever before, came into the foreground among the Anabaptists.

We need to take a closer look at this chiliasm. On the foundation of an allergorical Scriptural exegesis which provided the opportunity for the most extravagant fancies, Hoffman preached that the coming of the Lord was at hand. He believed that he was the second Elijah, whose calling was to awaken men's hearts to piety and love in preparation for the coming of the Bridegroom. When he appeared in his glory nothing would be lacking to the faithful. But in his preaching Hoffman was concerned no longer with temporal circumstances or relationships. All this would hasten quickly to its end and he was already far beyond it. Even if tyrants or Satan himself held power, they should be obeyed in all matters that did not involve disobedience to God; the people of God were in, but not of, the world. The condition of the pious in this world could only be one of oppression: was it not revealed that in the last days Herod and Pilate would live in luxury while the cross was laid upon the shoulders of the elect? But finally the Day of Judgment would come.

Then a new heaven and a new earth would appear; there would be no more sorrow and every tear would be wiped away.

. . . .

In addition to all this, there was the misery of economic decline. Because of obstructions to Baltic commerce there had been a great slowing down of business in Amsterdam and the Waterland cities. The textile industry in Leyden was undergoing a depression. Prices were rising due to debasement of the coinage. Strikes were common, in response to low wages. This is described for us by Dr. Thiessen in his useful book about Charles V; at the same time he remarks with laudable caution: "In general it was the little people who eagerly adopted the Anabaptist beliefs. Material need *may* have been a contributing factor." Certainly, material need had its effect on the outcome of the tragedy which was soon to occur.

Such were the prevailing circumstances when Anabaptism quietly and noiselessly came to the Netherlands. Jan Volkerts Trijpmaker, a disciple of Melchior Hoffman driven out of Emden, established the congregation at Amsterdam, which before long was to become the center of the whole movement. In 1531 the leader himself came into the metropolis where he "moved about in public" and baptized fifty persons; in the next year he must also have visited Frisia.

We know only a little about these earliest Melchiorites, but the little that we know is remarkable enough. They sought the Kingdom of God; hence they were convenanters entirely in the sense of Hoffman's teaching. Moreover, "they were accustomed in their gatherings to read the gospel and discuss it, after which one of them broke bread, distributing a piece to each, although they knew that it was no sacrament but solely a commemoration of the passion of our Lord." On all these points we discover a striking agreement with the congregational life of the South German Anabaptists.

But was this movement merely sporadic? Only a superficial appraisal could come to such a conclusion. When Trijpmaker spread his teaching both inside and outside Amsterdam, he remained undisturbed for a year. He was able to baptize "many, diverse individuals" before the new sect drew the attention of the Court of Holland. Immediately thereafter the persecution began. The Amsterdam magistrate tried to save these Anabaptists, who did no harm to anyone or anything; but, however much he warned them and gave them the opportunity to get away, nevertheless nine of them were arrested, taken to the Hague and executed. The severed heads were brought back to Amsterdam with the command that they should be exhibited on stakes beside the gallows, with the preacher's elevated in the middle and the others in a circle around it. By this means the court hoped to introduce an atmosphere of terror. It succeeded but in a different manner than had been expected. The effect was that the threatened group became more cautious, more on their guard. Moreover, on account of this persecution Melchior Hoffman gave the command in 1531 to stop baptisms for a period of two years. Many desired baptism, to be sure, but Hoffman decided that there should only be private teaching and admonition. Obbe Philips, the writer to whose trustworthiness Vos devoted an article, recorded this for us. Hoffman kept to this position so as to prevent renewed bloodshed, as more than one of his statements from 1533 shows. He could not have shown more clearly that a religious disposition was his chief concern and that baptism was only a sign or confirmation of that disposition.

. . . .

For about three years Anabaptism spread silently in this way; then suddenly something happened that brought abour a radical change. Great things were expected towards the end of 1533. Melchior Hoffman lay in prison at Strassburg, but, after a half year, according to the word of a prophet, his glorious deliverance would come. This was about the same time as the end of the two-year period in which no baptisms could take place; and then, finally, the great transformation would be at hand. Jan Matthijs appeared in the midst of the feverish tension of those days. Shoving Cornelis Polderman aside, he declared that he was Enoch, the second witness of the Apocalypse. His command was that baptism must be resumed immediately. He disposed of Hoffman's objection that the time was not yet ripe, in view of the persecution, by invoking the decisive argument that nothing could be put ahead of the truth. Indeed, he did encounter resistance when, with an invocation of his divine mission, he presented himself to the leading group at Amsterdam; but Jan Matthijs was not the sort of man to allow himself to be turned aside. He at once cursed and damned all the unbelievers who would not recognize him. Seized by intense terror and fearing to become guilty of blasphemy, they devoted themselves to fasting and prayer. The outcome was that they recognized the new Enoch; and he, making immediate use of his authority, sent his apostles in groups of two to all regions of the country so as to get things started by baptizing the brothers and everyone else who desired salvation. From that moment forth the quiet in which the sect had previously lived was over; it stepped forth from secrecy into the light of day.

In doing all this Jan Matthijs regarded himself as the follower of Hoffman and wanted to continue his work. For the moment the violence in his character had not yet expressed itself. Also he resumed baptism without introducing any great change in its significance. For Hoffman. . .it meant a spiritual marriage with the Bridegroom, so that the pious would be found pure and thus saved at his Second Coming. Jan Matthijs developed the second idea in particular; he regarded baptism as the means of preservation during the coming Judgment. Further he, no less than Hoffman, taught that the Lord must be awaited in patience. This may sound strange, but we know it with absolute certainty from Obbe's account. It was precisely this preaching—that no more Christian blood should be shed but that the beginning of God's Judgment was imminent—which enabled Jan Matthijs to be so successful among the peaceful Melchiorites.

There is something else that sounds still stranger: Matthijs' emissaries to Münster preached the same message of nonresistance to violence in January 1534. We still possess the records of judicial hearings that prove this. Later, when the Anabaptists in the New Jerusalem had rejected this teaching of nonresistance as an error, and Rothmann, their well-known spokesman, had become an apologist for violence in his "Restitution," he felt it necessary to state: "When we were baptized in January 1534, we all laid down our weapons and prepared ourselves for the sacrifice of our lives. We thought that it was not permissible to resist the godless, but that we must patiently accept suffering, even death. Then the godless were well satisfied and thought that they could easily accomplish their will with us."

Perhaps it will be remarked that it doesn't make a whole lot of difference whether a revolutionary disposition comes to the fore a bit sooner or a bit later. But anybody who says this is overlooking something significant. Certainly Jan Matthijs finally concluded that only the sword would settle things. He sent new emissaries to Münster with that message. However, when the revolution took place in the holy city—and there only—he himself left the Netherlands at the first opportunity, only a few weeks later, never to return. In the meantime all the preaching here in the Netherlands was peaceful until January 1534; it was an insistence on patience and long-suffering in the spirit of Hoffman. Obbe and Rothmann, who oppose each other in every other respect, confirm this through their unshakeable testimony. What was new in the preaching was the appeal to special revelations, the threatening with hell and damnation. Yet this did not make the Anabaptists into revolutionaries, but rather into "fantastic melancholic people," just as the royal councillor, Van Assendelft, concluded about most of them in his investigation a month later (February 1534). There has been no keener or more precise description of their mental and spiritual orientation.

Naturally what brought Jan Matthijs to the point of revolution was in the first place his impetuous fanaticism, which blazed higher and higher, spurred on by circumstances. Also present as an external stimulus was the fact that the prophecy of Hoffman's miraculous deliverance went unfulfilled. Now Jan Matthijs could wait no longer. A new revelation came to him: the Kingdom of God must come through other means, with more forceful cooperation from the faithful. Therefore he took the sword.

The Anabaptists took up arms not because of a desire for a just society, for riches or power, or any other social motives that Pastor Vos might name. The object of *all* Anabaptists, peaceful or revolutionary, was a religious one, the Kingdom of God. We are dealing with a persuasion which wanted to conquer heaven before earth, at first through purity of heart and conduct, through sacrifice and self-denial: in a word, by doing what they thought of as good. When the prophecies failed and the persecution of the children of God continued to be oppressive, there arose a parallel, second way looking at things: the Day of the Lord could not dawn unless the elect first punished and rooted out wickedness. Now the worst fanatics seized the sword in order to institute a kingdom of righteousness. But this was not their final goal, as with the revolutionaries of our time, it was just a means. Only after this preparation by them would God be able to intervene in order to bring perfect blessedness. "No, dear brothers, he will come, it is true, but *first* God's servants must carry through the vengeance as he commanded:" so it said in the last manifesto from Münster, in response to the objection that one must await the coming of the Lord with resignation. Naturally it was impossible to put such a principle into practice without the fanatics, who imagined themselves to be instruments of God, becoming ordinary rebels whom the government had to curb and to punish as a danger to public order. Equally natural was the fact that this ill-fated teaching unchained all the passions, even the lowest, and that the movement, now that a part of it had become rebellious, drew fanatics and discontented individuals to it with magnetic power. The government feared rightly that the socially discontented would join the Anabaptists. And, finally, it is true that the Münsterites, in their despairing struggle to maintain themselves, often seemed the only Anabaptists in the fray. But all this, however enlarged upon, must not close our eyes to their essential goal. No one can find his way through the maze of their confused and over-excited spiritual life unless he is able to distinguish the real motive of their actions from all the incidental factors. In this respect Pastor Vos continuously misses the mark. He has not accurately presented the driving force behind what these Anabaptists did, the aim of their striving; and, consequently, he has also misrepresented their factional spectrum. He dresses the revolutionaries of our time in sixteenth-century costumes, wraps up their very modern beliefs in pious language, and then he says, "Here are the Anabaptists!"

In the ensuing years of crisis the baptist movement appears to us as a bewildering chaos. The spotlight is on somber tableaus of religious excitement, fanaticism and bloodshed. Surrounding them we see the turbulence of the variegated masses in a half-light which shades by degrees into darkness. There is much that we cannot bring into focus or that we can make out only with difficulty.

The confusion was heightened by the fact that in this early phase the peaceful and the revolutionary lived among and beside one another in an often ingenuous intermingling. When the rebellious orientation arose there was no sudden, magical division. For the moment their sense of community, the ties that bound them together, were still most sharply felt. Living together in a world which lay under the power of darkness and persecuted the children of God, hoping together for the coming of the Lord, the Melchiorites of various shadings were still brothers. Nevertheless they became increasingly conscious that they did not belong together. First there was a chastisement of the rebellious as false brothers; finally came the schism which occurred in 1536 after the great assembly of Bocholt.

In the nature of things the revolutionaries attracted the most attention. Their principles pushed them to the fore, in that they sought for battle. On the other hand the peaceful preferred to remain in the shadows, to live and work in silence. But the continuous incitements from Münster were addressed to both groups alike. From this center of agitation repeated attempts were launched, aiming to involve the Dutch in the rebellious movement. The fatal propaganda could be spread with the most potent means, since, despite the siege, the communication of the city with the world outside remained practically unhindered until January 1535. Emissaries from the New Jerusalem set out for the Netherlands; they gave their agitating harangues, delivered letters and summons, distributed writings and handed out money for the purchase of weapons. Hence Münster is the best vantage point from which to gain an overview of everything that occurred in these turbulent years; what took place in the Netherlands becomes more comprehensible to us to the degree that we keep in mind the course of events across the border.

Nothing can give us a better comprehension both of the effect of Münster and of the mentality of the covenanters than the great trek to Overijsel, which took place as early as March 1534. Some thousands of Anabaptists participated in it, but it is by no means certain that they constituted the whole movement. The government saw clearly when, in the midst of their overwhelming excitement, they wrote that there were still others who were silent and remained quiet. These unknown persons in both city and countryside were the continuers of the original persuasion, followers of Obbe Philips, who remained firmly opposed to any form of incitement of rebellion.

But what of those unfortunate people who boarded ship with wives and children and all their possessions to journey into a strange country—what did they really want? If we are to believe Vos they were committed revolutionaries. They set out well equipped with weapons; the spark had now fallen into the powder; the latent disposition was transformed into the deed.

But we find no trace of this conclusion among the officers who arrested the trekkers, or among the judges who passed sentence upon them. And these, nevertheless, were the men who came into closest contact with them, and whose reports, moreover, are the chief source of our knowledge. If we rely on the reports of these individuals, most of them fierce adversaries of the movement, then we get an entirely different perspective on that ill-fated exodus. We find not rebels but a variegated multitude of "fantastic, melancholic people" seeking for a good end. Their great fear was that they should be lost with the irrevocably doomed world. They thought that theirs was such a narrow escape that they imagined that they saw the towers of Westzaan collapse as they journied off. Only one hope remained to them: if they reached Münster in time they would be saved.

To grasp this we must, as I remarked, begin by focusing upon Münster. There a whole new situation prevailed as of the end of February. The prophets had wiped the slate clean by driving all the unbelieving out of the city with unvarnished force. Now they ruled absolutely, but over much too small a flock. There were fewer than sixteen hundred men left behind, and with this scanty population they had to face the Bishop and all his allies. Threatening thunder clouds were already hanging over them: the first preparations were made for the siege, the first outposts occupied by the enemy.

For the new Jerusalem it was a question of life or death. Help must be procured from the outside; otherwise in the long run the city could not hold out. Able-bodied men were needed, preferably well armed. Hence the spasmodic efforts, from the beginning to the end of the events there, to increase the population of Münster.

The manner in which the prophets sought to attain this object showed how much they combined fanaticism with cunning. They told their congregation, which had no need to know how desperate the situation was, that they were performing a deed of mercy on behalf of the Dutch brothers. One must invite these unfortunates, so bitterly persecuted in their own land, to come to Münster where they could live in freedom. They kept their real objective secret from the Netherlanders also: they did not indicate with a single word that they wanted their help for the defense of the city. Moreover, it was not an invitation that was extended but a crass command full of threats. And the prophets understood very well what sort of impression this would make! The situation in the Netherlands was extremely critical. A short breathing spell had arrived after a persecution in which many Anabaptists had spent the severe winter nights in the open field. The government had promised mercy to anyone who would be converted within twenty-four days. Precisely in the tense days when the deadline was elapsing the prophets circulated their letters throughout the whole country. It is easy to imagine what sort of panic must have arisen among the already alarmed Anabaptists when they received the following as a divine command: "Come to Bergklooster on March 24th, at noon. Make sure that you do not remain behind or the wolf will devour you. I will say no more, but I command you in the name of the Lord to obey without delay. Don't tempt God: everyone should think of what happened to Lot's wife and not look back for any earthly thing. Under the dragon of this world no one shall remain free from physical or spiritual death." It went on in this tone for a considerable time, and then finally there followed the command to buy weapons and bring them along. Naturally, an unarmed multitude would be of no use to the prophets. They counted on the blind obedience of the faithful to the divine command. In fact they were not wrong: the motley throng boarded ship and brought along all sorts of armament. But here I should recall what Cornelius said: "These people had weapons with them, indeed, for they were commanded to do so; but all military order, all leadership, even the thought of using the weapons was lacking. Not a single measure was taken in this direction." That is the way it was; the outcome confirmed it. If the whole subject were not so sad, we would be amused by the story, confirmed by all sources, of how twenty-seven ships with their three thousand passengers were halted without the least resistance taking place. It was no more than a large-scale arrest. "When the ships came into the Zwarte Water and thought it was safe to land there, there were persons on hand who observed their arrival. The bailiff with the captain of the cities boarded the ships and took some of the leaders as prisoners. . . .They discovered a great treasure of money which, together with the weapons, was taken away from the travellers. The shipmasters were ordered to stay there, and instructed that none of the Anabaptists should be permitted to land." With this sizzle the explosion of the "powder keg" fizzled out. The government did not regard their prisoners as rebels but as "poor people sadly misled." And how were they misled? "Through threats of the Last Judgment, which the founders of the aforementioned sects said was imminent." It is obvious, of course, that, had they succeeded in reaching Münster, there they would have been putty in the hands of a demagogue like Jan of Leyden and would have participated in all the later atrocities. These misled people were not yet dangerous, but they could easily have become so. Primarily they are greatly to be pitied: as victims of their own religious excitement, of an unfeeling persecution, and of unscrupulous or irresponsible leaders.

The majority of the arrested people on the ships came from Waterland, which together with Amsterdam was the center of the baptist movement. Hence I should make a few remarks on their social position. According to Pastor Vos the Anabaptists were the proletarians of the sixteenth century, driven to revolution through social distress. He continually describes them as a group assembled from the dregs of the population, "the poor and the unemployed, the wharf workers and sailors and manual laborers," although he has to admit that there were a small number of exceptions. By contrast, let me remind the reader of the comment on Waterland by Dr. Thiessen, one of Vos's favorite authorities: "Waterland seems to have been baptist at nearly all levels of its population." On this point, if I am right, Dr. Thiessen could have expressed himself even more positively. It is true that we must generally base our judgments on miscellaneous remarks and indirect evidence, but this time a letter from the Court of Holland does cast adequate light. Immediately before the departure for Münster "*many* persons from *all* quarters" were occupied with selling their immovable property; they could only take ready cash with them to their new fatherland. Were these people, then, the poor, wharf workers and sailors? What we are told here is also communicated elsewhere in pictures. As is known, after the failure of the putsch in May 1535, the Amsterdam government commissioned the painter Barend Dirks to produce eight paintings to preserve the memory of the Anabaptist riots. These works were destroyed in the burning of the city hall in 1652, but we still possess good copies of them in the book by Hortensius. Of course they are trustworthy: produced with such a purpose by a contemporary for contemporaries, they express not fantasy but reality. One of these paintings is devoted to the journey to Münster: little ships ready to sail stand in the background, and in the foreground is a scene explained by the inscription: "They sold jewels and clothes, land and property, in every nook and corner; hurrying on board ship with great desire, prophesying the quest for a new God." We actually see two women selling jewels and other valuables. Also there are two men, the one negotiating, the second receiving a money purse, and further up a few groups boarding ship. All are well-dressed; obviously the majority belong to the estate of propertied burgers. So much is certain, that Berend Dirks, who knew the baptists from his own observation (although he was not their friend), had another view of them than Pastor Vos.

We can guess that after all that selling a good deal of money was taken along to Münster. Doesn't this tally with the report cited above, that the government of Overijsel found "a great treasure of money" in the ships? It confiscated everything without scruple, to the vexation of the authorities in Holland who felt themselves seriously injured by this. Thus there was something to be gotten from the unfortunates. When Vos, in order to prove the opposite, cites the very small yield from the confiscations, again a statement from the Court of Holland is the only answer: "In Overijsel everything was taken from them, so that *now* they have nothing or very little for us to put our hands on."

So much to demonstrate how one-sided and exaggerated is Pastor Vos's conception. Naturally no one can deny that there were also less favourable elements. How could it be conceivable that the restless and discontented should stand aloof in such a violent disturbance? For them every change tended to be an improvement. Probably many of them weren't even baptized—so little feeling did they have for the real Anabaptism; for among the imprisoned we encounter also unbaptized individuals. Even less could the poor and destitute have been lacking, their lot worsened by the multifaceted depression. The bleaker their world, the more passionate their desire for its end. The Münsterite temptation was doubly dangerous for them. But also propertied people, even prominent individuals, allowed themselves to be dragged along into the maelstrom of religious fanaticism. And, if it is true that in a city like Amsterdam the great majority of the Anabaptists were "little people," they did not for that reason belong to the dregs of the population. Many notables were craftsmen in the sixteenth century; surely there were quite a few sold citizens among the rebaptized goldsmiths, shoemakers, bakers, ship-masters, whom we find mentioned in the documents. But for Pastor Vos they fall all together into a given social class; when he reads of goldsmiths in his sources, he turns them arbitrarily into unemployed goldsmiths' journeymen. It is in this way that they are degraded into proletarians!

After the aborted trek things remained relatively quiet in the Netherlands for the remainder of 1534. Surely the fermentation continued and it was evident on various occasions how tense the situation was, but there were no real uprisings until 1535. And throughout, even during the most violent part of the crisis, the peaceful party maintained itself, whatever the attempts made from Münster to drag it along into the abyss.

In the center at Amsterdam, where we find traces of Obbe's stay, there are all at once circles of the peaceful of various coloring. In the first place I would mention Jan Pauw, deacon of the congregation, and thus a man of significance among the brothers. For him "the covenant was nothing else than that one promises to walk in the ways of God without straying." There was to be no force of arms: a priest from Münster might assure him that self defense was permitted, but "his heart did *not* bear witness that he should defend himself with the blade." There is no doubt about it, Jan Pauw, although he had participated in the general excitement of his time, was a Melchiorite of the original, peaceful persuasion. He did not stand alone. From a letter of Reinier Brunt, solicitor general of the Court of Holland, we learn that this deacon "with the other brothers" patiently awaited the coming of the Lord, at which all persecution would end. This was also the teaching of Obbe Philips.

More to the left, but still on the side of the peaceful, stood the well-known bishop, Jacob van Campen. Hortensius described his activity as "admonishing vainly that they should not attempt to bring about any innovations through rebellion." If anyone wants to talk of a "legend of the peaceful Jacob van Campen," then the honor of its invention is not due to Scheffer but to Lambertus Hortensius, who, it needs hardly be said, was one of the most partisan anti-Anabaptist writers. Certainly Jacob van Campen approved of the purchase of weapons, but he maintained the emphatic reservation that these weapons might only be used for self-defense in case of persecution. Beyond that one must patiently await God's command. He disapproved of the trek to Münster, he condemned every conspiracy. He sought by instruction and example to check the Münsterite tendency among the numerous members of his congregation, with what result we shall see presently. It is obvious that Vos does him an injustice to characterize him as "not a peaceful but a fearful man." Acquoy, whom no one, certainly, will suspect of Mennonite prudishness, came to a very different conclusion! On the basis of the same sources to which Vos referred, he wrote: "Everything goes to show that Jacob van Campen was in fact a moderate among his coreligionists. Besides, the character of this thirty year-old man inspires respect involuntarily. He left behind a pregnant wife, cheerfully went to his death and courageously endured the most atrocious tortures." But very many of Vos' assertions do not stand up to examination. Even the sixteenth-century Hortensius, however fiercely embittered against the Anabaptists, is fairer to Jacob van Campen than he.

It is however not sufficient that we may be certain of the existence of a peaceful group. Much more important is the question: what was their numerical relation to the revolutionaries? Did they form only a minority, or were they a group of similar size, perhaps even greater than the Münsterites? Alas, we have no direct evidence upon which to decide this point. Therefore, our best method is to follow the further course of events by examining two Anabaptist conspiracies against Amsterdam, the first merely plotted, the second brought to execution, but failed.

. . . .

It was now clear that the revolutionaries did not have the peaceful at their beck and call. If in the future they wanted to undertake a conspiracy against Amsterdam they would have to do it themselves. But then it would at the same time become apparent what they were capable of by themselves and which party had the majority.

Yet again we must turn our glance to Münster. There the frightful drama was coming slowly but surely to its end; the encirclement of the city was finally complete and want stood before the door. The greater the pressure of necessity, the fiercer the propaganda directed outward. It was no accident that precisely toward the end of the siege uprisings broke out in the Netherlands.

The notorious Jan van Geelen was staying in Amsterdam as an emissary from Münster. He was able to work unhindered because he had deceived the government by presenting himself as a turncoat. Earlier perhaps a hundred or more persons had been baptized here in public meetings on a single day. . . .According to one statement, given on 23 January 1535, there were no less than thirty-five hundred Anabaptists in Amsterdam. Although this may be exaggerated, beside it the number of the rebellious is significant. For, despite the activities of Jan van Geelen, fewer than forty fanatics could be found for the adventure. As is well known, on the late evening of 10 May 1535 they staged a surprise attack and seized the Dam and the city hall.

But disenchantment followed. The unfortunates had trusted in a promise that, for all its absurbity, sets one thinking: many of the militia and also others of the best and most prominent persons in the city would support them. But when nothing of the sort occurred and they themselves were soon besieged in the Dam, they began to perceive their critical situation. First was the veteran soldier, Hendrik Goedbeleid. "I was always afraid," he said, "that our small number would bring our ruin." And that was the way it turned out. None of the other Anabaptists was willing to join Jan van Geelen; the citizens at their watch-posts had no problem with some group attacking them from the rear. The rebels were left to the fate that they had brought down upon their own heads. Help appeared only from outside the city, and it arrived too late.

We should consider that the better part of the group executed after the uprising appear to have been non-Amsterdamers, and that the large local congregation was led by two men both of whom condemned the conspiracy and kept totally apart from it. Hence we can come to no other conclusion than that these forty rebels formed a small minority, or—to use Scheffer's formulation—that "the majority had an aversion to violence." Is this latter statement an assertion without any proof, as Vos would have us believe?

It is understandable that after these uprisings the government extended no further mercy and punished all Anabaptists without distinction with the death penalty. Nevertheless, it was not this severity but the fall of Münster, occurring soon afterward on 25 June 1535, which broke the power of the revolutionary movement. The blinding light of the new Jerusalem was darkened. Many who were still in doubt, and asked themselves whether there was not some truth in the miraculous stories emanating from Jan of Leyden's kingdom, now came to their senses automatically. All writers from the sixteenth century, as well as from later periods, recognize this as a turning point. Cornelius knew this; and so did Pirenne: "The crisis was too violent to last a long time. It ended after the fall of Münster, and since then Anabaptism lost its revolutionary character." Disturbances took place afterward, at Hazerswoude and Poeldijk, but the center from which the power emanated had been taken away. "It is certain," Dr. Thiessen remarked, "that the interlude of turbulent Anabaptism had more or less run its course with these last tableaus." This picture is entirely correct. Anabaptism, which had begun peacefully, now continued its development along peaceful lines. The revolutionary deviation was an interlude which had no consequence for the future.

Naturally not all revolutionaries were converted at a blow. There remained quite a few Münsterites who simply waited for a second Jan of Leyden. But such a prophet did not appear again and the rebellious movement presents us with a picture of rapid degeneration. It split into two parties. On the one side were the genuine Münsterites, still dreaming of violent intervention; on the other were the Batenburgers, deteriorating into common criminals, of whose robberies, murders and acts of arson we still hear for a period of years.

The future belonged to the peaceful Anabaptists. Immediately after the fall of Münster Obbe Philips was able to assert himself more powerfully and successfully among the covenanters. However painful the course of events, they had a reinvigorating effect upon him personally. His eyes were opened. The outcome had given the lie to all of Hoffman's prophecies, so that they could be nothing but fanaticism. Together with his followers, named Obbenites after him, he concluded that there was no condition of the Kingdom of Christ to be awaited other than the present one, namely the condition of persecution. We can be certain of this. Blesdijk tells us this in detail with emphasis; as son-in-law of David Joris he was exceptionally well informed, as a renegade from the baptist movement he was its declared, albeit honorable, enemy. He wouldn't have given such a favorable description of Obbe if he hadn't felt obliged to do so, because it was true. Nevertheless, Vos, in order to advance his peculiar standpoint, argues that Blesdijk was in error: Obbe supposedly came to this insight only about 1540 and consequently abandoned the movement. But Vos forgets to bolster his "finding" with any proof and he forgets, moreover, that Obbe himself in his "confessions" (always so reliable) presents an entirely different reason for his withdrawal. The leader had arrived at a new belief. Hence there originated two parties among the peaceful, just as among the revolutionaries: the Obbenites and the gradually disappearing adherents of Melchior Hoffman.

. . . .

In conclusion we have still to show Menno's place in the baptist movement. By the exceptional position it assigns him, the new interpretation judges him favorably, perhaps more favorably than it intended. Given the odd mixture of elements which has been presented as constituting the circle of the oldest Anabaptists, Menno would seem to have performed an admirable conjuring trick indeed to have been able to transform them into the baptist brotherhood. But Menno was in no sense an exceptionally gifted man; strength of character, originality or even a semblance of genius are not among his attributes. He called no new brotherhood into being. Rather, continuing the work of Obbe, he advanced the already existing group which had weathered every sort of storm.

Menno first appeared with a bold protest against Münster. He branded Jan of Leyden as the greatest Antichrist and awakened all *true* convenanters to be on guard against the "venom" of his teaching. This happened in the period when the new Jerusalem was still in existence. A few years later he wrote his *Foundation Book* (1539). The situation was then changed, in that the parties had moved apart and the Münsterites were distinguished from the others as "covenanters of the sword." He condemned the "accursed, godless action," the "devilish error" of the false prophets, just as vigorously as before, although he had faith that the unfortunates, who had been led astray by them and had erred unknowingly, would "have a gracious God." He is aware that the rebellious persons emerged from the peaceful circle of those "who placed themselves under the cross of Christ;" he refers to a minority, to "some," yet another confirmation of the interpretation I have demonstrated above.

Menno was occupied exclusively with spiritual and religious concerns. Never did he "longingly anticipate a total transformation of social life." As with Melchior Hoffman I ask: out of all his numerous writings, show me one single passage that even remotely confirms that opinion. It is most absurd, that these two prominent leaders should have been possessed by an ardent wish, without ever having expressed it in any way. The characteristic link between the two men is precisely that neither the one nor the other had the least concern with social relationships.

Chiliastic impulses retired more and more into the background for Menno, and thereby also the belief about remaking the congregation into an earthly kingdom of Christ. Moreover, experience taught Menno one other thing particularly: he had seen what extravagances necessarily sprung from an attachment to special revelations and he retained a permanent fear of them. He clung with scrupulosity to the letter of Scripture, "the express, simple command of Christ." He placed his emphasis upon practical piety; he adopted various general Christian dogmas, but for him a doctrine came to life only if it could be reduced to moral exhortation. Baptism on confession of faith was not for him the centerpiece of doctrine, although it served as the first and most convenient distinguishing mark. There is no salvation for anyone outside of the true congregation of the reborn, separated from the world. Only there can mature persons believe and be reborn, and they alone can be incorporated into the congregation through baptism. Baptism is the representation of inner purification, "the sign of the new life," through "this outward sign of the water covenant we join ourselves in obedience to the Lord." If this is compared to what I wrote of Hoffman's view of the same subject, it is obvious how closely Menno corresponds to his predecessor. We have before us here a process in which the changes proceed automatically from the development of religious ideas and the effect of events.

The brotherhood went further along this path. There was a dark page in its history: the going astray of a portion of the members in connection with Münster. The black spot cannot be washed out, no one imagines it can—but on the other hand neither may anyone magnify it contrary to justice and reason. When the lamentable interlude had been played out, the brotherhood continued its development in harmony with its original character, purified by numerous ordeals, bearing the cross of persecution. In this manner it took to heart the new questions of the future. It would, however, not emerge again into historical prominence; it had become the brotherhood of the "still in the land."

IV

Thomas Müntzer:
Theologian and Revolutionary

Theology and Revolution in Thomas Müntzer

Thomas Nipperdey

There are two respects in which Thomas Müntzer is of historical significance: indeed, of world-historical significance. First, as a theologian he was the greatest power at the beginning of the fanatical deviation within the Reformation. In him the antithesis of the *"Schwärmer"* to Luther first became "clearly self-conscious." In spite of all the inconsistencies of his personality he is the rough draft of an Anti-Luther. The Spiritualists, especially Hans Denck and through him in turn Sebastian Franck, were deeply influenced by him; and his influence continued through followers of Weigel into radical Pietism. Similarly, through Grebel, Hut and Rinck (perhaps through Hubmaier, too) he exercised a lasting effect on practically all Anabaptist groups, both the activists and the suffering pacifists. By way of the Netherlands he probably had an impact on the Puritan Revolution, particularly upon the chiliastic and social revolutionary movements whose offshoots merged to form the Quakers. Second, as a revolutionary, Müntzer was the key figure of the Peasants' War in Central Germany. This fact accounts for Luther's particularly harsh attitude towards the rebellion and also for the hardening of his theory of government. . . .

Historical research has only recently illuminated Müntzer's life, thought and career. Nevertheless, the question of the relation of theology and revolution remains in dispute; and this is, after all, the question of the unity of his career, indeed of the unity of his personality.

. . . .

It seems appropriate, therefore, to examine once again the relationship of theology and revolution. In the process, however, one encounters a new difficulty: namely that the interpretation of Müntzer's theology remains in dispute, even if the issues of its later revolutionary effects or revolutionary extensions are left aside. The debate about Anabaptists and Spiritualists is projected back to Müntzer. Thus either Müntzer's subjective religiosity is highlighted, with stress on the spiritualistic and mystical Inner Word; or conversely his objective religiosity is stressed, the fanatical legalism of absolute sanctification, the chiliastic separatism. The opposing tendency is noted in each of these interpretations, but there is no express consideration of the combination of the two currents or of their distinctive unity. Hence the state of theological research also points to the need for a new effort to grasp the possible unity in Müntzer's thought and to make it understandable. It is possible to speak of Müntzer's theology because his sermons and polemical writings were undergirded by a quite distinct Christian self-understanding, even though his writings present no explicit, well-considered or systematic theology. These sermons and polemics are not expositions but rather they take the form of personal address and demand. This peculiar character of Müntzer's theological expressions must be an essential test of whether an interpretation is accurate.

The fundamental theological problem and a point of departure for a suitable understanding of Müntzer lies in his relationship to Luther. Müntzer was not, as has often been alleged, a temporary fellow traveller of Luther, belonging really to the world of late medieval sects and mysticism. On the contrary, Müntzer fully accepted Luther's original Reformation standpoint. And his opposition to Luther, his distinctive revolutionary starting point, did not originate from late medieval undercurrents, but precisely from his original acceptance of Luther and an agreement with him assumed by Müntzer as a matter of course. This is still evident in his explanation of his personal role in opposition to Luther. Even in his last writings Luther appears as the first messenger from Noah's ark, the malicious raven who did not return with the message of peace. The truth had dawned on Luther, but then he had neglected and abandoned it. Müntzer appears as the "dove" who properly continues the work now begun and completes it. The thesis is here set forth that the Reformation had been brought to a standstill. Müntzer becomes the opponent of Luther precisely because he begins on the ground won by Luther. His questions originate in Luther's questions: in this sense Müntzer belongs to the second generation of the Reformers.

The most noticeable element in Müntzer's theology has always been its antithesis of Spirit and Scripture—inner and outer Word. . . . Spirit is contrasted with Scripture and the letter, with the Word, and particularly the outer Word; as a concept it has a polemical rather than a complementary function. Müntzer's opponents were the learned "scribes." He understood his theology of the Spirit as the antithesis of the theology of the "scribes." The intention of this concept of Spirit must be understood through its polemical function.

In the polemic against Scripture two themes are closely intertwined. The first theme is intellectual or rational and raises the issue of the criterion of Christian truth. The appeal to Scripture and to its authority can only satisfy the "invented" faith. The obvious, unquestioned authority of Scripture is gone for Müntzer. Scripture in itself cannot demand a binding obligation beyond which one cannot question. Turks and heathens do not submit to an assumed authority of Scripture; and it cannot be expected that they should do so, as long as no other criterion for truth is provided. In the same sense the Christian is expected to question beyond the authority of the Bible. He must "know" conclusively; this means, too, to be reasonably convinced "that God has spoken this and not the devil." The Christian cannot be satisfied with the conventional ignorance concerning the ground and foundation of his faith which barricades itself behind the appeal to Scripture. . . . Finally Scripture itself points beyond itself. The Biblical authors had no Scripture, but they, especially, were filled with faith. Scripture "gives witness, but gives no faith"; in itself it is not revelation. It is witness, namely witness to the faith of the faithful writers of its books, and to what these writers experienced as witnesses. As a witness Scripture is subject to the question of the criterion of its truth. Although Müntzer gives no evidence of particular reflection on what he is doing, he has begun here the classification of the Bible within the tradition of testimonials to faith. In principle, the criticism of tradition includes the Bible itself. . . .

Here begins the second and dominating motif of the polemic against Scripture. It may be characterized as theological-existential. Scripture "as outer witness cannot produce a substantive change in the believer." Outer witness cannot be appropriated in any real sense; it does not take hold of or transform the believer. Scripture and belief in Scripture are something dead. Their place is in the memory. Scripture "is drawn into the memory from the outside." Faith in Scripture becomes a mere holding to be true, something intellectually attainable. It is what the "Bible stealers" collect without the foundation of an existential experience.

. . . .

The heart is the only possible location of faith and the only possible criterion of its truth. God writes into the heart, he speaks in the heart. His Word and faith originate in the heart. Without the heart faith has no binding force and gives no assurance. The word of the Bible is made true only by the witness of the heart. "Christ wants his remembrance, essence, and Word in the soul of man." Faith is not doctrine but the "handicraft of God." It can be God's handicraft only as the most personal, original and genuine experience. Müntzer pleads for this with all his passion. The evidence of truth is therefore subjective. True faith proves its truth through subjective involvement with illumination, so that the "secret" of the heart is revealed, so that the conscience leads man to the ground of his being. This ground is suffering. Faith originates through suffering in which man experiences himself. Indeed such an existential experience can only be properly understood as the experience of God. That is indubitable and self-evident. Such internal evidence demonstrates its potency by transforming a person's life. Therefore a discrepancy between life and faith is a sign that faith has not experienced the truth nor taken hold of it internally.

Faith unfolds itself in experience, individual appropriation and transformation. This constitutes the personal structure of faith. The object of the concept of Spirit is to describe this structure of faith and to defend it over against an unattainable objective norm, which perverts faith into a mere assent to propositions and strips it of subjective seriousness. Spirit is, however, not a natural quality which a person has or lacks, freeing one from all personal responsibility. Neither does Spirit mean that the "speaking God" is minimized in favour of the "receiving person." Rather this concept aims to do justice to the dialectical relation between God and man, and to the dialectical position of the person between full independence and absolute dependence. Spirit means that God's action can be experienced and understood by man as an existential reality. Thus with the category, Spirit, Müntzer attempts to assure the personal quality of the Christian faith of the Reformation. He attempts to describe a faith in which the subjectivity remains pure, in which faith remains faith.

. . . .

It is necessary to ask, against whom is this whole argumentation directed? Does it not, at least in motif and tendency, correspond throughout to the starting point of Luther? What Müntzer called invented faith and experienced faith, Luther called *fides historica* and *fides fiducialis* respectively. Even Luther, who had a more self-evident and less questioning relation to the Bible, differentiated between Scripture and the Word of God: the Gospel is not really what is found in books. For Luther, too, the believer does not depend on another's faith. He does not rely on a testimony held to be true, but on the existentially encountered Word. The Christian truth is accepted as true not on the basis of Biblical authority, but because it convinces the conscience. "No one except God can put the Word in the bottom of my heart." For Luther, too, there is an immediacy of the Holy Spirit. The word of the Bible is effective only because, and to the degree that, the Spirit holds sway in it. For Luther this connection to the Spirit alone provides the Word with the essential quality of the *pro-me* [of being personally directed "for me"]. He seeks to explain the creation of faith without reference to magical miracles. For him, too, therefore, the Word of God is to be heard as if spoken yesterday, although there is a characteristic shift of meaning between him and Müntzer on this point. Like Müntzer, Luther can illustrate the Christian faith by reference to a non-Christian—Abraham.

Müntzer, it appears, did not see this side of Luther. There are reasons for this. Luther attempts to understand the relationship between Word and Spirit as a unity. For him truth is not established by the outer Word, but it remains connected to it, specifically to its temporal priority. The Word cannot be relativized or emasculated. Luther seeks to make faith personally explicable from the point of view of Word and language, as a hearing of and answering to Scripture. Thus he attempts to go beyond the objective as well as the subjective. But he did not solve the resulting problems clearly. The binding of the Spirit to the Word is based on the argument that God had ordained it so. Luther's love for the offensively anti-rational, his "positivism" (as J. Kuhn labels it), clings particularly to this factual argument. Müntzer did not grasp the dialectical and personal structure of Luther's understanding of Word and faith. He saw only the anti-subjectivist elements, and therefore held the whole to be unacceptably objective. With remarkable anticipation he saw in Luther's teachings the outline for a later Word orthodoxy which surrendered the unity of Word and Spirit to the predominance of the Word. He recognized that Luther emphasized more and more the objective elements against the radicalization of his own original position by the Spiritualists, repressing his own spiritualistic tendencies. Thus Luther's originally freer relationship to the books of the Bible hardened more and more, threatening the role of the conscience as the existential testing ground of faith.

Against this development in Luther, Müntzer radicalized the subjectivity of faith, dissolving its absolute bond to the letter of Scripture, which he saw as a "paper pope." He believed that the personal reference (the *pro-me*) in Luther's Word-centered faith could be protected against the predominance of objective Scripture only by an accentuation of the category of Spirit. *Sola fide* can be assured only if *sola scriptura* is given up. Thus two of the fundamental principles of the Reformation are separated, because for Müntzer the subjectivity of faith clashes with the objectivity of Scripture.

. . . .

However, Müntzer's attempt to assure subjectivity underwent a massive objectification because of the renunciation of the firm bond to the Word, because of the attempt to protect faith by denial of Scripture, and above all because of the passionate desire for the unmediated. For Müntzer the Christian experience of divine reality was objectified in the supposedly spoken word of prophecies, dreams and visions with which his period was so familiar. To be sure Müntzer rejected the demand of his opponents that he prove the validity of his Spirit-faith by miracles; to be sure he granted priority over visions to the inner Word; but the demand for an objective oral revelation remained. All the attempts to distinguish genuine visions and revelations wrought by the Spirit from those flowing from an arbitrary inner experience—the demand to examine them against Scripture, the requirement of simplicity, of preceding sorrow or distress, of a satisfactory account of the origin of each vision—all confirm and strengthen the tendency in Müntzer toward the objectification of the inner experience. Faith produced by the Spirit, therefore, becomes something objective—something demonstrable and proveable.

The same process is noticeable when one turns to Müntzer's understanding of the Christian experience of justification and redemption. First there is a radical subjectification of Luther's initial impulse and then a turning over into objective categories. Müntzer is in agreement with Luther in separating from the old Church. He rejects meritorious works and refuses all compromise between grace and human achievement, and he rejects altogether teachings of sacramental grace. "God did it alone." But he also turned against Luther's teaching on justification. He understood Luther's teachings on justification in the light of those tendencies which Melanchthon later formulated in the theory of imputation. Accordingly justification consists of declaring the unjust just on the basis of the vicarious satisfaction wrought by Christ. To Müntzer vicarious substitution and nonimputation of guilt appeared to be merely intellectual conceptions: perhaps he was thinking of the nominalist notion of acceptation. He thereby anticipated the critique of later Pietists against the Orthodox teaching on justification. "The godless accept with pleasure" that another suffered for them and that Christ's suffering was sufficient; because this does not affect them. It permits them to go on as before without changing their lives. The mercy of God, so presented, originates from an unbroken human self-confidence; it is invented, fictitious, depriving Christ of his relevance for life and turning him into a "cute" and "fantastic idol." Justification understood in this fashion is merely objective. It is not appropriated. It leaves the person essentially outside the process.

The starting point of this criticism, to be described more precisely below, is therefore the insistence on subjectivity. Müntzer attacks Luther for preaching a "honey-sweet Christ." On the contrary, he asserts the importance of the "bitter Christ," thereby introducing a fundamental theme into the criticism of Luther by religious radicals, both Anabaptists and Spiritualists. This theology shows dependence on Tauler's theology of discipleship, even though it is totally free from the *imitatio* of the Modern Devotion. The person wins his salvation by undergoing a difficult process of suffering and inner transformation through which he is placed outside himself, in that he becomes "conformed to Christ," and experiences "the cross" while Christ is formed in him. Only through acceptance of the cross of Christ does the truth of justification become personal. What is the cross? The cross is the place at which the conscience accuses us. In Christ we must "recognize every day and every hour the measure in which the self has been slain." Man must experience himself as a sinner "who all his life has acted against God's will," who has "fallen from God to the creatures," to the world and its lusts, who puts his trust in his own nature, seeks his own, relies not on God, fears not God but the creatures. Man is a sinner, and not because of the metaphysical fate of individuality, but because of personal guilt. He is unbelieving, and because of it has misdirected his life. The conscience consumes the person while that person experiences himself on the cross as a sinner. It "consumes" everything "that I am"; it shatters the invented faith and all natural self-confidence. All of man's "adopted manner is crushed"; deprived of every hold on the world, he despairs before God, believes himself forsaken by God and finds no comfort in any assumed eternal pardon. This is also the intended effect of Scripture: it kills, whether it preaches the law or the cross of Christ. The central concepts of this experience of the cross are terror and the fear of God. They relate quite clearly to guilt and conscience. Müntzer's mystical categories have to be interpreted with this in mind. When there is no longer any trust in God and the person is in despair, unbelief and sin are brought to their foundation. Here faith begins as hope against hope; in acknowledging the experience of judgement, the uncovering of his guilt as annihilation of the self, the person is justified. The cross itself is justification. This justification occurs in the confession of unbelief as the essence of sinfulness and in the longing for redemption expressed therein. This confession is no mere intellectual declaration, rather it is confessional, conceived of as a truly existential transformation. By confessing his sin, the person gives himself up and surrenders himself trustingly to the will of God. Through a "penitent heart" and "sincere sorrow" he gives up his self-affirmation and selfish nature which strive against God. He permits himself to be detached from the world. He becomes "composed," yes "estranged from life," so that his assurance rests "not with any creature but in God alone." By submission to and acknowledgment of the judgement of the cross man becomes estranged from sin. He can now live with an "assured," "good, clean and peaceful conscience." Expressed positively, this means that through the justifying experience of the cross the justified becomes the brother of Christ, a son of God. For, since he is crucified with Christ, he is also resurrected with him. The believers become "deified" so that "the earthly life is transposed into the heavenly."

Confession and the divinely wrought transformation of man are thus inextricably interwoven. They are not distinguished as two separate impulses but unreflectingly thought of as homogeneous. In this confession justification is also sanctification. In justification man is renewed. He is placed in a new estate before God and is brought thereby into a new relationship to himself and to the world. Justification is effective, it transforms man. How Müntzer understands this renewal needs to be discussed further.

. . . .

Müntzer opposes his subjective, experienced, effective justification against an objective, imputed justification. He emphasizes the process within us against the event outside us. Here, too, the essentials can be expressed in concepts of time: not an objective past fact, not a completed, petrified cross, but a present process is decisive. The believer becomes a contemporary of Christ. The eschatological promises, of blessedness and the kingdom of God, are not only for the future, but are already present in us. The Christ for us becomes real only as the Christ in us, Christ's suffering for us becomes real only as Christ's suffering in us. Therefore pedo-baptism can have no reality. It remains *opus operatum,* a merely objective and simply external act or a merely intellectual act on the part of the participants. True baptism can come only from faith, the confession of sin and the experience of renewal.

If justification does not occur through the mere acceptance of a past objective fact, if it happens as an inner process—not a psychological development but God's action on and with the person—the question arises as to the role of Christ in this process. Müntzer passed over the difficulties of this question without reflecting on them expressly. Nevertheless some things are clear. Christ is by no means an example, either in a moral or religious, Anabaptist or Enlightenment, sense. Imitation is totally alien to Müntzer's view of discipleship. Neither is Christ a mere mystical-metaphysical symbol, even though with the weakening of the objective act of salvation his historical existence appears to become less significant. Christ is rather the archetype and source of justification and of man's experience of salvation. Only in Christ does man experience himself before God; and thereby man comes into a new situation, which happens to be his true situation. The trust in God which arises in this situation knows itself as verified in and through Christ. In this sense Christ is saviour. It is impossible to differentiate whether salvation depends on the objective—the historical Christ—or the subjective—the personal experience of the cross. Such an alternative and such categories are simply unsuitable. For Müntzer the personal experience of the cross retains its unbreakable connection to the historical Christ, and the historical Christ in turn exercises his power through the cross of each individual. True preaching points always and only to the "slain Lamb" and his act of salvation. Christ is the first-born among God's sons. In keeping with the still unchallenged tradition he is of course God's son by nature, while the Christians are sons only by grace. The rudiments of a universal theism do not weaken the references to Christ. True, according to Müntzer the Turks, together with all human beings, have the beginnings of the Christian faith; but they have only the beginnings, the same foundations for experience and the same capacity for understanding as anyone else. Salvation, the transformation of the cross into justification experienced in Christ, lies beyond these beginnings.

. . . .

Müntzer's understanding of the cross is thoroughly Lutheran in its original intention. It, too, is an attempt to free man's relationship to God from any objectified character and from the clutches of a philosophical doctrine. Müntzer, too, stands on the ground of *sola gratia*. The preparation for faith, which Luther ridiculed, is not meant by Müntzer as a human achievement. It is not self-chosen asceticism and pious work. The acceptance of the cross of Christ is not imitation. The person does not create Christ within himself, but God places the person in the same situation as Christ, in view of Christ. It is God who sends him the cross. The experience of the cross is the experience of the conscience, which is never self-chosen, never esoterically meritorious. When Müntzer polemicizes against the juxtaposition of faith and works, his aim is to show that faith itself is a work of God, not a mere human mental affirmation but a divine transformation and new creation. As early as his Zwickau ministry Müntzer turned a blunt anti-Pelagianism against his opponents, and this point of view remained constant. Christ turns his chosen ones into lambs, and they must confess that he alone did it. Man has no faith unless God himself grants it. Faith is an "impossible" work. Faith makes impossible demands upon us. Faith is therefore in no sense at man's disposal. It is the power of God alone that rejects and breaks the invented faith and the secret unbelief which are part of man's natural constitution. The concept of "elect," however faded in its use by Müntzer, also points in this direction. Luther in his polemical writings held that Müntzer wanted to "tempt God with his own works and free will . . . and dictate time, place, and measure in which God is supposed to work with us." True, Müntzer had written that God could "not forsake" someone who confesses his unbelief and calls "to the physician" for help. God would grant a favourable hearing to the remorseful heart. He also polemicized against Luther's teaching on the bondage of the will, and his message of repentance places all its stress on the obligation of man. But in no way does he mean that by preparing himself for the cross man can compel God to act and therefore justify himself. Müntzer's statements are not metaphysical declarations. One cannot deduce from them any pretensions whatever concerning man's estate, for they are the confession of the believer about God's act of judgement and mercy upon him.

They are preachings which call upon the hearer to repent. They are a demand to give one's self up to the experience of judgement and to act accordingly. The polemic against the bondage of the will has the intention of making it impossible for the unbeliever to evade his guilt and sin by an appeal to the unfree will. The believer is elected through grace. The unbeliever is hardened through guilt. This Christian paradox is very real for Müntzer. The question here does not concern the natural or supernatural qualities of man, because freedom and grace are not given a metaphysical explanation. We are dealing here with a personal testimony, a confession of the believer and preaching to the unbeliever. It is exactly in this that Müntzer comes close to Luther. To be sure Müntzer has not reflected on the relationship between freedom and grace. This is why his contradictory statements cause misunderstandings. But the difference between Müntzer and Luther does not primarily concern the *sola gratia*.

Müntzer is in agreement with Luther on the personalness of justification and the cross, but he appears not to see the Luther of the *theologia crucis*. Instead he reinterprets Luther's theology in objective terms. He does not recognize the somber and deadly serious experience that underlies Luther's teachings of grace, an experience Luther presupposed for his listeners and expressly accentuated with his repeated linkage of repentance and grace. Müntzer sees only the Christ *extra nos* and the imputated righteousness, which according to his understanding cannot become the person's own. Against this view he asserts unconditionally and in all seriousness the subjectivity of justification. This implies being radically serious about one's status as a sinner, and signifies that forgiveness has to be existentially experienced as the taking away of sin; it cannot remain mere doctrine. In Müntzer's view Luther fails to meet the standard of this subjective faith; instead he preaches a cheap grace, a grace entirely without cost, a grace that consoles the conscience but leaves everything else as before, because it does not change anyone's life. But Müntzer is not concerned with the cheap grace of Christ; his focus is on discipleship. He does not assert discipleship dogmatically in terms of human effort over against the merit of Christ, but in such a way that the person is called to discipleship through preaching. The Gospel is not mere consolation, as Luther interpreted it, but it is essentially demand, or rather: consolation and demand are one. The demand of the law is consolation, precisely in the death-bringing experience of the cross. However, this truth of the Gospel is covered up if its character as demand is not made central. Müntzer sees, once again anticipating future developments, that in the application of Luther's preaching the severity of the cross is watered down in favour of the comfort of the Gospel, for fear of works righteousness and legalism. As a result the sinner's life remains unaffected, while in a false and passive humility he appeals to his status as a poor sinner incapable of any good works. Against this danger of appealing to an excessively joyous message of forgiveness, Müntzer emphasizes the seriousness of the Christian calling. Since Müntzer, all Anabaptists and Spiritualists have polemicized against Luther's: "Surely he suffered death for us, I know now that he's paid the whole bill." This cheap grace, grace that makes no demand on the believer, is for Müntzer something objectified. Against it he asserts the subjectivity of justification, as an internal not an external event.

But here again it is evident that Müntzer in struggling against Luther's objectivity was unable to retain the intended personal quality of faith, an intention that after all unites him with Luther. Müntzer reinterpreted and misunderstood this personal quality of faith by rendering it as subjectivity, and therefore failed to comprehend Luther's personal concept of faith and justification. Indeed the person or personality of the believer is something different for Müntzer than for Luther. For Luther, person is a relational concept. Faith is *fiducia*, it is constituted by trust, a personal relationship. Luther's seal, the heart under the cross, is symbolic of this relationship. In contrast, Müntzer's seal shows a heart pierced by a sword. For Müntzer it is not upon what the person looks, but how the person looks that constitutes the person. Only in this is the person not mere object. He is incapable of understanding the essence of the person in mere relational terms; because for him the person is substantive, personality is nothing more than subjectivity. Therefore a mere change of relationship between God and man, being looked upon by God as righteous as expressed in the theory of imputation, is not redemptive or justifying. It does not change the substance of the person. It does not provide the possibility of transformation of the person as required by the seriousness of subjectivity. Therefore everything Luther said about the effect upon the person himself of a changed relationship to God remains inaccessible and unacceptably objective to Müntzer. Against the relational character of the person he stresses the importance of the substantive character of the subject. Müntzer's focus is not upon the Word that establishes the relationship in and for the believer, but on a substantive distinctive inwardness itself.

. . . .

In that for Müntzer the experience of faith does not place the person in a new relationship, but transforms the person in substance, it changes from a continually renewed occurrence into a process that is in principle terminable. The confessional formula *simul iustus simul peccator* does not adequately describe the position of the Christian. Müntzer adds a theology of being made righteous to the theology of justification, which is the only possible theology for Luther. Forgiveness in itself is no longer central, but the essential foundation and prerequisite of discipleship. The justified is no longer a sinner in the radical sense that Luther meant this. The unity of confession of sin and renewal is dissolved. Confession of sin becomes in principle terminable, while renewal is elaborated and undergoes objectification. The justified, the true believer, becomes characterized by a number of qualities. He is a changed person, he has a new disposition, which is no longer "fleshly." Müntzer insists that the presence of the new disposition is demonstrable, although he acknowledges, of course, the difficulties of recognizing faith by way of words and deeds. The "elect" can be separated from the "godless." Müntzer contradicts Luther's theory of justification, because the *imputatio* appeared to separate the *justificatio* from the *vivificatio* or *sanctificatio* and therefore remained incurably objective. However justification is above all attaining holiness, hence *sanctificatio* or *vivificatio*. Only so can the absolute ethical seriousness of Müntzer's notion of subjectivity express itself. However, by taking the *vivificatio* and *sanctificatio* into the *justificatio* and by concretely coupling them to the *justificatio*, Müntzer falls into a new and more massive objectivity which corresponds to his substantive conception of the person. Not only does attaining holiness move to the centre of his preaching, but holiness becomes tangible, objective, and secure, impossible to lose. It demonstrates itself in the life style of the person. Therefore it is possible to make inferences about faith from the conduct of life. Because, for Müntzer, Luther's faith necessarily stands in an unresolveable discrepancy to conduct, it is idle faith. Justification as mere doctrine of *imputatio* leaves faith without works. It merely unshackles the person for the liberty of caprice. Only from the standpoint of an objectified holiness is it possible to fight against the sinners as the guilty unbelievers.

The theology of being made righteous has therefore extraordinary implications for the organization of Christian life. Because the central process between God and the soul has become terminable, the topic, soul and world, God and world, moves into the foreground. Here, too, a noteworthy shift takes place. The category, Spirit, and the special formulation of the experience of the cross accentuate the personal relationship between God and man. This is the anthropological, Lutheran trait of Müntzer's theology. Conservative theologians can actually see in these statements of Müntzer a belittling of the omnipotence of God. However, since the completed act of justification is characterized as attaining holiness, the glory of God and his sovereignty over man and the world move forcefully to centre stage. Here we have the chasm between man and God in a form characteristic of Reformed theology.

From the theology of having been made righteous follow further consequences. For Müntzer the Gospel as demand not only shapes the special structure of justification, understood as renewal, but it also maintains its character as demand. Attaining holiness is not only an experience but also a duty; not only indicative but also imperative. The dialectical unity between indicative and imperative characteristic of the New Testament message undergoes a shift; indeed it undergoes dissolution. In Müntzer's hands it becomes sequential in time. Because the indicative, justification, undergoes objectification, the corresponding imperative becomes isolated and is set free. It becomes the dominating theme in Müntzer's theology. Because, as has been repeatedly observed, Müntzer is incapable of keeping together the indicative and imperative, which in Luther's thought constitute a dialectical unity—and because Müntzer dissolves this unity—Luther is seen by him as the champion of the mere indicative.

Thus Müntzer developed the doctrine of the law as a centrepiece of his theology. He questioned Luther's interpretation of Paul as an enemy of legalism. It is the work of scribes. Christ does not abolish the law, he fulfills it. Law and grace are one. The law terrifies through pangs of conscience. It brings the person to the ground of his being, to the confession of sin and through it to grace. Thus Müntzer replaced the dialectical relationship of law and Gospel with an undifferentiated unity. To be sure one is not justified through keeping the law, but through a confession of one's sin, which is brought about by the pangs of conscience resulting from one's inability to fulfill the law. There ensues a subsequent turning away from sin. Thus the law itself is grace, is justification.

The fact that justification is a process capable of completion makes it possible for the elect to follow the law. However, the law remains valid for the elect in all its severity, without losing its character as law. For Luther, on the other hand, the life of the Christian is determined by the spontaneous action of love. Only in this fashion can every appearance of personal achievement be prevented. For Müntzer, too, the works of the law follow salvation rather than produce it, but he is less concerned than Luther with warding off self-righteousness and pretentions to personal achievement. Luther's concern was that the law should not obscure grace and trust in man's relationship to God. Müntzer believed that he had destroyed all notions of meritorious works through his cross-theology, and hence he believed it possible to establish the significance of works on a new and different foundation. Only after justification does the imperative come into effect properly and decisively. The elect must "honor God's work with discipline." Without the law man withdraws from the demand of the Gospel and, like Luther, becomes "soft-living flesh." The chosen one has to live in contradiction to all worldliness. That is the core of the law. From it all individual norms receive their meaning. To be sure Müntzer's ambivalent attitude to the Bible results in certain oscillations. Some norms are grounded in Biblical literalism and in that way elevated to law, while other specifically Biblical norms fall away. Generally Müntzer's preaching of the law is marked by a strong ascetic, puritanical ethos.

Thus the severity of Christian subjectivity and the objectivity of Christian law blend into each other. The belief that the Spirit and faith are visible in and demonstrable through works unleashes an intense Christian activity. It is understood as a self-evident consequence of justification, as a necessary accomplishment required by obedience. Sanctification can be seen as a duty because being made holy is already a fact in justification. Therefore sanctification is not as in Erasmus or Calvin essentially progress toward an ideal goal, rather it is already present in totality. It is a radical transformation, the working out of a consumated and completed inner revolution. Hence stems the intensity, the un-Lutheran but not really anti-Christian character, of Müntzer's activism.

The theology of being made righteous is thus also a theology of demanded holiness under the law. The Christianization of the world is the telos and ethos of this theology, a matter of decisive significance for the problem of revolution. A Christianization of the world is impossible for Luther, because the condition of being a sinner cannot be abolished and the condition of being a Christian remains invisible. Moreover, existence in the two kingdoms, person and office, existence *coram deo* and *coram mundo,* are separated from one another. Müntzer protests against this separation. For him the existence of individual Christians may be demonstrated, hence a demonstrable mode of Christian life exists as well. Moreover, for Müntzer the debate with Catholicism about comforting the conscience and peace with God is no longer central. It has been replaced by the problem of the second generation, the establishment of an evangelical order of life. The release of reason from theological tutelage for action in the secular order initiated by Luther is impossible for Müntzer. Just as he had perceived in Luther's teachings concerning Scripture and justification the shortcomings of subsequent Orthodoxy, so he foresaw in Luther's teaching of the two kingdoms the decay of Lutheranism into a Christian inwardness,which with its faith and justification makes itself quietistically at home in an un-Christian world. This is a rejection of the anticipated secularization of Christendom, a protest against the toning down of the Christian contradiction to the world, against compromise with the world. Because of it, too, Luther is considered the "soft-living flesh at Wittenberg."

The sanctification of life is not limited to the individual realm, but includes, of course, the social and political relationships. Sanctification does not take place aside from the world, but in it. There is no withdrawal to a private sphere. The formation of a Christian life is the formation of a Christian world. The world is not to be accepted in a Lutheran sense as creation, either corrupted and to be left to the devil or to be loved with a spirit of forgiveness. It is to be changed, so that God's lordship becomes real in it. This transformation cannot be postponed to an indefinite world to come, but it must be realized here and now. And this claim cannot be pushed into a sectarian mold as the Anabaptists were to do later, making it relevant only for part of the world, the separate sphere of the elect. The claim is universal. It is total and radical, hence different than in the Reformed tradition of Zwingli and Bucer. The Christianization of the world is a revolutionary event.

The revolutionary character of Christianization is particularly accentuated by a further and new theological argument. For Luther a Christian order is impossible, among other things, because Christians are "rare birds." The relationship is inverted for Müntzer. There are only a few

Christians because the existing social order prevents it. It binds a person to the business of the world, so that he cannot come to salvation. According to the traditional Christian critique of riches, clinging to goods and honors leaves no place for faith in God. Beside this critique Müntzer placed a more decisive critique of poverty. The economic pressure by the princes and landlords, their "skinning and scraping," enslaves the poor, and particularly the peasantry, to "anxiety about nourishment" and worry about obtaining a mere subsistence. Thus the poor do not learn to read the Bible. (The Bible, as noticed above, retained its significance for Müntzer, too.) Outer suffering kept the poor preoccupied and hindered the experience of suffering in the conscience. Precisely because, unlike his descendants, the Anabaptists, Müntzer did not build an ideology from outer suffering, precisely because his cross-theology does not refer to everyday suffering but to suffering from inner failings, could a critique of poverty emerge from it. For Müntzer *theologia crucis* is no longer primarily *theologia pauperum,* in the sense that the poor *per se* are especially close to the cross. Poverty entangles the person in the world, making it impossible for him to "estrange himself from the lusts" of the world. Thus through poverty the person is potentially alienated from salvation. Therefore, only a Christian renewal of social relations creates the possibility for a majority of Christians to exist. The new Christian society must thus first of all create its own preconditions. Only a minority can bring about this renewal. This points to the necessary revolution. Of course, Müntzer turned reality into ideology. Particularly the situation of the Central German peasants belied the thesis that Christianity had become impossible for them. But it is extremely characteristic of Müntzer that he pushes social problems into the category of alienation. Thereby social and economic upheaval receive a theological foundation and goal. Thus the theology of the cross does not exclude revolution but actually demands it.

The Christianization of the world, which Müntzer's theology demanded, is finally directed against the political order. The "regents," at least in their majority, reject Christ. They have no true faith, but want to "rule" over it. Thereby they favour unbelief, indeed impede true faith and cheat the world of Christ. It is out of this train of thought as well that Müntzer gradually forms the conviction of the necessity of revolutionary renewal, which is to provide the possibility for Christian life.

. . . .

The final reason for the transmutation of Müntzer's theology into revolution, or rather for the actualization of his revolutionary theology, lies above all in his eschatological expectation. Because of it the new order for which he aims remains undetermined in its content. His concern here is not with specifics or with a planned future, but with the beginning of the kingdom of God, an order that is really different and entirely new. His aim is not the restitution of the primitive church, but the real freedom of God's children, so that the "earthly life may be transformed into heaven." This trait reappears in the modern revolutionary consciousness. According to Hegel, for example, the French Revolution in an eminent sense "transplanted heaven to earth." This heaven is the salvation and real truth of temporal life. Müntzer's concern is not with better days but with the end of days. This end, however, does not transcend history but is immanent in history, and in this sense Müntzer sets himself apart from the eschatology of his contemporaries, including the Lutherans. God will usher in the new world with the aid of the true Christians. Since his eschatological expectations and his eschatological despair grew more and more intense, Müntzer was possessed by a sense of urgency, very much like the one Campanella later experienced. This sense of urgency finally drove him into chiliastic revolution. The utopia of the peaceful Kingdom of God then justified once more the final holy war, the execution of God's judgement, the carrying out of his vengeance upon his enemies and the annihilation of the godless. For Müntzer the outbreak of the Peasants' War was an eschatological sign, the *kairos* of his mission. He did not bring the rebellion to Central Germany. But he decisively influenced its spirit by consistently interpreting "divine justice" (the peasants' slogan) to mean equality, and by radicalizing the immediate aims of the peasants into fundamental principles of chiliastic revolution. However often the realistic traits of Müntzer's final struggle may have been misunderstood in past history, in the final analysis it retains the strangeness of an enthusiastic-chiliastic faith, bent on the impossible, and passing all understanding.

A number of modern elements may be found in Müntzer's thinking, among them subjectivism and the critique of alienation, the will to revolutionary transformation, inspired by a utopian design, and the destructive application of what had been taken as an ultimate good. Historically, Müntzer's spiritualism stands at the beginning of a tradition which extends through the free churches, Pietism and the Enlightenment to the modern secularized world, with its principles of reason, tolerance and human rights. Objectively, however, Müntzer's universal totalitarian theocratic program with its destruction of the individual is further from modernity than is Luther's conservative outlook. The latter, relativistic in temporal matters, basically permits reason autonomy to shape the world; and, with its personal concept of faith, Luther's view first makes it possible to regard the individual as a person rather than as some sort of object. In this respect as well, historical conditions, the princely institutionalized church and the free church, have had more impact than theology in determining the different roles of the churches of Germany and Western Europe in the creation of the modern world.

The Mystic with the Hammer: Thomas Müntzer's Theological Basis for Revolution

Hans-Jürgen Goertz

. . . .

[Thomas] Müntzer's ideas take us into the world of medieval mysticism, out of which, wrestling with the problems of the incipient Reformation, he surprisingly struck revolutionary fire. That is the meaning of my title, "The Mystic with the Hammer," which brings together his intellectual tradition and his self-understanding. Müntzer uses the language of the Prophet Jeremiah: "Do not my words scorch like fire? says the Lord. Are they not like a hammer that splinters rock?" (Jer. 23:29)

1. THE PROBLEM OF INTERPRETATION

. . . .

Müntzer has thus fallen between the millstones of the quarrel between Christianity and Marxism; and this fate has had a baneful effect on the interpretation of his writings. Christian theology is in general not favorably inclined toward revolution, and Marxism is in general theologically illiterate. But Müntzer was both revolutionary and theologian.

Karl Holl says of Müntzer's soteriology: "It is an absolutely clear and logically articulated train of thought." But in his opinion Müntzer's ideas of social reform could not be fitted into that train of thought. Holl felt that the mystical piety he observed in Müntzer was basically "selfish" and not socially oriented. He lets the matter rest as a contradiction between mystical piety and socio-political agitation. From this Robert Friedmann concludes:

> Though he (Müntzer) is today still a profound disciple of German mysticism, by tomorrow he will have forgotten all his teaching of resignation (*Gelassenheit*) and cross-bearing, and will merely be striving egotistically for the success of his personal fantasies.

Then he adds the comment that Müntzer was a revolutionary because of his natural drives. It was apparently not possible to harmonize his theological argumentation with his revolutionary agitation, at least not on the plane of systematic thought.

Marxist historiography takes a different approach. It proceeds from the idea that Müntzer's thought develops logically into the "Early Bourgeois Revolution." Whereas the Holl school of thought discovered the key to Müntzer's personality in contradiction, the Marxist begins with its unity. This unity can, in any case, not be a theological unity, but solely an ideological one, for in Marxist thought theology is merely a mythical form which presents a distorted and disfigured picture of objective social reality. The Marxist regards Müntzer's intention as directed toward this objective reality and his theological statements as only a means to communicate it. Not until the advent of Marxist doctrine was the instrument available for understanding Müntzer as he wanted to be understood but was unable to communicate himself because of the limitations of his era. This attempt at interpretation does violence to Müntzer's thought because it does not deal with his theology in its own terms. And so in recent times it has been Müntzer's fate to be misunderstood by some because they do not want to understand revolution, and by others because they cannot understand theology.

Anyone who hopes to find the clue to Thomas Müntzer must avoid both misapprehensions. And it is no accident that an age which shows increasing sympathy for a "theology of revolution" also meets this first Protestant "theologian of revolution" with greater understanding. The decisive problem of interpreting Müntzer today consists in discovering how he provides a *theological* basis for revolution. For neither the psychological nor the ideological basis has up to now proved satisfactory as a device for revealing the man.

. . . .

2. THE MYSTICAL FOUNDATION

Not every page that Müntzer wrote and not every work he published is saturated with revolution. Nor, as is occasionally assumed, had he begun in Zwickau to prepare and propagandize for the Peasants' War when he identified himself with the poor of the city. The attempt to grasp his theology only in the context of social disorders renders impossible any balanced perspective on it. The part he played in stirring up the Peasants' War was less significant than Luther's. The peasants most often called upon the Reformer of Wittenberg. In his *Liberty of the Christian Man* they perceived a heralding of their own freedom. Müntzer did not attach himself to them until later. Ever after his *Sermon to the Princes* of 1524, when he failed to win the government's support to overthrow the current social order and set up the Kingdom of God, it still took some time before he could issue a stronger and more definite call for a violent upheaval. He was by no means the man who, long beforehand, planned and organized the rising at Frankenhausen. Many factors came together here. For the peasants there was objective exploitation as well as a subjective unrest, which kept erupting out of their long suffering into constantly increasing activity. They had experienced a bitter disappointment from the social ineffectiveness of the Reformation. On Müntzer's side there was an incapacity to realize that he had failed to rouse the masses with his sermons and writings, despite his incessant attacks on the clergy's attempt to hold the laity in tutelage, and his sharp exposure of the powerlessness of the Reformer's doctrine of justification by faith to raise the moral standards of the day. His rage at Luther's strong invective against his person was joined with a growing awareness that his own theological insights and the signs of those stormy times pointed with greater and greater urgency to the apocalyptic climax of the world. Shortly after the defeat of the peasants in May 1525 Müntzer hid in an attic somewhere or other, was accidentally recognized by a bag of copies of his own letters and writings, "recanted" on the rack, and was put to death with his colleague Heinrich Pfeiffer. He cannot be made solely responsible for the Peasants' War, even in its Thuringian version. It was a piling up of inextricably entangled ideas, emotions, hopes, unsatisfied yearnings, exhausting suffering, Bible-reading, prayer, sermons and deeds that exploded into the catastrophe before the gates of Frankenhausen.

Hence it would be unreasonable to try to find Müntzer's theological foundation by judging from the final results. The opposite way, i.e., observing the development of his ideas in a quieter period, is more promising.

Anyone who starts out on a search for Müntzer's theological beginnings will, to be sure, be confronted by new difficulties. First, the sources shed little light on his biographical or educational development, and second, his earlier expressions have an inevitably Lutheran intellectual context. It has therefore frequently been assumed that Müntzer built his theological structure with materials borrowed from Luther. To begin with, a piece of biographical information seems to point in that direction. After a debate between Luther and John Eck at Leipzig, which Müntzer most likely attended, Luther was happy to recommend this former Father Confessor of a convent for a pastorate in Zwickau. There, as a loyal and dependable comrade in arms in a post of strategic importance for the Reformation, he was to strengthen the moderate Reformation of the Erasmian Egranus, who had obviously disappointed Luther. Thus Müntzer took up his struggle against the Franciscans in Zwickau as a conscious "Martinian." Only later—so it was assumed—did he come under the influence of the Spiritualist Nicholas Storch and gradually forget what he owed to Luther in his theology. But an analysis of the arguments that Müntzer marshalled against Egranus shatters this assumption. The theological perspectives of his critique do not point back to Luther's basic Reformation theology, but to a mystical-spiritualistic tradition which made intellectual comrades of Müntzer and Storch before they ever met, and with which Luther, too, was conversant, if only during a transitional stage in his development.

This biographical datum, which definitely detaches Müntzer from Luther, is followed by a second. Until the present it, too, has been used to support the opposite assumption. Müntzer was unable to stay long in Zwickau and in 1521 secretly slipped off to Prague. In order to find entrée there he probably sent ahead under his own name the disputation theses of Melanchthon to the theologians of Prague. That, too, has been taken as evidence of his Lutheran standpoint. His later development has been explained as a one-sided rigidification, a legalistic exaggeration, of Reformation theology. Müntzer's theological basis for revolution, as it gradually crystallized, was attributed on the whole to a misunderstanding of Lutheran fundamentals. But a closer look reveals what Müntzer had in mind with these theses. He used them solely as a line of demarcation over against Catholic theology and as proof that he was in the Reformation camp. But they offer no *a posteriori* conclusion about his theology. For in the Prague Manifesto, which appeared soon afterward, his words are indeed directed against the Catholics, but the intellectual content implies a decisive rejection of Luther. None of the substance of the Manifesto was later retracted or altered, once Müntzer had begun his public polemic against Luther, "the soft-living flesh at Wittenberg." Against both pope and Reformers the Manifesto cites the "living voice of God, when the Father addresses the Son in the human heart." It is withheld from the chosen ones by the Scribes, as Müntzer calls them. Faith can be experienced only through the living voice of God in the depth of the soul, without external means—neither through the letter of Scripture, nor through the sacraments, nor through the institutional church or ecclesiastical hierarchy. This criterion recurs as a stereotype; it is identical with the statements on the free working of God in the human heart. It does not emerge from Martin Luther's theology. Rather it is reminiscent of German medieval mysticism, e.g., that of Tauler and the *Theologia Deutsch*, or the *Book on Spiritual Poverty*, formerly erroneously ascribed to Tauler.

Karl Holl pointed out Müntzer's mystical piety; in my book *Innere und äussere Ordnung in der Theologie Thomas Müntzers* I have gone a step further and have attempted, by drawing upon medieval mysticism, to derive a mystical theology from Müntzer's writings. He did not simply copy the mystical tradition without making it relevant to his times; he incorporated it into the distinctive conceptions and the vivid language of the Reformation debate. Lutheran influence upon Müntzer can be taken for granted, and it has a certain significance for his theological development over and beyond the subjective feeling of liberation which it conveyed. Likewise Hussite-Taborite and eschatological or apocalyptical elements from other medieval movements conditioned his thought. However, the structural elements of his theology were derived from the practical (not the speculative) mysticism of the Middle Ages. My only objective in *Innere und äussere Ordnung* was to demonstrate this derivation, not to deny the presence of other influences. They also contributed important content to his theology, but only within the framework of its basically mystical pattern.

Müntzer took great pains to explain in what manner a person could attain faith. Individual appropriation of faith and the assurance of salvation, the "arrival of faith," are in the center of almost all his writings. In opposition to the "contrived faith" of the Reformers, who allegedly pieced it together out of the letter of Scripture, he set "experienced faith." He insisted so strongly on this contrast because he believed that only experienced faith could offer theological insight and direction for the Reformation. Here he found the justification for his increasingly revolutionary preaching. "Everyone chatters whatever he wishes about faith; the sensual and the ambitious cannot be believing in anything, for they preach what they have never tasted themselves." He pointedly attacks Luther's constant allusion to the Word: "Even if you gobbled up whole Bibles it would do you no good, you must suffer the sharp plowshare. You will still not have faith unless God gives it to you himself and teaches it to you himself."

Only he who is taught of God can claim the right to renew theology, the church, and the society. This theological justification of the Reformation by means of a new authority built upon the mystical process of salvation by-passes the Lutheran doctrine of justification at the very outset, and cannot be explained as a later distortion of this doctrine.

Drawing upon the conceptual arsenal of medieval mysticism, Müntzer describes in detail the process that leads to the experience of faith. Fundamental for him is the assumption of the *Seelengrund* (abyss of the soul). Nowhere does he give an exact definition of this phenomenon. As with Tauler, it can probably best be understood as the "organ of experiencing God." The Seelengrund is dirtied and besmirched by longings, wishes, desires, and human reason, all of which draw man away from God, distract him from concentrating on God. The "world" has gained entry into his heart and soul and rules over him.

Within this Seelengrund the Holy Spirit does not work in the fullness of his gifts, but is at first concealed as the "Spirit of the fear of God." He sets the process of salvation in motion. Man becomes restless and afraid, is assailed by doubts about God and himself. He falls into an unendurable distance from God to the point of despairing of himself so that his will to live is broken. In an unutterable process of suffering—a mysticism of the cross—man is separated from his worldly desires. He loses his being (*er entwird*); his abyss becomes "empty"; he permits the Spirit working in him to have his way; "yielded" (*gelassen*) he awaits what comes. This process begins anew again and again. The Spirit of the fear of God demands the self-mortification of man; he accomplishes his work ever more thoroughly; and in the "night, when wretchedness is at its highest," says Müntzer, "then Christ, true Son of God, descends" into the depths of the soul. Here Christ is born. The divine birth in man takes place in suffering and pain and the infilling of the Holy Spirit. The "Kingdom of God" begins in the heart of the elect; this step corresponds with the medieval *unio mystica*, the uniting of man with God.

. . . .

This brief description of Müntzer's understanding of salvation (which Müntzer himself never describes so concisely and rigorously, but only in a fragmentary fashion, sometimes focusing on one stage, sometimes on another) certainly demonstrates that this theology cannot have grown on the rootstock of Lutheran theology. Nor can it be simply disposed of by judging it to be a legalization of Luther's doctrine of grace. To be sure, the Lutheran dialectic of Law and Gospel is done away with by Müntzer in the gradualistic work of the Holy Spirit; but the grace of the divine work of salvation is not thereby sacrificed to human manipulation. Within his mystically oriented basic insights (which in their systematic entirety would certainly not suffice to express the Reformers' theology of Law and Gospel), Müntzer definitely tries to present the divine work of salvation as a human appropriation of a grace which is, nevertheless, grace, free of human contamination or usurpation.

Müntzer's theology is a descriptive theology which has as its object the spiritually progressive human experience of God which presses toward the fullness of the Holy Spirit. And it is amazing how adeptly Müntzer succeeds in drawing all the important theological problems of the Reformation into his descriptions of the process of salvation. He treats the significance of Scripture, the role of the Law (both are connected with "the Spirit of the Fear of God"; Law and Scripture kill but do not make alive), the teaching on justification and the sacrament of baptism (justification is a suffering submission to the divine work in man) and, finally, discipleship and imitation of Christ. This can only be suggested here. We must keep in mind that Müntzer had a deep pastoral concern for the individual person and tried to assist him in the achievement of an "experienced faith." Thus his theology and his proclamation have exclusively missionary traits. Whatever he says or writes is directed toward the process of salvation and is realized only within that process. He says hardly a word about the period following the birth of God in the human soul, which is the period of the testing of faith. As soon as experienced faith has to be tested it is once more connected with the process of salvation, so that Christ may grow within the individual and the "world" decrease, Christ become larger and the world smaller. Here too mystical terms and conceptions shine through.

Compared with the mystical tradition on which Müntzer drew, he laid greater stress on the efficacy of divine grace in man, even if the mortifying demands of "the Spirit of the Fear of God" occupy the verbal foreground. At least in part he broke through scholastic conceptions of infused grace, which medieval mysticism generally taught. (His progressively articulated relationship between Law and Gospel is, admittedly, not on a par with Luther's dialectical and eschatological interpretation.) In his own way Müntzer found himself on the road to the Reformation as did Luther, too, when he passed through the stage of a mystically oriented theology. His view of the "arrival of faith" (which gives assurance of salvation) was not more radical than Luther's doctrine of justification; it was indeed more moderate, if the radicalness of this teaching is measured by the release it produces in man. It is all the more surprising that his mystical preoccupation afforded him a more radical insight than Luther's into the need for change in the social structure and relationships of authority of his time. It might be appropriate to remark here that the topic of human liberation is not exhausted by the anthropological application of Luther's teaching on sin and salvation. A social dimension must also come into the picture. This will be discussed at the end of the next section.

3. THE EXTERNALIZATION OF MYSTICAL EXPERIENCE

Müntzer's concentration on the process of salvation that controls communication between God and man, i.e., on the "inner order," is so intensive that it is hard to imagine how the "outer order"—church, government and social order, history, eschatology and apocalyptics—can find room in his field of vision.

. . . .

To explain the transition from the inner to the outer order we must proceed from Müntzer's judgment of the social situation of his time; the man who is called to faith is put into this social situation or even subjected to it; to change it is his task. The conditions of social life conspicuously resemble the nature of the "fictitious faith." Love of gain and fame, ambition and unbridled hedonism, seeking one's own advantage, etc., not only usurp the place of revelation but also affect the lives of other people and impair the common welfare; they bring about an "irreparable harm to all Christendom." Fictitious faith, the opposite of experienced faith, controls public life. What made it so dangerous was its claim, based on pretensions of biblical legitimacy, that it was true Christian faith; and what made its effect on public life so dangerous was its usurpation, with Christian motivation, of political and social power. It was this mutual reinforcement between political-worldly and spiritual-Christian power, between secular government and church, which Müntzer constantly denounced. This is the root of his anticlerical passion. And insofar as he shared this position with the spreading Anabaptist movement, as well as with the humanists and other groups, it must be admitted that in this respect he, like them, stood opposed to an evil—not a fiction—of his time. He was committed to the total destruction of the medieval *corpus Christianum.*

It is now clear that he sees the outer order from the point of view of the inner. Indeed the analysis of the social situation has its point of orientation either in the fictitious or in the experienced *faith* and as a whole proceeds from the perspective of the inner order. "The destructiveness of the uncomprehending world must first be recognized with its entire *origin*, otherwise it is not possible for the allwise Father to apply his gracious rod." We can proceed one step further: Müntzer develops his conception of the "world" directly from his conception of faith. At first glance the conception of the world, as well as that of fictitious faith, seems to have an exclusively moral derivation. The principal characteristic of the "world" is the decline of morality. But if one considers further that the aggressiveness of the "world" is basically directed against God, against all that is of God and against his work in man, it becomes clear how powerful also is the theological evaluation of the "world." This conception of the world, which was ultimately derived from Müntzer's conception of faith, explains why his attack on the fictitious faith (i.e., Luther's doctrine of justification as Müntzer understood it), and its alleged incapacity to elevate deteriorated moral standards, had to be at the same time an attack upon the "world," specifically upon the existing social order. In his makeup there was a compulsion to reform a half spiritual, half worldly faith and likewise to reform a society based upon a half spiritual, half worldly law. The two were inseparably connected.

Müntzer articulates his program most strikingly in the struggle against government (*Obrigkeit*). For, with the failure of his attempts to raise up the Kingdom of God with the help of the Obrigkeit, it very soon became for him the advocate of the "world." In its pinnacles of authority is to be seen its radically ungodly nature. It harasses and fights against those who are awaiting the "arrival of faith" and those who have experienced this faith, thus preventing the "true" Reformation by keeping the populace dependent and dominated. Müntzer did not develop a firm teaching about government but preserved for himself full freedom to approach the government with direct demands according to the situation. James M. Stayer makes the point effectively: "About the sword and about tyrants, Müntzer had a teaching, but about rulers and government, only an attitude." Thus he could write as a loyal subject to his sovereign, Frederick the Wise, at the same time threatening a tyrannical local government that he would overthrow it by all conceivable means. His criterion for evaluating a government was its willingness to serve the people—in other words, not to suppress the experienced faith. But under the pressure of events Müntzer came closer and closer to the realization that he must equate the government with the "ungodly world." As soon as this became clear to him his call for resistance resounded radically and unambiguously:

> Forward, forward, strike while the fire is hot! Don't let your sword become cold or blunt! Smite, cling, clang, on Nimrod's anvil; cast their towers to the ground! As long as they remain alive you can never rid yourselves of the fear of men. No one can speak to you of God as long as they reign over you. Forward, forward, while it is still day; God is leading you; follow, follow.

Müntzer bases his right to resist on his concept of faith. If faith is above all concerned with radically breaking and overcoming sin in the inner life, it is at the same time the revolutionary principle that attacks and overcomes the existing order of authority, which is an outgrowth of sin.

The revolutionary conquest of the "world" must be examined a little more closely. His very concept of the world reveals how much Müntzer is concerned with the predominance of the inner order over the outer. He admonished his readers above all to pay attention to and to overcome the "world" in their hearts, since it is present there "many thousand times more than outside." He is obviously afraid that a hyperactive attentiveness to the outer "world" could deflect people's attention from themselves (i.e., from the obstacles they themselves have erected against the arrival of faith). He fears that the change in social, economic and political conditions—which must be far more than simply removing some acute abuses—could issue from selfish and self-interested motives, hence from the fictitious faith and not the unself-interested faith that is produced by God.

Faith and "world" become mutually contradictory concepts, each of which stands in the other's way and seeks to crowd it out and eliminate it. This is true in both the inner and the outer order. Like faith, the "world" also extends its influence from the inner order to the outer. Nevertheless, this should not be interpreted to mean that the inner order must first be brought into a right relationship with God before the reformation of the outer can be undertaken, even though Müntzer himself on occasion fosters this misunderstanding. Only in an intellectual sense is the one derived from the other; in actual life, however, the two are intertwined. The defeat of the "world" within means at the same time and in the same process the defeat of the world without. This logic becomes continually more prominent under the pressure of events and the increasing adoption of apocalyptic impulses. Although Müntzer occasionally complained that governmental pressure and wretched social conditions prevented the peasants from reading the Bible and experiencing faith, I cannot agree with the Marxist historiography that his stress lay chiefly on altering social conditions in order to make a place for faith (which is certainly not conceived of in a mystical sense by these historians). From this complaint of Müntzer one can only perceive that he does not separate the outer order from the inner—indeed, precisely in the reverse direction from the Marxist interpretation, he conceives of and demands the change in society as something proceeding from a change in the individual man. This occasional expression by Müntzer, which we characterized as open to misunderstanding, can, in fact, be turned against the Marxist interpretation. Only the "elect" who has already undergone the inner change has the insight and power to call for and contribute to a change in external conditions.

The right to resist is established together with the concept of faith and is founded upon the demand that the government be given to the people. At first glance Müntzer's argument seems to be incompatible with its mystical context. It can only be correctly understood if one sees in the "people" a concept basically corresponding to faith. As faith exhibits the basis of God's dominion in the soul of man, so the people—in the context of the prophecy of the outpouring of the divine Spirit upon all flesh in the last days (Joel 3:1) and the eschatological reversal of relationships of authority (Luke 2:52)—exhibit the basis of God's sovereignty in the world. Authority and power that do not provoke rebellion and insurrection can only be based upon a people experienced in faith, for thus the original relationships of authority and obedience (Gen. 1:28) are reestablished. The people delegate authority and examine the way it is exercised. Whoever possesses authority serves the people with it and does not dominate them. It therefore follows that theocracy and democracy are one and the same thing. Democracy is theocratically based, and theocracy is democratically exercised. The argument for the sovereignty of the people which was handed down to Müntzer out of medieval tradition, and for which he could cite Daniel 7:27, is integrated into his concept of faith. Thus, the pre-eminence of the inner order is once again demonstrated. Previous attempts to interpret Müntzer have been unable to connect the mystical and revolutionary elements in his theology into an acceptable unity of thought. This unity, previously observed in connection with his understanding of faith and the "world," can be demonstrated, finally, in the concept of man's cooperation with God. In the inner order, where salvation is effected and the assurance of salvation is attained, this cooperation is limited to mortification and suffering submission to the divine work, but outwardly it appears in man's activity in resisting oppression by the "world"—that is, in transforming, changing, or even annihilating the existing "worldly" conditions.

The inner process of the birth of God is revolutionary, cleanses the inner man through and through and destroys the power of sin; the outward process can be no less revolutionary. As sinful resistance in the soul is broken and destroyed under the revolutionary action of God in the dark night of despair and the destruction of self-will, so also the same resistance in the "world" must be broken by the same action and the "world" itself destroyed. Only then will the Kingdom of God come into existence on earth. However determinative the eschatological-apocalyptical interpretation of the Old Testament, especially the prophet Daniel, is in Müntzer's argumentation, it must not be forgotten that the Kingdom of God on earth is derived from the kingdom that has its source in the human heart. Like the concept of the world, so also the concept of the Kingdom of God is internalized, receives its structure thereby and is then once again transferred out of the inner man. Expectation of the end and apocalyptic argumentation, which breathes the common spirit of centuries permeated by Joachimite and pseudo-Joachimite speculation (itself always connected with mystical Spiritualism), lend warmth and fire to his preaching. Nevertheless, the inner consistency and intensity of his message are derived from the basic mystical idea, into which the apocalyptic images are fitted and the external aspects of which they strengthen. Müntzer is the mystic "with the hammer." For him the hammer, like the sickle, symbolizes eschatological radicalism.

Müntzer's revolutionary mysticism finds comprehensive expression in the imitation of Christ. This *imitatio*, or discipleship, is a component part of the process of salvation and unites the inner cooperation between God and man with the outer, which has as its goal a transformation of the "world" or its annihilation. The distinctiveness of this discipleship lies in the conjunction of these two aspects of cooperation. Discipleship is a mystical-revolutionary act. In it, not only man, but God and man are active. In other words, in discipleship God acts in, through and with man. It is misunderstood if it is described simply as the ethical consequence of a mystical understanding of faith. Discipleship or *imitatio* is basically another mode of expression for the process of salvation itself. Thereby the old opposition between the mysticism of the cross and revolutionary agitation (which has in any case never been adequately accounted for by the traditionl historiography) is removed. The combination of the two elements is an independent achievement of Müntzer. He takes the Kingdom of God into man's mystical experience; and the divinely-guided initiation into mystical experience is like building "dynamite charges into the social structure."

Only an impetus from the outside was needed to compel Müntzer to think, to speak, and to act, and from the moment he received it the revolutionary consequences of his doctrine of salvation were evident. No situations or opponents *changed* his thinking, but simply brought it to expression from occasion to occasion with different degrees of intensity. Thus, Müntzer reformulated mysticism for the early Reformation, which was on the point of becoming an individualistic Reformation, but not at the same time a fundamental and comprehensive social Reformation. Ironically, in his case religious individualism prepared the way for a social Reformation—Müntzer's description of the process of salvation cannot be interpreted as other than individualistic. Müntzer is a rare example demonstrating that the social engagement which arises out of the realm of inwardness must not necessarily be an affirmation of existing power relationships, but can conceive itself summoned to the task of changing or even annihilating illegitimate structures of rulership and injustice. Here we can pick up the point made at the conclusion of the last section and pose the question of the comparative "social relevance" of the theologies of Luther and Müntzer. Let us compare the two theologies from this point of view and ask if it is true (as it first appears) that Müntzer's understanding of sin and salvation is more shallow and less radical than Luther's. (Perhaps in answering such a question we must distinguish between Müntzer's evident theological intention and its insufficient articulation.) Müntzer's linkage of individual and "social" sins corresponds to the intertwining of individual and "social" salvation and of the renovation of the inner and outer order.

4. THE TENDENCY TOWARD WORLD-ANNIHILATION

Thomas Müntzer's struggle for the release of the peasants from serfdom, for the initiation of a democratic social order, for revolution (to the extent that the uprising before the gates of Frankenhausen in May 1525 deserves that name) ended in failure. But that does not necessarily justify a condemnation of his theology, although his theological interpreters have often assumed that it does. The failure of its realization is not a proper criterion for the evaluation of a theology. Too many superindividual and extratheological factors come together here. How, then, is one to judge his theological theory, which pressed toward revolutionary practice and indeed was first and foremost articulated in practice?

Manfred Bensing combines his evaluation, which follows the traditional lines of Marxist interpretation, with a positive judgment of the failure. He believes the failure did not reflect upon the theory. Defeat became unavoidable when "within the revolutionary camp the moderate and narrow-minded local forces were able to strengthen their influence and only the 'elite of the available revolutionary elements' (Engels) presented themselves for the battle," whereas the princes succeeded "in uniting in Thuringia and for the moment in overcoming their own inner conflicts." Müntzer "wanted too much too soon," since the objective historical process, under the conditions of early capitalism, was focused on the "necessary form of the achievement of the individual" (Karl Marx) and had not yet achieved a breakthrough to the creative involvement of individuals on behalf of a socialistic society. Three characteristics of this verdict are worthy of note. First, Bensing translates into the ideology of the Marxist philosophy of history the theological explanation derived from his general theory which Müntzer cited for the failure of the uprising: namely, that his followers had not yet been sufficiently freed of selfishness by the mystical process of salvation. Second, he turns his attention away from Müntzer's theology, remarking simply that he remained loyal to his program. Third, he gives an idealized presentation of Müntzer as a totally admirable human being:

> His human greatness stands out both in the battle, in which he led the people, avoiding no danger, and in the defeat, when he entreated for the people. A life that is dedicated until its final moment to the common people must truly be called great.

Bensing is obviously repeating a theme of Wilhelm Zimmermann, the radical-democratic historian of the Peasants' War.

> In Müntzer's soul there is much that is disturbed and savage, but through this wilderness and this darkness in him a brilliant red flower glows—his love for his people, for humanity.

Thomas Nipperdey, on the other hand, criticizes Müntzer for the "boundless pretensions of a theology of revolution and its inhuman logic." He says that a theology must lead to intolerance and violence when it undertakes to "identify a truth which it advertises as its own possession with the worldly goals of particular groups." Nipperdey also stands in a definite tradition of interpretation. Just as Karl Holl in his noted essay, *Luther und die Schwärmer,* had drawn conclusions from Müntzer's theology which he could turn against allegedly unacceptable ideas of contemporary opponents or against the increasingly influential affirmation of Müntzer's worldview, so Nipperdey opposes the new "clericalism of the theologians of revolution, who now arrogate authority to themselves in the name of the Christian Gospel" and also the inclination of the "Idealists" of the New Left "to limit or do away with tolerance and pluralism" in the name of *their* truth and *their* righteousness. This polemical tradition of interpretation often tells more about the theological and political stance of the interpreter than about Thomas Müntzer's theology.

Both of these interpretations are judgments of popular scholarship, which are nevertheless products of intensive study of Müntzer. It would be wrong to eliminate the theological basis of revolution from our area of judgment, since it is a weakness to show a lack of comprehension for the intellectual permeation of a revolutionary situation.

Whenever Müntzer takes up the problem of violence it is always with the awareness of having to meet a revolutionary situation in theological terms. Too little attention has hitherto been given to the fact that even at the climax of the controversy Müntzer never speaks of force, nor does he call for a show of force, but only of counterforce. After all, he discovers the cause of the Peasants' War neither in his theology nor in the demands of the peasants and of the common people, as though they were trying to use force to get something to which they had no right or which did not belong to them. He sees it only in the antisocial, exploitative behavior of the "ungodly rulers."

> Behold, the basic cause (*Grundsuppe*) of usury, of thievery and robbery are our lords and princes who claim all creatures as their property. The fish in the water, the birds in the air, the fruits of the earth must all belong to them (Isaiah 5). About these things they let God's command be promulgated among the people and say, "God has commanded, thou shalt not steal"; but it does them no good. Thus they provoke everyone and skin and scrape the poor field-worker, the craftsman and everyone around (Micah 3); but if he then steals the smallest thing he must be hanged. Then Doctor Liar (Luther) says Amen. The lords themselves cause the common man to become their enemy. They refuse to remove the cause of rebellion; how then can things get better? If I say that I must be rebellious, very well!

In the eyes of Müntzer God's command is abused as the justification for usurping possessions and suppressing the freedom necessary for life. This kind of abuse (detected in an early experiment with "ideology critique") is the cause of the rebellion. This "analysis" has a theological origin: "It is clear that the ungodly rulers themselves violate the peace of the country, and beat and punish the people on account of the Gospel, and our princes have not a word to say against it." The specific occasion that brought the situation to a head ("think about the transformation of the world now before the gate") was the threatened extradition of his followers who had fled to Allstedt from the surrounding area. In theological terms, this was the situation: In the battle of the "world" against the Gospel, hence against the "advent of faith" in man, the revolutionary character of the social situation was demonstrated. Force that is employed in this situation, exercised upon the basis of experienced faith ("then they must be throttled like dogs"), is counterforce, and to Müntzer it seems to be ethically required. He did not decide lightly to issue the call for counterforce. He tried to form an alliance with the princes who favored the Gospel or who refused to persecute people for their faith, to keep the "ungodly rulers" in check and thus to avoid a bloody insurrection while there was still time. "The Covenant is nothing but an instrument of self-defense, which is not denied to anyone in the natural judgment of rational men." Likewise he tried to make it clear to his followers that the government was instituted as a "broom," as the disciplinary rod of God—certainly not in the sense that the princes would be able to derive from this a justification of their authority (or of a ruthless violence against the revolting peasants such as Luther advocated later on), but in the sense that it would shove the elect onto that road of purifying suffering upon which the transfer of rulership to the common people would come to pass. These attempts at a relatively cool-headed procedure, which have only rarely been perceived in the research on Müntzer, were disregarded both by the princes and by the rebels.

. . . .

Thus, there were reasons for considering the violence of the rebels to be a necessary, unavoidable counterforce. But Müntzer's theological argumentation makes this finding problematical or even negates it. For in the final analysis it turned away from the revolutionary situation by forcing social reality into the confines of a theology of experienced faith, of the mystical process of salvation. It moulded its conception of the revolutionary on the "inner order" before carrying it over into the outer order. Sin in the inner order was the prototype of rebellion, or of force against God. The struggle against this sin, or mortification, thus became counterforce; and accordingly the struggle against sin in the social and political realm, against usurped authority and exploitative force, became an action of counterforce. Social reality, the "world," was seen only as a symptom of sin, and was indeed regarded as sin, rather than as an area for living, which is a gift entrusted to man in order that through it God may be served and faith tested, both individually and socially. Müntzer absolutized the negative traits of the biblical interpretation of the world and did not consider that God also loved the world and accepted it in his Son (John 3:16). The "world" had to be destroyed. Müntzer's objective, after its mystical anthropological beginning, received an apocalyptic edge, and was expressed as the annihilation of the ungodly. In this context what he conceived of as counterforce degenerated into pure force. His concept of counterforce was untenable within the framework of his mystically oriented theology; contrary to his intention it turned into violence and destruction from its very beginning. This was because it was the direct consequence of the shattering and violent transformation of the sinful, which was initiated by God within the elect man. This contradition did not develop only as his apocalyptic expectations assumed increasing power over his thinking and acting; it was imbedded from the start in the mystical foundation of his theology. Here it becomes apparent once again how Müntzer succeeded in integrating apocalypticism into the mystical framework of his theology. It also becomes apparent that his attempt to construct a careful "politics of the covenant," which was pointed out above, was bound to check rather than to promote the logical consistency of his theology.

In order to avoid misunderstanding, the integration in Müntzer's theology of mystical with eschatological-apocalyptic elements, to which reference has been made a number of times, must be examined a little more closely. It is by no means the case that my interpretation of Müntzer's theology together with its social-revolutionary consequences overlooks the large part played by eschatological-apocalyptic thought in the traditional current of medieval mysticism. . . .

Müntzer's writings resist a one-sided mystical interpretation, but they also resist a one-sided eschatological-apocalyptical interpretation. They are rightly dealt with only when considered from both the mystical and apocalyptical standpoints, which after all, have their points of correspondence. There is a correspondence between the judgment to which suffering subjects human beings in this life and the final Judgment upon the ungodly at the end of the world. There is a correspondence between the need to "root out" unbelief from the human soul and the necessity to separate the elect from the ungodly in this world. The movement that can be perceived in the inner life corresponds to the "new movement in the present world," which signalizes a general transformation of power relationships. The reception of the Spirit corresponds to the eschatological Kingdom. In brief: the situation in the soul corresponds to the situation in the world and vice-versa. But there are other points of correspondence besides the ones mentioned. With his bold insight Müntzer had seen that mysticism and apocalypticism could be fused together. Thus, the language of mysticism deepens his eschatological conceptions, and the language of apocalypticism lends an urgency and earnestness to his description of the process of salvation. The content, as well as the vocabulary of the two realms, is merged. A particular clear proof of this is his statement:

> All the evildoers of the original wickedness of Christendom must be justified through the Law, as Paul says, so that the severity of the Father may clear away the ungodly Christians who resist the saving teaching of Christ, so that the just may have time and space to learn the will of God. It would never be possible, amidst such tyranny, that a single Christian could give heed to his meditation if evil were to be free of punishment by the law. . . .

His *Hochverursachte Schutzrede,* which is a politically relevant polemic against the Lutheran doctrine of justification, reveals not only the fusion of mystical and eschatological-apocalyptic traits in Müntzer's argumentation; it also shows that the mystical conception of salvation, the inner order, is the source of this fusion. That becomes clear in other places as well. In the *Prague Manifesto* Müntzer is most of all concerned that the Bohemians learn "how kindly and how very gladly God speaks with all his chosen ones." For this he is willing to stake his life. The emphasis is placed on this more than on the instruction of the Bohemians about their functions in the final Judgment. And in his letter to his followers in Halle, which Maron also cites, Müntzer ties the cleansing process in suffering caused by his exile with his preparation for the harvest time. The sickle within him is being sharpened as the abyss (*Abgrund*) of his soul is cleared. The letter does not clarify whether Müntzer is referring to his preparation for a function in the final Judgment or in the inner purifying process of the elect, but it is unmistakable that the eschatological action is motivated and authorized only by the salvation experienced in the mystical process. The mystical doctrine of salvation plays the leading part in the integration of mystical and eschatological-apocalyptic conceptions.

The integration of apocalyptic notions into a mystical framework, here referred to, can also clarify a problem that has created a fundamental clash between the Marxist and non-Marxist interpretations, and has determined the positive or negative verdict on Müntzer's program. In Marxist historiography there is stress upon Müntzer's intention to raise up a new, democratic-socialistic society by means of revolution. The non-Marxist view is that he intended to destroy the existing society completely and to transform it into the Kingdom of God, which knows no government (or self-government!). Neither of these interpretations can be verified clearly and comprehensively by the sources. The one overlooks the theocratic strain in the establishment of Müntzer's democratic social order, a strain that is incorporated into his apocalypticism, insofar as it is God who exercises authority in his Kingdom. The other overlooks the democratic trait of the Kingdom that will finally and permanently arrive when the ungodly, in the persons of the rulers who enslave the people, are annihilated. (In general when Müntzer refers to the "ungodly" he really means only persons possessed of ungodly authority.) These two traits are united, hence neither is neglected, by the interpretation of Müntzer's theology that has as its object his mystical-anthropological understanding of the world and the Kingdom of God. But therein lies the decisive weakness in this theology. It is not capable of seeing social reality under the aspect of divine freedom which leads to a comprehensive freeing of mankind. It constricts the world and the Kingdom of God into the "inner order" and loses sight of the actual situation. Thus it succeeds neither in freeing the peasants from serfdom (or at least indicating a way to freedom), nor in producing a proclamation on judgment and mercy from the standpoint of the approaching Kingdom of God. Certainly, Müntzer had realized with keen insight that medieval society, with its characteristic mixture of the spiritual and the secular, had need of an ecclesiastical and social reformation, and even that the Reformation of the church would have to bring with it the emancipation of the suppressed classes of society. But he did not transcend the corpus christianum. His attack on the existing social system and his draft of a new society (i.e., of the Kingdom of God), based as they were upon the spiritual experience in the mystical process of salvation, instead radicalized the corpus christianum in an anthropological direction. A free co-ordination of the spiritual and the secular was thereby made impossible, the secular was swallowed up by the spiritual, and the concrete value of the secular in the struggle against sin was diminished if not completely destroyed. Thus Müntzer robbed himself of a positive result from his—for that time— unique insight that faith can be properly grasped only if its social dimension and form are considered. Thus, the charge made by Karl Marx against Luther's theology really applies to Müntzer's theology: "At that time the Peasants' War, the most radical fact of German history, was shipwrecked by theology." Of course, one should not see in theology more than *one* cause of the failure of the Peasants' War. Müntzer's theology became ensnared in a fateful dilemma: the mystical teaching of salvation, which unleashed in him a tremendous urge to transform and renew the world, at the same time thwarted this transformation and renewal by its inherent trait of world-negation, in his case even world-annihilation.

The dominance of the mystical-anthropological understanding of the outer world, which ultimately leads to depriving all social relationships of their reality, makes it impossible to proclaim Müntzer as the founder or executor of the "Early Bourgeois Revolution" in Germany. Likewise it makes it impossible to warn against all theology of revolution by pointing to his theology as a terrifying example. Müntzer conceived a theology of revolution which contains on the one hand embryonic elements of the Marxist theory of society and revolution, and, on the other hand, the elements of a theology of revolution as it is developed today in the ecumenical movement. The mystical framework into which these elements are bound ultimately makes it illegitimate to claim Müntzer either for Marxist theory or for the ecumenical theology of revolution, at least beyond incautious statements about "embryonic elements." Nevertheless, his theology is suitable for pointing out the difficulties and inadequate solutions of the early Reformation. The theory of rebellion, which did not exactly make of Luther a peacemaker in his role as counselor of princes, the rise of the princely or territorial church constitutions, the social and political failure of the governments, and the post-Lutheran doctrinal conflicts give belated confirmation to Müntzer's early criticisms. But Müntzer's theology could not have mastered the theological and social problems of this period. Nor can it help a period that is obliged to face a revolutionary world situation under different philosophical, social and political conditions. Still its example is instructive. It spans a bridge over the chasm that today divides those who want to change the world into two antagonistic camps: those who want to begin with an alteration of structures and those who demand a transformation of people. Müntzer recognized that the human heart is a problem of structure (the inner order) and that the structures (the outer order) are a problem of the heart.

When the heart is alienated from its origin in God, it disturbs the "order established in God and the creation." He is unworthy of imitation in his co-ordinating the movement of the inner order with that of the outer order. This theology inevitably got in the way of its own promise: "The people will become free, and it is the will of God that he alone shall be their Lord." This promise is not yet fulfilled. Whoever adopts it as the basis for his thoughts and deeds will certainly accept the suggestion that the lordship of God is inconceivable without the inner and outer liberation of the people. It is not because of the results of his theology, but only because of this insight that Thomas Müntzer has a place in the history of the emancipation of mankind.

Thomas Müntzer in the Research of the Present

Max Steinmetz

For a long time now the beginning of the German Reformation, which tradition assigns to October 31, 1517, and the birthday of Martin Luther, November 10, 1483, were the occasions for centennial celebrations. Now the anniversaries are observed by Lutheran churchmen every fifty years; and since the nineteenth century they have taken on more and more historical, political and secular overtones. In contrast, the German Peasants' War and Thomas Müntzer in particular are still excluded from such celebrations. This side of the German Reformation is not willingly called to memory; and certainly it does not offer suitable material for the poets, historians and theologians of the princely courts. Indeed, in 1625 when Martin Rinckhardt, archdeacon of Eilenberg, dedicated his "The Turbulent Müntzer or . . . the Müntzerite Peasants' War" to the councils of Mühlhausen, Langensalza and Eisleben, naturally expecting a suitable remuneration—the honorable city fathers spurned this unsolicited reminder and left the author go away emptyhanded. Hence it is hardly surprising that in 1725 and 1825 no one took the effort to conjure up the spirit of this unloved past, even though from the end of the eighteenth century there were several significant biographies of Müntzer, such as the one by Georg Theodor Strobel, brought out in 1795, which enjoys a good reputation even today.

In 1875 the official German historiography, still drunk with victory in the Franco-Prussian War and more overbearing than ever, took no notice of the Peasants' War and Thomas Müntzer. Instead there appeared in this year the third edition of Friedrich Engels' *The German Peasants' War*. Its first publication in 1850 in the final number of the "New Rhineland News. Politico-Economic Review" was not widely circulated; the unique success of this work began only with the independent editions of 1870 and 1875. Even today it is one of the most widely read works of its author. Here for the first time historical materialism was applied to earlier German history and at the same time a classic character sketch of Thomas Müntzer was drawn. In 1876 it was August Bebel who—like Engels—reminded the German people of their revolutionary tradition. His book on the Peasants' War with its wideranging and absorbing narrative supplements Engels' analysis.

With the 1925 centennial new conditions had set in. It took place, as would the 1975 anniversary, against the background of the development of historical thought and research initiated by the great Socialist Revolution of October, 1917. In 1925 the Peasants' War and Thomas Müntzer moved for the first time into the center of the ideological struggles which were shaped by the revolutionary workers movement and its scientific world-view. Bourgeois historians contributed a mass of publications, particularly local historians from Mühlhausen and Zwickau, who could not, however, break loose from local legends. The only representative biography, that by J. Zimmermann, stood totally under the spell of the Lutheran tradition in its most conservative version. Only one publication, dating from 1921, was not in this framework: namely Ernst Bloch's *Thomas Müntzer as Theologian of Revolution*. Here Bloch first raised the question of the relation of theology and revolution, since then analyzed repeatedly, and tried to resolve it in terms of the example of Thomas Müntzer. However, the historically and philosophically subjectivist manner in which Bloch treated his problem invited disagreement. With Karl Holl, the initiator of the Luther Renaissance, theology began to take Müntzer seriously, albeit somewhat reservedly and entirely in a conservative spirit. Heinrich Boehmer, the eminent Leipzig church historian, was every bit as conservative as Holl but he went a step further than Holl by placing his great heuristic talent at the disposal of Müntzer research. His enduring contribution is the edition of Müntzer's correspondence, which P. Kirn published four years after Boehmer's death. Bloch, Holl and Boehmer have all left their personal marks on bourgeois Müntzer historiography right up to the present: Bloch and Holl through providing the conceptual framework and Boehmer through his energetic application of the method of textual criticism to Müntzer's writings.

However, it was the workers movement that set the tone of the 1925 anniversary. It alerted a wide public to the legacy of the Peasants' War and particularly of Müntzer through many pamphlets, books, newspaper articles and public meetings. Engels' work on the Peasants' War remained constantly available, newly published in 1908 by Franz Mehring and in 1925 by Hermann Duncker. In the meantime new [socialist] studies had appeared by K. Kautsky, E. Rosenow, V. Loewenberg and the Englishman E.B. Bax, just to mention a few.

. . . .

When one turns to the content of [current West German] Müntzer research, the great prominence of theology and church history in this field becomes immediately obvious. . . . Secular historians seldom had anything to say on the subject. Günther Franz, too, in the new editions of his study of the Peasants' War only listed the more recent work without revising his text to take it into account. This shrinking back from interpretation of Müntzer among historians has a natural connection with the fact that Müntzer was a theologian. But that does not explain why, at least since 1960, it has been largely left to the theologians alone to fend off the incursion of the Marxists into the previously well-defined realms of Reformation history. Could it not be that this task was gladly handed over to the theologians, who have always earned their reputations in defense against heretics? Perhaps it was thought that, with their special expertise, they would be in a stronger position than the "profane historians" to refute the Marxist outlook and to bring uncertainty and irresolution into the ranks of Marxist historians. However that may be, there were good grounds for the church historians to devote themselves to Müntzer: they had to perform a work of restitution for past injustices, for their intemperate anathemas, their stubborn defamation, their persistent misrepresentation. There was a lot of scholarly catching up to do after the long period of neglect— and in addition there was and is the theme of "bringing the heretics home" into ecumenical Christianity, the broad utilization of their ideas and conceptions for a "modernizing" of Christianity, the so-called *aggiornamento*. This reception of elements of Müntzer's theology must be viewed as one of the numerous attempts to modernize Protestantism. It is closely connected with a simultaneous defense against the Marxist view of Müntzer and an immunization against what the West Germans refer to as the "Müntzer euphoria."

Marxist historians, of course, have no wish to involve themselves in theological questions: since they reject all metaphysics, they have nothing to do with matters of faith. Real history is another matter, however. Here the dictum of the Czechoslovak music historian Z. Nejedly is valid: "There is only one history." The history of religions is part of this broader history. The premise of the historical materialist method is that religions, too (particularly religions!), are not phenomena *sui generis*, not causes but products of a particular level of human social development. They are not contingent upon supernatural powers but dependent upon actual historical and social conditions and relationships.

Our critique is directed therefore against any perspective which abstracts itself from the material basis of the historical process, the direct production process that is essential to people's lives. Such an approach necessarily leads to an absolutizing of theology and metaphysics. The result is always an uncritical dehistoricizing, a loss of real history, a flight into irrationalism and mysticism. Marxist historical science views the majority of church historical studies as substantive contributions worthy of serious attention, to the extent that they represent a genuine increase of knowledge and are not merely apologetics and polemics. However, it is not blind to the close connection between church history and history in capitalistic countries, a connection which has developed towards full integration and in many fields has led to a division of labor.

. . . .

All Marxist Müntzer research works from the assumption that Müntzer's theology developed under the historical conditions which ripened the German Peasants' War, that it was accordingly a decisive contribution to the Early Bourgeois Revolution in Germany, that the theological ideas contained the social and political program of the People's Reformation, and that it is necessary to uncover and extract the social and political content and pertinence of the theology.

Accordingly no full explanation of Müntzer's teaching can be achieved by merely reducing it to its individual elements or their combination. Only the development of his teaching in the context of the class struggles from 1521 to 1525 produces a reliable picture. Only social praxis produces the preliminary form of a class ideology from elements of theology and sectarian viewpoints. The *Prague Manifesto*, which already contains essential elements of Müntzer's teaching, was ineffective, led to no action, but to complete failure—since the preconditions for action of the popular masses were not yet present either in Bohemia or in Germany. The writings of the second half of 1524, however, contain the mature program of the People's Reformation and constitute an ideological preparation for the Peasants' War: thus it is praxis which lends effectiveness to ideology.

Very early Müntzer recognized the regressive elements of Lutheran theology as one of the chief barriers to continuation of the Reformation. He saw its tendencies toward social passivity, its efforts to prevent the common man from actively helping himself and to bind him to the prevailing exploitative order, thus preventing the Reformation from becoming fully effective in his life. All of this was rooted in Luther's social limitations and social ties, things which Müntzer sensed without clearly understanding them. He battled against these tendencies with theological means. Against the teaching of Luther he set up his own theology with its three chief components: 1. the teaching of the Spirit as the constant divine revelation, tied to or limited by nothing whatsoever, which not only avails itself of the Scriptures but constantly discloses itself to men through the inner voice; 2. the teaching of the cross as a person's purification through suffering, which is indispensable for the attainment of a "tested" faith and consequent assurance, through which the poor, bearing their crosses, prepare themselves for the reception of the Spirit; 3. the teaching on the sword or the government, consisting in a right of resistance against godless overlords, in the duty to resist godless rulers and to take their sword from them, in a summons to the poor and oppressed to wield the sword and to take power into their own hands.

On these three points the contrast to Luther is expressed with particular clarity: 1. Luther recognized the Scriptures as the sole and definitive source of revelation—*sola scriptura*—and is therefore attacked by Müntzer as a scribe, a literalist and an externalizer; 2. Luther proclaimed justification *sola fide et gratia* without any human contribution, i.e., without works as an expression of human activity; 3. Luther demanded the "pathos of obedience," suffering obedience, the recognition of every government, since all governments were established by God and the individual human being must subject himself to their will.

Both in his point of departure and in his evident goal Müntzer differed from Luther. Luther matured within monasticism and was able to break away from it only quite late. Müntzer was a secular priest, although acquainted with the cloistered life through extensive, though not exclusive, experience as a spiritual counselor to nuns. While Luther wrestled for a long time with the Ockhamist version of late scholasticism, scholasticism had no effect on Müntzer—just like Melanchthon, Zwingli and Calvin, who were all strongly oriented towards humanism. While Luther won his theological conviction from the study of Paul's epistle to the Romans and developed the teaching of justification *sola fide et gratia,* Müntzer turned early to the sources of Christendom and of church history but also to the Old Testament. Both had very intimate contacts with mysticism; Luther edited the *German Theology*, at first partially and then completely; Müntzer immersed himself deeply in medieval mystical thought, which left an enduring stamp on his manner of expression. When Luther wrestled with the issue of indulgences and thus with the Roman curia, Müntzer retired to quiet study in Beuditz cloister. He assimilated an entirely different tradition and consciously drew upon other sources. His mind was shaped not by Ockhamism or Augustinianism but by the prophets of the Old Testament, the Taborites, medieval mysticism and heresy, humanist literature, as well, of course, as the publications of the early Reformation movement—besides Luther, especially Carlstadt. He appropriated and reshaped these materials within a framework of activism, not disposed to a quietistic contemplation of divinity or to religious introspection.

Only in this way could Müntzer become the representative of different class powers than Luther, namely classes and strata which wanted to carry the Reformation further and apply it to the social sphere—the lower classes in the towns and in the countryside, the plebeians and poor peasants. That enabled Müntzer to criticize Luther, to grasp the limits of Lutheran thought and the bearing of Lutheran ideas. It permitted him to fulfill the historically necessary break with Lutheranism. Only in this way did it become possible to advance the Reformation and to bring the Early Bourgeois Revolution to its high point, i.e., the decision to attempt with revolutionary force to clarify the contradictions from the bottom up.

In the first place, Müntzer had a different Scriptural understanding from Luther. Indeed he built upon Luther's understanding of the Bible as the Word of God, so as to reject and destroy the fundamental Catholic teaching according to which the priesthood was the mediator between God and man. Müntzer, however, carried these conceptions to their radical conclusion: the universal priesthood makes everyone an independent Bible reader, abolishes the guardianship of the church and allows each to hear the Word of God directly. God's revelation is not limited to the written word of the Bible; the Spirit is not chained to the Scriptures but is superior to them, having made them possible in the first place. God's revelation is a still continuing process; God writes with his finger in the hearts of the faithful and speaks to them. Müntzer rejects Luther's conception according to which God is hidden, his plans incomprehensible, so that he plays with men like a puppet master without rendering any explanations whatever. According to Luther this God, whose will remained a *mysterium tremendum,* must simply be glorified. It was Müntzer's view that God revealed himself to his servants, the faithful, constantly—hence there was no need of the Wittenberg theologians, who only harmed things, since they obscured the Gospel. God revealed himself constantly to those who wanted to hear him, who were ready to perceive his voice. In this way Müntzer developed a new conception of revelation and the Spirit. In the final analysis it was a universal spiritualism which left the frontiers of Christendom behind it, broke with the idea of a Christian monopoly on revelation to seek and find the divine Spirit not only among Christians but also among the heathen—the Moslems, for instance. The whole Bible is the Law of God, the New and Old Testaments are understood as a unity, and there is no opposition between Law and Gospel. Moses and the prophets are not opposed to the Pauline Gospel but viewed within a unified framework of divine revelation extending from Moses to Christ. The line from Paul to Augustine, which Luther renewed and continued, fades into the background. Müntzer rejects the reductionism that assigns continuing validity only to New Testament norms; he interprets Paul's epistle to the Romans in a revolutionary manner. For him, Romans 13 provides the foundation of a right of resistance, for Luther the foundation of a teaching of obedience, with Müntzer stressing verses 3 and 4, Luther verses 1 and 2, as well as 5 through 7. Spirit, Scriptures, revelation and Law were interpreted in a revolutionary manner, not without contradiction, to be sure, as in the matter of spiritualism and legalism, but very effectively, delivering the rationale for the People's Reformation.

The Spirit of God is alive and revelation not tied to the Scriptures; but the Old Testament Law is nevertheless valid and the struggle against the godless a constant task, not just an obligation of Old Testament Israel. For Müntzer there is no contradiction between revelation and Law: spiritual faith and divine law are ultimately identical, bound together by the same divine will, but this connection is only possible as revolutionary teaching. That means likewise a premium placed upon prophecy, visions in dreams, the Old Testament prophets, the apocalypses of Daniel and John, the shepherd of Hermas—right up to the visions of Mechthild of Hackeborn, Hildegard of Bingen and Elisabeth of Schönau. That also meant an overvaluation of dreams, since Müntzer believed that they could be the vehicles of divine revelation.

Müntzer's sacramental teaching was to a great extent Lutheran: abolition of celibacy, monasteries, indulgences, pilgrimages and endowed masses, no more veneration of Mary and of images; he retained baptism (as the baptism of older children) and the Lord's Supper; but all sacraments were made less prominent, weakened in their significance. Müntzer had a different position from Luther on the doctrine of the Trinity, the basic Christian teaching, hence also on Christology and the Lord's Supper. Johann Lang drew him into the battle over the Lord's Supper in 1525, in that he applied a writing of Urbanus Rhegius to Müntzer as well. A certain closeness to Erasmus is likewise unmistakeable; the *Editio princeps* knew nothing of the *"filioque"* clause, nor of the "coma Joanneum" (I John 5:7), the only Scriptural proof for the Trinity, since the passage was lacking in all of the older Greek manuscripts. Müntzer placed a remarkably slight stress on Christology. Perhaps he was inclined to Anti-Trinitarianism, perhaps only to Unitarianism; his emphasis upon the unity of God would seem to point in this direction. Already in 1525 Agricola reproached him for devaluing Christ and his work of redemption. Certainly the stresses on the Old Testament and the Law, which offered no starting point for a Trinitarian doctrine, were part of the picture here. Possibly the conception of universal revelation was important, too, since it counteracted any overemphasis upon Christ and his work of redemption, understanding the latter neither as the central doctrine of religion nor as the central event of history.

In the second place, Müntzer teaches another road to salvation than Luther. The purification of man is not a consequence of justification alone, not *sola gratia, sola fide*, but a product of his active cooperation. Müntzer decisively rejected the Lutheran teaching on justification and the passivity to which it led. The purification of the individual resulted from cooperation, through suffering, distress and the cross. This "imitation of Christ" is a maturing process for the person, which occurs through a taking up of the cross. Müntzer sharply rejected any underestimate of works, of the activity of men. An active response to redemption is necessary in his view. His teaching on the cross was coupled with ethical activism: man must not simply wait for God to act—here Müntzer deviated strongly from Judaism, too. With the aid of mysticism he developed a procedure which perhaps foreshadowed the *Spiritual Exercises* of Ignatius Loyola. From this resulted a different conception of predestination with reference and application to the poor, for the poor alone are the predestined tools of God in the struggle against the godless. Indeed excessive poverty was just as great an obstacle as excessive wealth, both hindered reception of the Spirit. But, while the poor must be enlightened and freed from their struggle for subsistence and their torpor in order to fight for life, there is no help for the hardened rich. Hence Müntzer knew no false assurance of faith but demanded a "tested" faith. Faith became a transforming, revolutionary principle.

Connected with this is a different picture of humanity, a different ethic. The human being is not a lost sinner, hopelessly ensnared in his sins, but a bearer of active responsibility, a shaper of society. Müntzer strongly emphasized the freedom of the will against the Lutheran *servum arbitrium*. The human being is able to change society—not without or against God, to be sure, but following the divine summons, in accordance with the Law.

This conception is closely related to Müntzer's teachings about government and obedience, to his rejection of a passive role for man within the framework of divine providence and of history.

However, there were limits. Although Müntzer rejected the asceticism of compulsory celibacy, nevertheless he advocated an ascetic and rigorous conception of marriage which has a certain relation to Luther's. All pleasures were rejected as self-seeking and sinful, diverting the person from suffering and the cross, from the path of reflection and insight into himself. Müntzer embodied the greatest conceivable antithesis to Renaissance paganism; in him there is no Renaissance posture as with Poggio or *The Letters of Obscure Men* (as was thought by Bebel among others), no emancipation of the flesh.

Thirdly, Müntzer had a different teaching on government from Luther. The state is no organ above social classes but a revolutionary instrument for the realization of the divine will. The princes are agents of God, the sword is not given to them to gratify their arbitrary wills nor to suppress the people, but in connection with, and bound to, a clear commission: the prince is not *legibus absolutus*. The sword is held conditionally upon the fulfillment of the divine commission, otherwise it will be taken away and given to the common man. Müntzer does not regard princely power as holy; he rejects the right of lineage, the claim to the grace of God, as pretext and deception and is in no sense a glorifier of princely power. It is linked to a commission and can be overthrown should that commission be betrayed. Hence there results a legitimate resistance, the revolutionary right of the people to take the sword in case the government does not fulfill its duty. Here there is no room for a "natural" subordination of the people, for a justification of the "organic" order of estates, as we find in Luther. Possibly in dependence on Marsilius of Padua,

Müntzer further develops the medieval conception of rulership from *pax et justitia*. All of this is connected with a different conception of the people, which is not the negatively stereotyped "Mister Everybody" as in Luther's view. It is the group called and predestined to fight and destroy the godless, to overturn the old order, since the nobles, the princes and the rich are neither able nor willing to give up their soft lives and the suppression of the poor.

His conception of "the people" separated Thomas Müntzer most decisively from Luther, the Wittenbergers, the Lutheran governments, whether princely or municipal, and also from the humanists, from Mutian, Erasmus and their conceptions of an elite, their estrangement from the common people, their arrogance, their cultural pretentiousness. This was true even though Müntzer derived his conception from the Old Testament notion of God's "chosen people" and then concretized it and filled it with social content, applying it to peasants and plebeians.

Luther's theology was for Müntzer a theology without the people and against the people, not in its beginnings but in its regressive development since 1521. Müntzer viewed Luther as the representative of a theology of passivity, of pure reception of grace without any contribution from the human being, who has fallen under sin and cannot raise himself up through his own powers. To be sure, the teaching of the justification of the sinner *sola fide et gratia* destroyed the structure of the papal church and rendered superfluous both the mediatorship of the priest and the majority of the previous sacraments. But, since Luther denied the cooperation of the human being in the work of salvation, in the winning of God's mercy, since he derived passive obedience [to human rulers] from passivity towards God in the reception of salvation, he arrived at conclusions which Müntzer totally rejected. With magnificent acumen Müntzer saw through Lutheran theology to its final consequences—in modern terms, he recognized its class character—and rejected it. Müntzer demanded from people an "imitation of Christ," a "tested" faith, i.e., a faith proven by deeds. He called for a bearing of the cross, an affirmation of suffering, since only after a man had been purified through the cross and become Christlike was he ready to hear the voice of God. And, as he realized with growing clarity, only the poor could do this, since the rich were ensnared in sensual pleasure and creature comforts and could not turn away from the abuse of power for their own selfish purposes.

Luther's teaching stressed man's passivity, his incapacity to raise himself up, passive reception of grace, suffering obedience, the Holy Scriptures as the single and complete divine revelation, the justification of the sinner by faith alone. Against this Müntzer opposed a very different group of fundamentals: the Spirit of God as a constant revelation, source of knowledge and principle of transformation, independent of the letter of Holy Scripture; the cross, as the precondition for the reception of the Spirit and the test of knowledge in pain and poverty; the obligation to resist godless governments and the necessity of creating a revolutionary power of the people; the character of the government as divinely commissioned to destroy the godless and to initiate a just order; the common people, alone predestined by God to rule, the only power which can execute God's Law and fulfill his will.

. . . .

What has been presented is not intended to be a full enumeration of the components of Müntzer's teaching, but is rather an attempt at a systematic statement. No one has as yet undertaken a "theology of Müntzer." Here the problems connected with the development of Müntzer's thought have also been deliberately put to one side. They call for further discussion.

There is no doubt whatever that Müntzer was a theologian, or that as a theologian he was a revolutionary in the full sense of the word. That is to say, he was someone who saw the goal of his struggle in the solution of the problem of power. It is equally certain however that as a revolutionary he always continued to be a theologian and was doomed to shipwreck upon theology. In interpreting Müntzer and the time in which he lived and played an exemplary role, the chief problem is to demonstrate the relevance of Müntzer's teaching for the course of the Early Bourgeois Revolution, and particularly for the German Peasants' War as its high point. It may not yet be determined with certainty whether a linear development brought Müntzer into the Peasants' War and made him the ideological leader of the revolutionary forces among the peasants, or whether there were contradictions in this process of development. Nevertheless, the socio-political program of the People's Reformation cannot have been, in Müntzer's eyes, a deviation from, or surrender of, his original teaching. It can have been nothing less than the fulfillment and crowning of his aspirations.

. . . .

Müntzer's self-assurance is recognizable from early on in the strong polemical tones he sounded. The fact that he remained only briefly in any one place, repeatedly expelled or dismissed, was the consequence of his falling out with his superiors again and again. From his youth (that is to say, as far back as our sources reach) Müntzer was filled with a sense of mission, with a pronounced self-assurance bordering on eccentricity. We constantly encounter him as a blunt person, intolerant and unbending. He saw the precondition and confirmation of his own calling precisely in his path of suffering, which he consciously followed and consciously provoked. The cross of suffering and persecution was for him the content and reality of life, no mere figure of speech growing out of wide reading.

Great men do not make history, but neither is it made without them: they have a definite and necessary role in it. Especially in periods marked by spontaneity and a limited mass consciousness, a particularly important task can fall to the lot of the great personality—he comes close to substituting for the missing hegemony of a class. But Müntzer demanded too much of his followers and their level of consciousness. Precisely for this reason he was in continual danger of not being fully understood—whether in Prague, in Allstedt or in Mühlhausen. He tried to meet this danger by intensifying his agitation, his words and preaching, through a violently exaggerated and over-excited tone. Precisely this exaggeration of his activity, his revolutionary activism, magnified the danger of his pressing people beyond the possibilities of their current mode of life and thought. That was Müntzer's tragedy. He had a clear insight into people's immaturity, how they were largely unsuitable for realizing his goals because of their egoistic, "fleshly," narrow-minded, "parochial" manner of thinking. But he underestimated the requirements of the maturation process. He believed that he could use the resources of theology to prepare people for revolution—what else should he have done? He was a popular educator in the grand style, working, of course, with the resources of the period: through the worship service, liturgy, sermon, Bible reading, the practice of mysticism, the sacraments. Through them he wanted to purify the people and prepare them for reception of the Spirit. He wanted to mature them for action in accordance with the divine Law, to make them ready for the revolutionary deed: at first in a covenant with the Saxon princes, then however against all princely power. He had, as E. Werner convincingly showed, a pronounced messianic sense of mission. Müntzer considered himself, and called himself, a servant of God in many of his letters—sixty-two such passages can be pinpointed. He saw his own life depicted in the songs about the servant of God in Deutero-Isaiah (so called because Isaiah 40–55 is known not to have been written by Isaiah). Indeed the "Law and the prophets" (the so-called "Old Testament") in general were of the greatest importance for his sense of mission.

This brings us to another important problem area—Müntzer's sources. Smirin did pioneering work in this area: he first showed the significance of Luther, mysticism, the Taborites, Joachim of Fiore and medieval sectarianism as sources of Müntzer's ideology. The chief sources have been well-known for a long time now but insufficiently investigated. That applies particularly to the whole Bible, about whose fundamental importance to Müntzer there can be no doubt; even the most cursory glance at his letters and writings substantiates this. The peculiarity and distinctiveness of his understanding of the Bible has in no sense been clarified. In reading Smirin, as in reading the 1968 edition of Müntzer's writings and letters, numerous questions emerge. What affected Müntzer: only Tauler, or other mystical writings as well, the Tauler apocrypha, or still others? Was he influenced by Joachim of Fiore, or by pseudo-Joachite writings? What was the extent of his reading? . . . For instance, it is unclear to this day what was the source of Müntzer's knowledge of Taborite ideas.

On the subject of Müntzer's achievements—beyond his writings and letters, his revolutionary ideology and his political role—recently his accomplishments in church music and language have been investigated more intensively by music historians and Germanists. K. Honemeyer has cast an entirely new and surprising light upon Müntzer's liturgy, particularly his *Kirchenamt*. The first two hundred pages with musical notation in the complete edition of Müntzer's works point to the extent of his efforts to create a popular liturgy in the German language, the first of the German Reformation. In addition to that there is the composition of songs in these liturgical works, newly interpreted by S. Bräuer. Indeed the role of Müntzer's work of liturgical composition needs to be investigated further in the context of his ideological and political aspirations.

Müntzer's application of the ideas of humanism and the Renaissance seems also to belong among his special accomplishments. This statement in itself rejects the widespread tendency to underestimate or misunderstand the function of humanism as a source and component of Müntzer's thought. There is no absolute opposition between Müntzer and humanism, only a relative one; and the affinities may well be greater than the points of contrast, although such a matter is difficult to measure. Furthermore, humanism—like the Reformation—was not a homogeneous movement in its social goals or its class basis. Humanism is not identical to the Catholic-conservative bloc, since it contained ideas which were common currency of the time: the return to sources, criticism of the church, rejection of scholasticism, etc. With humanism Müntzer shared the appeal to sources, a stress on free will, an emphasis on education and human educability, a social and ethical teaching, a doctrine of community of property, a theistic universalism, a disposition to relativize revelation and dogma, an antipathy toward princes, and a high estimate of the role of woman in society.

The proposition that community of property is the proper form of human society—*omnia sunt communia*—was the theoretical consensus among Erasmus and the humanists. It originated with Plato and the primitive Christianity of the New Testament, but only among the heretical movements did it become the goal of a transformation of social relationships. Universal theism, too, is a humanist idea which includes the pagans of antiquity within the revelation of God and consciously goes beyond the sphere of the Judeo-Christian Bible. The distinctions between paganism and Christianity were fluid at that time: Seneca passed as a Christian, Socrates and Plato were transposed into the Christian heaven. However, at the same time there was a separation of Müntzer from humanism on decisive issues. Müntzer was opposed to the sort of humanism which set learned culture against the popular masses, applied knowledge in order to maintain exploitation and capitalized on the ignorance of the masses, the better to keep them in check. To Müntzer, Johann Sylvius Egranus was the representative of this undemocratic, overbearing humanism, a person who gave expression to the same overbearing manner in the way he lived. Therefore Müntzer rejected such humanists together with the scribes of Wittenberg. He wanted culture for the people, education of the people, of a sort that could not, certainly, be achieved through the instrument of Latin erudition. For this goal an entirely new path must be tried.

But Müntzer rejected not only the cultural arrogance and elitist delusions of the humanists, he also rejected their moral laxity and dissolution of religion into morality and enlightenment, as it occurred in Erasmus. He would have nothing to do with all the undemocratic traits of humanism; for the illiterate are the moving power for change, a power which he took into account more and more and with whom he allied himself.

Still, it must be kept in mind that the controversy between Luther and Müntzer was not the only thing happening in those years. This was likewise the time of humanism's rupture with Luther, of the controversy between Erasmus and Luther, which expressed itself in a memorable debate about human nature. Müntzer's standpoint was entirely independent, in no way identical with the position of Erasmus, although influenced by it. For Erasmus and Müntzer, man was educable, capable of development, qualified to receive the Spirit. For Luther, reason was a whore and man was ensnared in sin. To Erasmus the princes were no inviolable powers; he had a negative attitude to princely authority and was a republican at heart. Luther justified the existing princely overlordship by saying that it was ordained by God; for him the government was a scourge of God for the chastisement of men. Müntzer came closest to a correct understanding of the society of that time. Not allowing himself to be blindfolded, he progressed to a revolutionary humanism, which would not content itself with mere words or aesthetic forms, but tried to lead the poor man from an unworthy bondage into freedom.

In the midst of our high esteem and appreciation of Müntzer, his teaching and his role in history, we may not overlook his self-contradictions and his limitations. Historical understanding would not be served if these contradictions and limitations were concealed; rather to grasp them precisely and to explain them is an important task of Müntzer scholarship. What Müntzer was striving for was not attainable, given the potentialities and limitations of his period. But his greatness lay in the fact that he did not shrink from the supreme, final effort. In the situation of 1524/25 he placed himself in the forefront of the movement of peasants and plebeians and dared the ultimate, to the point of sacrificing his own life.

Ideologically Müntzer was shipwrecked upon theology, a worldview unsuited to the process of emancipation, the liberation of the people by their own efforts. For it contained the constant danger of a relapse into mysticism, into waiting and hoping for God's direct intervention. Chiliasm, messianism, prophecy, the whole conceptual world of religion, limited Müntzer, for this world of ideas did not permit a complete understanding of man and history. It makes relapses possible at any time, it keeps open a line of retreat, since in the final analysis God remains the determining power. The biblical conceptual world does not allow a scientific comprehension of the world and history. It came into an increasing contradiction with the emerging natural sciences precisely during the Renaissance. But Müntzer suffered shipwreck not only because of theology, but also because social developments were not yet ripe and the bourgeoisie still too weak. Accordingly the failure of Müntzer was also an expression of the fact that there was as yet no suitable power available for the consistent, forceful leadership of the struggle.

. . . .

Müntzer was the exception, not the rule. He founded a revolutionary tradition, which however could not triumph in the sixteenth century, since it could not be carried through to a conclusion with either the intellectual resources or the class powers of the time. Nevertheless, in contrast to a great number of heretical ideologues of the previous period, Müntzer accomplished the alliance of heretical ideas with the tradition of peasant and plebeian class struggle. He rose above sectarianism and united messianism and prophecy with practical effort for the concrete goals of the class struggle. The result was a necessary connection of revolution and utopianism: the struggles against the aristocracy and their church, against the princes, against the notion of a holy Empire were all revolutionary; but the desire to leap over early capitalist development to the creation of a realm of equality and freedom was utopian. In his alliances Müntzer created the beginnings of an independent political organization with its own leadership; but he overestimated the strength and self-consciousness of the strata which he thought to be predestined for the work of deliverance, and he expected too much of his adherents, given their state of development. Nevertheless, he had a dim presentiment of the revolutionary role of exploited and suppressed strata, particularly the role of the proletariat as a class of the future. The seizure of political power was his theoretical demand and practical objective: together with the Saxon princes while he was in Allstedt, against all feudal powers when he was in Mühlhausen and Thuringia. But Müntzer was no politician like Cromwell, his organization never got beyond its beginning stages and was shattered before it had the opportunity to expand.

V

The Anabaptists, Thomas Müntzer, and the Peasants' War

The Zwickau Prophets, Thomas Müntzer, and the Anabaptists

Harold S. Bender

A perusal of the reference works of today as well as of the general works on church history reveals the surprising fact that there is, in spite of all the scholarly research done in the last several decades on this subject, still no unanimity of opinion regarding the origin and character of the early Anabaptists. This lack may be due in part to the failure of the writers of these articles to acquaint themselves with the results of Anabaptist research; theological and denominational prejudice is also very likely responsible for a share of the misrepresentation. But until recently not even the Anabaptist specialists have been in complete agreement. Now, however, in the light of the most recent investigations in the field, we are in a position to answer the question of the origin of the Anabaptist movement with nearly complete assurance. The reasons are clarified in the following.

The earlier conception is still current, which laid the origin of the Anabaptists in Zwickau (1521) and considered them in the early days to have been merely fanatics, men of the "inner light," equipped with personal divine revelation, fanatical, revolutionary, and dangerous to the state, and which supposed that from there their ideas were carried throughout Germany and beyond, and that the peaceful phase gradually developed from this, especially after the sobering effect of the terrible catastrophe of Münster (1535) . . . . The more recent conception places the origin in Zurich (1525) in the bosom of the Zwinglian Reformation, where the first Anabaptists, zealous adherents of Zwingli, after Zwingli had rejected their demand that he set up the church as a brotherhood of earnest Christians, went about the task of establishing the church as a completely peaceful, holy church built on the New Testament and in no wise fanatical or revolutionary and not at all connected with Zwickau or Thomas Müntzer . . . . A third view sees the Anabaptists as a double movement, arising in both Zurich and Zwickau, the revolutionary branch finally dying out and the other developing into a Protestant sect . . . .

Walther Köhler, who was initially (RGG, 1913) and also at the end almost completely of the second opinion (that of the exclusive Zurich origin), in RGG's second edition (1931) presents a variation of the third view in the following words (Vol. V, col. 1915):

> The controversy on the origin of the Anabaptists that has flared up between Karl Holl and Ernst Troeltsch has this solution: Zurich (as in Troeltsch) was the scene of the first Anabaptist congregation and performed the first adult baptism in 1524 (Grebel, Manz, and Blaurock), but the idea of rebaptism and the separation of the brotherhood of the believers from the mass church appeared first in the circles of the Wittenberg fanatics (Karlstadt, Zwilling, Münzer) 1521–22 (as in Holl), with whom the Zurich brotherhood maintained contacts without having been called into existence by them.

The question of the origin of the Anabaptists is not a simple matter of mere geography or even biography. For if it were actually historically true that the Anabaptist movement began in Zwickau, in principle fanatical rather than Biblicistic, revolutionary rather than peaceably constructive, that it was always pregnant with a Thomas Müntzer revolt or a Münsterite kingdom, we would find it necessary to condemn it with Holl.

But in view of the historical facts in Zwickau and Zurich one must ask how the assumption ever arose that the Zwickau prophets or Thomas Müntzer were Anabaptists or that there was an Anabaptist movement in Saxony and Thuringia in 1521–22. There is no longer any doubt but that the baptism performed in Zurich in 1525 was the very first adult baptism in the Reformation period, at least as a baptism upon confession of faith; it was certainly not performed in Wittenberg or by Karlstadt, Storch, or Müntzer. Luther and Melanchthon did not call the Zwickau prophets "Anabaptists" until later, after they had heard of real Anabaptists elsewhere. Before 1525 the word *Wiedertäufer* was not used, and in 1525 first in Zurich. Mühlhausen, the Müntzer city of 1525, which was accused in 1552 by an imperial ambassador of harboring at the time of the Peasants' War the "disgraceful, unspiritual sect of Anabaptism . . . in full swing in the city," assured the envoy that at that time "the sect of the Anabaptists was still unknown." Annemarie Lohmann in her thorough study asserts that adult baptism "actually is counter to Müntzer's basic belief." In September, 1524, on the occasion of his visit to Oecolampadius in Basel, Müntzer related that he was still baptizing newborn infants, and at this time he published a baptismal liturgy for infant baptism, *Von der Taufe, wie man sie heldet.* Nor was Müntzer an Anabaptist on the point of the church of believers and saints, which was even more basically characteristic of the Anabaptists than baptism upon confession of faith. Until the end of his life he was the pastor of a state church congregation, his being the one in Mühlhausen, where he was engaged as preacher of the Marienkirche in the middle of February, 1525. His final goal was to build the kingdom of God upon earth, by force if necessary, not, however, in the form of a separated brotherhood of believers, but in the form of a Christian state, in which the elect of God were to compel the ungodly with the sword. Since rebaptism is necessarily practiced only in connection with a separated brotherhood it cannot be asserted that there was in Zwickau or Mühlhausen any such idea. There is also not one bit of evidence in the court records that adult baptism or a separated brotherhood of believers was at that time practiced or even considered in Saxony or Thuringia.

As late as 1524 Müntzer published several church disciplines (*Ordnung*) quite in agreement with Luther. Nor does he become the originator and leader of an Anabaptist movement through the fact that he preached a mysticism of the cross and then later, partly in express contradiction of his previous peaceful position and stress of the requirements of the Sermon on the Mount, began to confuse radical social and political ideas with religious-chiliastic ideas, and finally for three weeks even took part in the Peasants' War in Thuringia (which he, however, did not instigate). Hence the continued designation of Müntzer as an Anabaptist is historically completely untenable. Müntzer was in no sense an Anabaptist. Whether his ideas influenced the Anabaptist movement which was later to arise in Zurich remains to be examined.

Nor was Nikolaus Storch, who in the winter of 1520–21 with his spiritualistic-taborite ideas, as Lohmann proves, turned Müntzer from his Lutheran course, an Anabaptist. For a time (1520–21) there was in Zwickau, especially among the numerous textile workers (*Tuchknappen*) and the lesser guild masters of the trade guilds a "conventicle" Christianity, which is probably to be ascribed to the influence of Luther's reformatory writings of 1520; however, they were not Anabaptists but evangelical Lutherans. Indeed there were in the 1520's in many places small groups who took Luther's message and writings seriously and began to study the Bible for themselves, thus introducing in practice the general priesthood of all believers. The worship services of these people in Zwickau were, however, conducted by the parson of the Katharinenkirche, vis., Thomas Müntzer, who was at this time a zealous follower and friend of Martin Luther. After Müntzer had been deposed from this position in 1521, the leadership fell into the hands of laymen, especially Nikolaus Storch, a master cloth cutter, who served until his departure for Wittenberg at the end of December. It has not been proved that Storch really organized his followers into 12 apostles and 72 disciples as is asserted in a contemporary document cited by Seidemann. At any rate the *secta Storchitarum* in Zwickau and later at Hof was not a brotherhood. With his spiritualistic interpretation of the Scriptures and his emphasis on the inner illumination of the spirit, Storch was indifferent to the outward means of grace of the church. He seriously questioned infant baptism, indeed he rejected it, and some of his associates even did not consider baptism necessary to salvation. Storch's "movement" (from April, 1521, to February, 1522, Storch was in Bohemia) degenerated into a strong subjectivism, but died out completely after his departure in December, especially after Luther's four powerful sermons against radicalism in April, 1522. Storch himself led the life of a wanderer, and died in a Munich poorhouse in 1525. The fact that the present unjust judgment of Storch will have to be revised in his favor has nothing to do with his supposed Anabaptism.

. . . . Karlstadt, who had already previously begun a radical reformation and renovation of the worship services, agreed with the "prophets" in their rejection of infant baptism, but never demanded or attempted to introduce adult baptism. Martin Cellarius, who was also won over to the rejection of infant baptism, was persuaded by Luther to change his position, but throughout his life, especially in Strasbourg, where he went in 1525 or 1526, took a friendly attitude toward the true Anabaptists, though of course never joining them. To stamp him and Karlstadt as Anabaptist is completely misleading; both ended their careers as professors at the university of Basel.

Thus the (later so-called) "Anabaptist" movement in Zwickau disappeared, although doubts remained among the populace regarding infant baptism. The fact that later, from 1526 on, real Anabaptists appeared in Saxony and Thuringia does not alter the facts, for as Wappler points out in his thorough work, *Die Täuferbewegung in Thüringen von 1526–1584* (Jena, 1913), this movement was brought in from South Germany . . . .

. . . .

In view of these facts the question must be seriously asked: How did it come about that the short spiritualistic movement in Saxony in 1520–22 and Müntzer's very short ensuing revolutionary movement in 1524–25 were called Anabaptist movements and that Thomas Müntzer was even regarded as the originator and promoter of the entire movement, as has been the case for nearly four centuries? The responsibility for this state of affairs is borne by Luther, Melanchthon, and Menius, for ecclesiastical church historiography has followed them completely on this point. The first mention of the assertion that the beginnings of Anabaptism must be sought in Saxony is found, so far as I can see, in a letter written by Melanchthon in February, 1530, to Friedrich Myconius, in which he says, "Storch and his following, to whom the entire Anabaptist tribe owes its beginning." Note that he also has the Zwinglians originate in Storch: "Thus from one stork have arisen all those factions of Anabaptists and Zwinglians." Luther even, in his foreword to Menius' *Von dem Geist der Wiedertäufer* (1544), connected the origin of the Anabaptists with Karlstadt and Zwingli. It is clear that the historical theory of Luther and Melanchthon rests on mere assumption. In his first work against the Anabaptists, *Von der Wiedertauffe an zwen Pfarherrn, ein Brief* (1528), Luther granted that his information about the Anabaptists was slight. "We here in our prince's lands have not yet anything of the rubbish of such preachers, God be thanked and praised in eternity." And in Melanchthon's first book, written in January, 1528, *Underricht Philip Melanchthon wider die Lere der Widerteuffer,* it is clear that he was not writing from a personal acquaintance with the Anabaptists or with their writings. It is barely possible that the two men in Wittenberg had in their possession the book of Urbanus Rhegius, written in Augsburg in September, 1527, *Wider den Newen Taufforden,* but this says nothing of a Zwickau origin of Anabaptism. Melanchthon's second book, 1535, *Etliche Propositiones wider die Lehr der Widerteuffer,* is a direct attack on the *Restitutio* of Bernhard Rothmann in Münster. From this time on, Münster of course plays a chief role in the polemics of Protestant authors against the Anabaptists. Nevertheless the information of the Wittenberg polemicists concerning the Anabaptists was usually of a secondhand nature, especially in the case of Luther. Walther Köhler wrote, "Apparently Luther does not have an exact acquaintance with Anabaptist writings, as surely as he has 'heard' and 'read' and 'knows' about it."

. . . .

The reformers really had considerable difficulty within themselves regarding the Anabaptists, and were clearly, because of their prejudice, no longer able to do justice to them. In the second edition (1535) of his *Propositiones* of 1528 Melanchthon added an important comment in asserting that there was no value in attempting to distinguish the good from the bad Anabaptists. It was not necessary to say that the Anabaptists were not always as bad as Münster, for the devil had perverted them all, and one devil was no more pious than any other devil. Therefore all Anabaptists were alike, only they did not all have the same good opportunity as the Münsterites to start a revolution. And in his *Verlegung etlicher unchristlicher Artikel, welche die Wiedertäufer vorgeben* (1536) he strengthens this judgment further by characterizing all Anabaptists as of the devil and against God; Münster is only one case of what the Anabaptists always will turn into.

In the sixteenth century the word "Anabaptists" denoted simply the enemies of the truth, opponents of God and His cause, the greatest threat to the existing order, the state, and Christendom. They were considered to be a devilish sect of satanic origin to be mercilessly eradicated.

This was the advice of Luther, Melanchthon, Zwingli, and others to their princes and city councils, and this was the procedure actually followed. (Philip of Hesse was a notable exception.) The representatives of the church, and the theologians and historians of later times, apparently simply copied these concepts and if possible strengthened them, without considering the sources or the Anabaptists themselves. Nikolaus Storch and Thomas Müntzer were the first to attack the Protestant cause from within, and they rejected infant baptism; ergo, they must have begun the Anabaptist movement. No evidence of factual connections with the later real Anabaptists was needed.

This common conception was strongly supported by Heinrich Bullinger, who was considered authoritative and who invented a direct connection between Münster and the first Anabaptists in Zurich. He claimed that Anabaptism began "down there in Saxony" in 1521–22, and that the Zurich Anabaptists imbibed their Anabaptism "from Müntzer." Grebel, Manz, and other "restless heads" had not only read Müntzer's writings, but had also called on him personally while he was staying in Griessen not far from Waldshut in late 1524. All of this Bullinger wrote in 1560 (*Der Widertöufferen Ursprung*) and in 1572 (*Reformationsgeschichte*) as facts, but without any proofs or sources. (Others said the same of Hubmaier, viz., that he had visited Müntzer and received his Anabaptism from him, but without giving proof.) Actually the only possible connection between the Zurich Brethren and Müntzer would have been Hans Huiuf, cosignatory of the appendix of the September 1524 letter to Müntzer (by Conrad Grebel and associates), who had just (since the writing of the body of the letter) returned from Halle, "who was with you [Müntzer] recently."

The statements by Bullinger I have carefully investigated in my book on Conrad Grebel and am convinced that we have here to do with a pure invention. Bullinger arrived at his construction of history late and only gradually; only in the *Reformationsgeschichte* (1572) does he report on the visit of the Zurich Brethren with Müntzer in Griessen. Jakob Berchthold, in his book *Das Zwinglibild und die Zürcherischen Reformationschroniken* (1929), explains how this came about. He shows that Bullinger was not an objective, scholarly historian, but the protector of the fair name of the Zurich church and of the city itself, and was anxious to remove the smirch of responsibility for the accursed Anabaptist sect. In the section "Tendenzen in Bullingers Geschichtsschreibung" Berchthold states Bullinger's position thus: "Bullinger's basic position in this: the good has developed in my own country of Switzerland: the evil has come into the canton of Zurich from the outside, thus Anabaptism, and thus the peasant unrest."

Another alleged proof of the dependence of the Swiss Brethren on Müntzer is the letter of September 4, 1524, which Conrad Grebel and his associates wrote to "the true and faithful proclaimer of the Gospel, Thomas Müntzer at Alstett on the Harz, our faithful and beloved brother in Christ." But a careful reading of the letter makes it clear that the Zurich Anabaptists were, on the contrary, quite independent of Müntzer, that they freely criticized and admonished him, and that they repudiated him precisely on those points on which he differed from them. The letter indicates that they had only recently become acquainted with Müntzer, and only by means of the five pamphlets which he published in 1523 and 1524—pamphlets that are above criticism with respect to revolution, etc.—that they had already previously established their position, that on essential points such as the use of violence and the founding of all ceremonies and principles solely on the Scripture their ways parted. The letter offers no support for the theory that the Zurich Anabaptists were dependent upon Müntzer. Furthermore, the letter never reached Müntzer, for it was incorrectly addressed (Müntzer was no longer in Alstett). The original is now in the *Vadianische Briefsammlung* in St. Gall; no copy was made, as Grebel expressly says in the letter.

Finally a comparison of the ideological and theological position of Müntzer with that of the Swiss Brethren reveals valid reasons for differentiating so sharply between the two movements that the leading ideas cannot be assumed to have been transmitted from the one to the other. Note the following points.

1. The Swiss Brethren were a "church of radical Bible readers" (Cornelius), Biblicists (W. Köhler), quite different from persons who like Storch and Müntzer lived from direct Spirit-given revelations. On this very point they sharply attack Müntzer.

> Therefore we beg and admonish thee as a brother by the name, the power, the word, the spirit, and the salvation, which has come to all Christians through Jesus Christ our Master and Savior, that thou wilt take earnest heed to preach only the divine word without fear, to set up and guard only divine institutions, to esteem as good and right only what may be found in pure and clear Scripture, to reject, hate, and curse all devices, words, customs, and opinions of men, including thine own . . . . Go forward with the word and establish a Christian church with the help of Christ and his rule. . . . There is more than enough of wisdom and counsel in the Scripture, how all classes and all men may be taught, governed, instructed, and turned to piety . . . . Once more we admonish thee, . . . do not act, teach, or establish anything according to human opinion, your own or that of others, and abolish again what has been so established; but establish and teach only the clear word and practices of God, with the rule of Christ.

The author of such lines is not a mystic or spiritualist.

2. The Swiss Brethren were pacifists in the sense of the Sermon on the Mount, standing for absolute nonresistance and rejecting all use of force.

> The brother of Huiuf writes that thou hast preached against the princes, that they are to be attacked with the fist. Is it true? If thou art willing to defend war, the tablets, singing, or other things which thou doest not find in express words of Scripture. . . . Moreover, the gospel and its adherents are not to be protected by the sword, nor are they thus to protect themselves, which, as we learn from our brother, is thy opinion and practice. True Christian believers are sheep among wolves, sheep for the slaughter; they must be baptized in anguish and affliction, tribulation, persecution, suffering, and death; they must be tried with fire, and must reach the land of eternal rest, not by killing their bodily, but by mortifying their spiritual, enemies. Neither do they use worldly sword or war, since all killing has ceased with them; unless, indeed, we were still of the old law; and even there (much as we consider it) war was a misfortune.

Is it possible that a Conrad Grebel who writes thus could have imbibed his Anabaptism from a Müntzer who had taken the red cross and the naked sword as his symbols (symbols which were to indicate that the elect had the right and the duty to exterminate the ungodly) and who demanded that the ideal of a new and perfect church must be achieved by violence on the part of the laity if the government should fail at this task?

The very formulation of the question suffices to give the answer. In the solution of social questions Müntzer favored the application of force, whereas the Swiss Brethren, following the apostolic pattern, would relieve the misery of the poor by voluntary aid. The Swiss Brethren, although granting the state its right of existence as an institution of God, would not occupy a governmental office; Müntzer, on the other hand, mixed politics with religion and sought to realize the kingdom of God in a Christian state on earth.

The mere comparison of the principles of the early Anabaptists with those of Thomas Müntzer shows that the former are not at all dependent on the latter. We grant that later a Hubmaier was ready to march against the Turks with the sword, that a Hans Denk can be found among the spiritualists of the Inner Word, that a Jacob Hutter inaugurated community of goods among the Anabaptist Brethren in Moravia, that a Jan van Leyden set up an earthly kingdom in Münster and defended it with the sword, that individual Anabaptists here and there boasted of visions. But these were later developments and had nothing to do with Storch and Müntzer.

We know also that some who were under the spell of Müntzer later became Anabaptists, that, e.g., a Hans Hut, who as an itinerant book dealer participated in the distribution of Müntzer's writings (but also of the Wittenberg writings) and was in Frankenhausen with his books, later, in 1526–27, united with the Anabaptists as an apostle of the peaceful faith and accomplished much for the movement. Also a Melchior Rinck, a former Lutheran preacher, who had even taken part in the battle of Frankenhausen, played an important role as a zealous Anabaptist apostle in Middle Germany in 1527 and later. Certainly there were others who had been swept away by the Peasants' War and by the Müntzer movement, as well as by the Münster kingdom of 1534–35, and who were later won for the Anabaptist movement. Whether as Anabaptist apostles or as simple Brethren it is possible that they did not all at once and completely cast off all Müntzerian ideas. But the Swiss-German Anabaptist movement, as well as the Moravian and Dutch, led by such men as Conrad Grebel, Michael Sattler, Pilgram Marpeck, Jakob Hutter, Peter Riedemann, Menno Simons, and Dirk Philips, which in spite of interminable persecution survived the sixteenth century and lives on today in world Mennonitism with its more than 400,000 souls, and which in 1952 held its fifth world conference, was born in the heart of the Swiss Reformation and belongs, even though as a "left wing," to the great mainline Protestant movement and to no other.

The Origin of Upper Austrian Anabaptism

Grete Mecenseffy

In his article, "The Zwickau Prophets, Thomas Müntzer and the Anabaptists," Harold S. Bender, the biographer of Conrad Grebel, strenuously resists any attempt to seek the origins of peaceful Anabaptism elsewhere than in Zurich. He was referring to the South German Anabaptism which lived in conscious repudiation of Thomas Müntzer after the Great Peasants' War. Bender was perfectly correct when he rejected the view that the peaceful line of Anabaptism emerged only after the catastrophe of Münster in 1535. He was right, too,when he made the writings of the Saxon Reformers, and particularly the history of Justus Menius, responsible for the view which connects the Anabaptists with Thomas Müntzer. However, I cannot entirely agree with Bender's assertion that the letter to Thomas Müntzer by Conrad Grebel and his friends on September 5, 1524, contains only criticism, rejection and opposition. It is true that it contains criticism of the retention of ceremonies and of the use of force, but it also contains the statement that the writers of the letter had been instructed, strengthened and wonderfully cheered by Müntzer's pamphlet, "Against the False Faith and Baptism." The Swiss were familiar with Müntzer's pamphlets, "On the Imaginary Faith," the "Unmasking of the False Faith," and his "Protestation." They were in agreement with Müntzer in their understanding of baptism.

If we compare statements made by Swiss Anabaptists with the religious teachings of Upper Austrian Anabaptists, a mystical-spiritualist trait is striking which we can scarcely find in Switzerland. To be sure, Grebel's letter cited above states that "True Christian believers are sheep among wolves, sheep for the slaughter. They must be baptized in anguish and affliction, tribulation, persecution, suffering and death. They must be tried with fire . . .," but such expressions are widespread. Nowhere in the congregations of Upper Austria do we find any mention of a connection with Switzerland, but there does appear repeatedly the name of a man who began his career in Müntzer's circle and who has been called the Anabaptist apostle of Upper Austria: namely, the bookbinder and bookpeddler, Hans Hut. There can be no doubt that Hut stood in a close relationship to Müntzer. The "Unmasking of the False Faith" was printed in Nuremberg during the late summer of 1524 by the journeymen of Johann Hergot on the order of Hans Hut from Bibra. The manuscript had probably been entrusted to Hut after Müntzer's flight from Allstedt, at about the same time when the Swiss entered into contact with Müntzer.

Even after the battle of Frankenhausen, which he witnessed, Hut in all probability clung to Müntzer's teachings on violent upheaval. Only in Augsburg was he converted to peaceful, nonresistant Anabaptism by Hans Denck. The fact is that during the disputation with Balthasar Hubmaier in the spring of 1527 at Nikolsburg, Hut represented nonresistance against the teaching that a Christian in authority could wield the sword. He was imprisoned because of this, made his escape from the prison and shortly thereafter baptized in Vienna. From here he began his successful westward campaign . . . and there can be no doubt that in the cities of Upper Austria, where he worked extensively, many persons accepted the sign of baptism due to the impression of his powerful preaching.

. . . .

The dependency of Hut on Müntzer is undeniable. It is not only evident through words like "creature," "Brother soft-life," "the tender scribes," and "inner composure" (*Gelassenheit*) or through Hut's rejection of the "false and invented faith"; but it is especially clear in the belief of the South German Anabaptists that man is prepared for faith in God's promises and becomes partaker of eternal life only through suffering. According to Hut no one attains truth unless he follows in the footsteps of Christ and of his elect through the school of tribulation. This teaching stems from Thomas Müntzer. Müntzer, too, called the great tribulation which must precede faith "the fear of God." The person to whom God wants to be merciful must fear God in the bottom of his heart, as did Abraham and Mary. In contrast the spirit of the fear of God, permitting the arrival of faith, was not revealed to Zacharias and Elizabeth. The arrival of faith must be endured with the greatest "fear and trembling." The Biblical foundation is Phil. 2:12: "Work out your own salvation in fear and trembling." According to Müntzer, "Even if you had devoured the Bible, it would be of no help to you. You must suffer the sharp plowshare." The introduction to Hut's tract "On the Mystery of Baptism," starting with the words, "I wish you the pure fear of God as the beginning of divine wisdom," is conceived and written in Müntzer's spirit.

The suffering of Christ is the prototype of human suffering. The image of people preparing animals as food is closely related to the picture of crushing and grinding grain. The Anabaptists may have taken this latter figure from Luther's "Sermon on the Sacred Sacrament of the Holy True Body of Christ" (1519), more likely than from the "Teachings of the Twelve Apostles" or the 63rd letter of Cyprian, since they do not cite church fathers. When the brothers were reproached with drinking from a bottle of which "not even the devil knows what is in it," Leonhard Schiemer replied: "The drink in this bottle is nothing else but a crushed, pulverized, ground down and grieving heart: crushed by the mortar of the cross; because the grapes in God's vineyard must all be pressed or crushed in the wine press or treadmill of tribulation. Otherwise they will not become wine."

The expression "abyss of the soul," borrowed by Müntzer from John Tauler, appears in the composition "On the Living and Written Word" by Ulrich Stadler, the Anabaptist from the Tyrol.

We return to the starting point of these short observations. Supported by the considerations above, which could certainly be added to, the assertion appears justified that in South German Anabaptism, within which Upper Austria plays a decisive role, the practice of adult baptism—which was probably but not demonstrably of Swiss origin—combined with teachings about the need to enter the new covenant, teachings in which an enthusiastic, spirtualist note echoed clearly enough. These teachings were taken from the ideas of Thomas Müntzer and mediated through Hans Hut to the Anabaptists in Austria.

Peasants' War and Anabaptism in Franconia

Gottfried Seebass

The relationship of the Peasants' War and Anabaptism to one another remains one of the unsolved problems in the historiography of the Reformation. Two matters of fact in particular will not allow it to rest. First, in many areas the Peasants' War and the Anabaptist movement are phenomena which occur at the same time and are in many respects interrelated. For this reason Bullinger's assertion that the Anabaptists were responsible for the peasant rebellion in the district of Grüningen becomes explicable. Secondly, since the beginning of 1527 both Catholic and Protestant governments warned again and again against the Anabaptists as rebels. Luther and Melanchthon found in Anabaptism a new edition of the ideas of Thomas Müntzer, the catastrophic effects of which they believed to see not only in the rebellion in Thüringia but, mistakenly, in the Peasants' War as a whole. For contemporaries, then, the relationship between the Peasants' War and Anabaptism appeared to be clear.

If in what follows I seek to answer the question of the relationship of Anabaptism to the Peasants' War in Franconia, there are three reasons for the limitation to a specific territory. First of all there are not yet enough investigations applying the problem thematically or systematically in a territory or region. At the present it is therefore impossible to answer the question comprehensively in a way that applies to all regions. This is directly connected with the fact that the editions of Anabaptist source materials (*Täuferakten*) contain few documents supplying information about the early life of those baptized. Thus the edited sources contribute little to a solution of our problem. Then also, the sources on the Peasants' War (*Bauernkriegsakten*) have either not been edited or edited incompletely for many of the areas. Therefore it is only with great effort that anything precise can be ascertained about the involvement of Anabaptists in the Peasants' War. Secondly, as was noted already by Engels, the peasant movement suffered from local narrow-mindedness. The causes, motives, beginnings, course and consequences of the Peasants' War were quite distinct for each German region. Contemporary scholarship agrees that the "great German Peasants' War" constituted the mere sum of its individual actions. Accordingly, it is not possible to establish the relationship of the Anabaptists to "the" peasant movement, but only to specific movements in limited areas. Finally in recent years it has become increasingly clear that when we speak of "the" Anabaptist movement we are surrendering ourselves to a fiction of denominational historiography. To be sure, from the beginning Anabaptism was a movement not limited to any single region; but for that reason it was not yet monolithic. Rather it consisted originally of very disparate groups stamped by a variety of leading personalities. Therefore Anabaptist scholarship still must face the necessity of abandoning morphological classifications and descriptions of types. Instead it needs to assume the task of examining the formation of diverse confessions within Anabaptism. For this reason as well the object of our study cannot in the first instance be the relationship of the Peasants' War to Anabaptism in general, but only its relation to a particular form of Anabaptism.

I

In Franconia signs of the Peasants' War were present as early as the summer of 1524. At that time assemblies of peasants began to gather under the influence of preachers committed to the Reformation in the southern district of the bishopric of Bamberg, as well as in the territory of Nuremberg. The meetings were directed against the clergy of the old faith and against the taxes paid to them. In Franconia the actual Peasants' War began in mid-March, 1525, and lasted until the beginning of June. There is no evidence of any Anabaptists anywhere in Franconia before or during that time period. This needs to be made clear against contrary claims found in older literature. It cannot be denied that in the circles affected by the mystical spiritualism of Karlstadt and Müntzer doubts existed already regarding the validity of pedo-baptism: indeed about the necessity of an outer act of baptism in general. However, there is no possibility that Anabaptists participated in the beginning or during the course of the Peasants' War in Franconia. For the Anabaptist mission in Franconia began only in the summer of 1526 with the activity of Hans Hut. In this region only persons who later became Anabaptists could have participated in the Peasants' War. Under no circumstances can Anabaptism in Franconia be considered a cause of the rebellion. It might perhaps, however, have been a consequence or result. In order to examine this possibility we turn to the other ways of looking at the subject mentioned earlier [geographical, ideological and prosopographical], and first of all to the geographical location.

. . . .

II

Because of the broad expansion of the peasant rebellion in Franconia it is possible to speak of an almost unavoidable geographical coincidence between the Peasants' War and Anabaptism, something Claus-Peter Clasen asserted for South Germany. Nevertheless, it is striking that the Anabaptists were found only in extremely small numbers in western Franconia, the main area of the rebellion. The centers of Anabaptism, if one can speak of centers at all given the small number of Anabaptists in Franconia, were in the southern area of Henneberg and Grabfeldgau, in the area of Coburg, Bamberg and Staffelstein, as well as the villages in the valley of the Regnitz around Erlangen. Here we have enumerated those areas in which the peasant rebellion proceeded in almost "orderly" fashion.

However, it would be premature to generalize and conclude that from the standpoint of geography there is little likelihood of a connection between the Peasants' War and Anabaptism. For, in contrast to South German Anabaptism, Anabaptism in Franconia found its supporters not in the large cities, but in the little country towns, small places and villages, as well as the out-of-the-way mills, namely in environs where the peasant rebellions, too, had been conceived and planned. Moreover Anabaptism in Franconia was the product of individual charismatic leaders who travelled through the area between 1526 and 1530. Their concern was not with the establishment of viable congregations but with sealing the 144,000 elect before the impending Last Judgment. Their mission carried less of a systematic, more of an *ad hoc* character. Thus Hut began his ministry in his home area of Henneberg, spreading his message along roads which he travelled as a book peddler. Only occasionally did connections of kinship, or other contacts of those baptized by him, lead him to remote places as well. He never visited western Franconia. His disciples Marx Maier and Georg Nespitzer as well as their followers Jacob Schmidt and Jörg

Gruber acted as missionaries in this area. From its beginnings Anabaptism in Franconia suffered under severe persecutions by the authorities. Therefore, it never possessed the opportunity of wider development. The reasons for this will become clearer below when we enquire after the causes and aims of the peasant rebellion and the teachings of Anabaptism in Franconia.

Meanwhile we can confidently assert that in Franconia the early Anabaptist movement spread primarily among the population in small towns and the countryside: indeed in those areas which did not belong to the center of the Peasants' War but nevertheless were touched by it. An inner connection between the Peasants' War and Anabaptism is therefore not improbable on the basis of geographical evidence.

III

One cannot give a mono-causal explanation of the Peasants' War in Franconia, any more than for any other area. Nevertheless, social and economic causes were obviously decisive almost everywhere. A strong more or less proletarian lower class, constituting almost thirty percent of the population, was found in the villages and towns. This layer of society was especially affected by manorial dues, the great and small tithe, the blood tithe, hunting services, and the infringement on communal rights by the steady expansion of sheep-rearing. The burden was increased by multiplying direct and indirect taxes imposed by the landlords: taxes on many foodstuffs, a tax on livestock in the form of hoof money, the territorial tax, and finally in the benefices of Franconia the inaugural tax, with which the newly elected bishop attempted to cover the enormous costs of his election. The hatred against the noblity and clergy, under whom the rural population suffered particularly, was stirred further because the first two estates were exempt from these onerous tax burdens and because they used their privileges shamelessly. Added to this were the Reformation sermons in which the small tithe, which could not be deduced from Scripture, and monasticism were depicted as socially worthless and un-Christian. The religious question often provided the impulse for rebellion, but then in most instances receded quickly behind political and social aims.

. . . .

The entire movement has been fittingly characterized by Endres as follows:

> In Franconia the aim was not to do away with the old order but to reconstruct or improve it on the basis of holy Scripture. Therefore the peasants demanded the removal of the burdensome intermediate authorities, the privileged clergy and the nobility, and the secularization of the monasteries and their rich endowments for the benefit of the 'poor common man.' The main aim of the rebels in Franconia was a socially uniform, centrally governed territorial state in which the Gospel could be freely preached and in which the subjects were exposed to fewer material obligations, above all, no 'new unfair burdens.'

What message did the Anabaptists have for men who had risked their property and life for such aims?

With this question one must turn primarily to Hans Hut, founder and leader of Anabaptism in Franconia. Hut's message can be recontructed very accurately from his writings and those of his students, with the aid of statements made by imprisoned Franconian Anabaptists. In his preaching, which began in the summer of 1526 after his baptism by Hans Denck, Hut was not concerned with particular social or political demands as the peasants had been. Neither did he aim at gathering small congregations of true Christians as did the Anabaptists in Switzerland. His concern was broader. Like Thomas Müntzer, who exercised the most lasting and pronounced influence on him, he expected the establishment of an absolutely pure Christianity in which there were to be no more sinners and godless. Like Müntzer, Hut identified the godless above all with the spiritual and secular lords. The clerical estate—Hut did not differentiate between the clergy of the Reformation and the clergy of the old faith—had spoiled Christendom with their "invented faith" and pedo-baptism. Invented faith appealed to the vicarious work of Christ and to the Word of divine forgiveness, seeking to avoid following Christ in suffering and the cross. Hence it was a faith without fruit. Through pedo-baptism everyone indiscriminately, whether he believed or not, became a Christian. Hut's judgment of the secular lords was particularly harsh. Since the doctrine of the two kingdoms was alien to him, the role of government could consist only in the Old Testament sense found in Deuteronomy, as the enforcement of the right worship and the elimination of sin and the sinner. But the political authorities failed to do their duty.

Under these circumstances help could not be expected from men, but only from God himself. He must bring to pass the Last Judgment over the godless spoken of in the Biblical apocalypse. Like Müntzer Hut had believed that in the battles of the Peasants' War the Last Judgment was being fulfilled, that the separation of tares from the wheat, of the godless from the pious, was taking place. This hope had proven illusory. The princely armies had destroyed the peasants. Christ had not come to their aid. History continued further without the appearance of the thousand year *Reich* in which there were to be no more distinctions between the estates and no more private property. Hut's disappointment did not last long. In his final letter to Mühlhausen Müntzer himself offered an explanation of the defeat of the peasants: They had not been God's chosen instruments who alone could have carried out the destruction of the godless, precisely because of their social demands, which showed that they had not sought God's honour but their own. Gradually Hut learned to reconstruct his apocalyptical schedule, which he had acquired by harmonizing Biblical texts, to fit the present situation. He learned from others, if he had not been an eye witness, that the bodies of Thomas Müntzer and Heinrich Pfeiffer had not been buried after their execution on May 27, 1525 but that they had been placed on stakes. What could have been more appropriate for him, therefore, than the identification of the two men whom he admired as his teachers with the two prophets, whose bodies according to Rev. 11:9 should lie unburied for three and a half years. According to Rev. 11:3 both prophets had preached for 1260 days or another period of three and a half years. Counting back from May 1525 takes us to the public appearance of the "Zwickau Prophets" who had prophesied the coming of a major transformation in seven years. The seven years, and the events in their mid-point, appeared to fit the passage in Daniel 9:27, which stated that the covenant would be strengthened for a week, but that in the middle of the week the sacrifice would cease. If the three and a half years, which are mentioned repeatedly in Scripture as the time of the last curse and tribulation, had been accurately calculated from the death of Müntzer, the result would have been the end of 1528. Since, however, according to Matthew 24:22 the time of tribulation was to be shortened, one could, on the basis of the parable of the fig tree, reckon with the End at the time of the blooming of the fruit trees—Pentecost of 1528. The "judgment on the house of God" mentioned in I Peter 4:17, would come to an end before then: for the plagues about which Luke 21:9–11, 20–24 and Rev. 9:1–11 inform us must according to Rev. 9:5 occur five months before the End. Nevertheless it remains open to question whether Hut calculated the five months from the end of the three and a half years, and therefore wanted the judgment of the godless to begin around Pentecost 1528; or whether he expected the final end on Pentecost 1528, in which case the last five months would begin around Christmas 1527. We encounter both dates among his followers. However, it was quite clear who was to punish the godless, that is, the lords and the clergy. Because since the beginning of the century the increasingly frequent Turkish invasions were generally understood to be God's scourge on the sins of Christians, Hut, too, saw in them the tool of divine wrath. What dimensions the Judgment would take he found in Rev. 14: 15 f.: (19): "And the angel thrust his sickle into the earth, and gathered the vine of the earth, and cast it into the great winepress of the wrath of God. And the winepress was trodden without the city, and blood came out of the winepress, even unto the horse bridles, by the space of a thousand and six hundred furlongs." At that time such descriptions were not understood as mere images or symbols! During the Judgment all the punishments that had been threatened in the Old Testament were to be meted out to the godless. The Prophets and Psalms furnished the visual images: "I will pursue my enemies and apprehend them, and not turn back until I have destroyed them." To be sure, the devout were to be spared from the Judgment. In accordance with the Synoptic apocalypse they were advised to flee into the mountains and forests. Hut designated Mühlhausen as one of the places of refuge where the faithful would be preserved. Above all, they were to participate personally in the Judgment. From Matthew 19:28 and I Cor. 6:2 one could gather that the godly were to be judges. And in Psalm 149:5–7 it stated that the saints are to rejoice and to have two-edged swords in their hands in order to carry out vengeance on the heathens. The time of passive suffering would then be over. Then the words of Jeremiah 48:10 will apply: that the one who holds back his sword in order not to shed blood will be cursed. Indeed, Hut recalled Psalm 58:11: the righteous will rejoice when he sees the vengeance on the godless and will bathe his feet in their blood. What enormous hatred must have been dammed up against the clergy and lords if such traditions were to be resurrected without the least amount of spiritualization!

After his baptism by Denck, Hut learned to understand in a new way who the faithful and just were. They were the Anabaptists; and so the adult baptism received through Denck became totally integrated into Hut's apocalyptical speculations. What in Switzerland represented true baptism—a repetition of an invalid baptism received as a child—Hut turned into the apocalyptical-apotrophical sign, the sealing of the elect. According to Ezekiel 9:2–5 and Rev. 7:3 it is given on the forehead to all those who will be spared from the approaching Judgment. Hut understood his own role as that of the man in linen cloth mentioned in Ezekiel 9:2–5 and Daniel 12:6; as the end-time Elijah, the new John and Moses, whose mission it was to seal the 144,000 elect. This gave Hut's mission that quality of restlessness that did not permit him to remain for long in one place, but which drove him further as soon as the signing had been accomplished.

What did Hut have to tell his individual hearer besides this vision of the future in which the events of the day were interpreted? According to Hut everyone lived in complete perversion of the order which God established in Genesis 1:28—the rule of man over the entire creation and the submission of man to God. Instead, man, particularly in his striving after security of life and possessions, had given himself to the creatures. From this original sin resulted not only the transgression of divine law but also the perverted relationship of man to man as it found expression in the domination of lord over servant and in the tax system that resulted from it. No one can free himself from bondage to the creatures. That occurs only when God Himself through inner and outer suffering frees man from the bondage. This action by God is witnessed to by Scripture. Scripture can only be understood, however, when the work of God—death and resurrection—has been endured personally. Otherwise one does not come to a harmonious understanding of the contradictions in Scripture but picks out isolated points here and there without fuller understanding. Besides visions and dreams, a more effective medium to hear God's voice is the "Gospel of all creatures," namely the Gospel preached by the creatures. The fundamental thought in this is as follows: instead of pointing people to the Scriptures, they must be rationally convinced by arguments that can be generally understood that the only possibility of redemption is suffering discipleship. This is possible by simply pointing to a person's everyday task. No matter what a person does—obviously Hut has the peasant and artisan working with his own hands in mind—he changes the material with which he works, the plant, the animal, in order to make it usable or enjoyable to himself. In each case the creatures suffer under man's action. Still, and precisely in this way, the animal comes to its God-appointed goal of service to man; for God has directed his creation to the service and nourishment of man. And the same holds true for man's relationship to God. Man, too, can only be prepared for the service of God through suffering which God inflicts on him. This "Gospel of all creatures" is equated by Hut with the content of Scripture. There is, therefore, no difference between Old and New Testament on this point. Rather the Old Testament is all that is and remains external to myself, while the New Testament is the existential faith received through suffering.

According to Hut an untried faith which brings man to the acceptance of the sign of the cross originates with the "Gospel of all creatures." Through it the person declares himself ready to take up the suffering of discipleship which conforms one to Christ. Beyond this Hut expected no special form of Christian life from the people he baptized for the time period preceding the Judgment. Above all, there was no rejection of the oath, no prohibition of war service nor any form of dress regulations. The emphasis on the Sermon on the Mount was entirely missing. Rather the concern was with the fulfillment of the highest commandment, which indeed found its best expression in the generous management of one's possessions. By this one's freedom from the creatures is especially evident. Hut, however, does not demand an immediate establishment of the community of goods. He does not form a congregational organization. Why should he, when the kingdom of Christ is imminent? . . .

In the broad compass of his theology Hut ascribed a central place to the Peasants' War and especially to the fate of Müntzer, in whom he saw one of the two prophets of the Apocalypse. By contrast he viewed the victorious power of the princes as the "beast of the abyss" and the "abomination of destruction." Müntzer, in spite of the debacle of Frankenhausen, received a clearly positive position in the divine plan of salvation. The relationship of Hut to Müntzer and the Peasants' War becomes even closer when it is remembered that Hut viewed Mühlhausen as a place of refuge for the faithful—the Anabaptists. Nevertheless, his references to the Peasants' War were not solely positive. When Hut accused the peasants of having drawn the sword not only at the wrong time in 1525 but also for false ends, he distanced himself from the Peasants' War. What high value this dissociation received from the recipients of Hut's message becomes unmistakable when it is remembered that the erstwhile peasant defeat thus appeared not as militarily accidental but rather as unavoidable because of divine providence. At the same time Hut announced the immediately impending destruction of previous and present enemies through Turks and Anabaptists. And those who dared to doubt Hut's expectations in the light of real experience were comforted by allusions to the expected divine aid, as those at Frankenhausen had been formerly comforted by Müntzer. The Anabaptists would fight with the "sword of Gideon"—a reminiscence of Gideon's miraculous victory over the Midianites. They would fulfill the prophecy of Deuteronomy 32:30, that one would pursue a thousand and two would put to flight ten thousand. If one adds to this that Hut's theology of suffering, fitting into the apocalyptical frame of reference, was well-suited to the often distressing situation of broad segments of society after the Peasants' War, and that the "Gospel of all creatures" was tailored to peasant and artisan circles, then it is easy to believe that Hut's message could expect a good resonance among one-time participants in the rebellion.

. . . .

IV

In an introductory fashion we have already drawn attention to the difficulties of ascertaining exactly who the individuals were who first participated in the peasant rebellion and later became Anabaptists. In spite of this Günther Bauer claimed that it was exceptional to find the same persons in the two movements; and Claus-Peter Clasen verified this indirectly, when he could name only seven former rebels among four hundred and sixty-six Anabaptists in Franconia. Nevertheless there probably were many more erstwhile peasant rebels among the Anabaptists. At any rate, this conjecture suggests itself after we examine the persons baptized by Hut.

Before we do so, it must be remembered that Hans Hut, born around 1490 in Haina, had been an enthusiastic follower of Müntzer since the fall of 1524 at the latest. At that time he signed himself into Müntzer's list of members of the "eternal covenant" before the gates of Mühlhausen. Shortly thereafter Thomas Müntzer, driven from this Thuringian imperial city, spent a night in Hut's house at Bibra. At that time Hut received Müntzer's manuscript, the "Express Unmasking," and together with Pfeiffer he brought the manuscript to the press in Nuremberg.

Between the fall of 1524 and the spring of 1525 Hut distributed Müntzer's writings, among other books, in Franconia. On one of his regular trips between Wittenberg and Nuremberg he became a witness to the rebellion in Erfurt, and thereupon he moved on to Frankenhausen. Possibly because of his books, which he had bought in Luther's city, Hut was at first imprisoned by the peasants. He was only released after Müntzer arrived at the camp and used his influence on behalf of his old friend. Hut heard Müntzer's sermon before the battle of Frankenhausen and participated in the battle itself. In spite of the terrible defeat and the fate of Müntzer, Hut remained in the grip of Müntzer's apocalyptical interpretation of events. Only a few weeks later he still called from the pulpit for the peasants of his home town to kill lords and priests because the divinely appointed time for this had now arrived. Like so many others he appears to have at first hidden in Nuremberg after the end of the Peasants' War.

Repeatedly the assertion has been made that Hut, before or at the time of his baptism by Hans Denck on Pentecost 1526 at Augsburg, experienced a conversion from the social revolutionary peasant-Saul to the religious, peaceful Anabaptist-Paul. Apart from the fact that with such a characterization one does not do justice either to the peasant movement or to Anabaptism, absolutely no evidence exists for such an assertion. Moreover, by such an assertion the modern division between religion and society is impermissibly projected backward upon the sixteenth century. Hut's dissociation from the Peasants' War was possible without any Anabaptist influence; for it came from Müntzer. And in Hut's theology only in a few unimportant points can an influence of Swiss and South-German Anabaptism be established. In reality, then, the significance of those days in Augsburg consisted in the fact that Hut made the acquaintance of a new "revolutionary subject," a group with which he could identify the truly devout in his apocalyptical scheme of history. This permitted him to recalculate and carry on with Müntzer's apocalypticism.

But is Hut [with his adjusted apocalyptic timetable] all that significant for early Anabaptism in Franconia? It is evident that in his home area Hut at first won those who, like him, had to remain in hiding because of their participation in the Peasants' War. Among them were Jörg Neuendorf and Georg Volk. Together with Hut these two were mentioned on a list of wanted persons as "among the important ones," thus indicating leading roles during the Peasants' War. Georg Volk was to become one of Hut's most important fellow workers in Franconia. In the area of Coburg as well, Hut directed his message first of all to former participants in the Peasants' War. When we are told that Kilian Volkamer, the sexton of Grosswalbur who had been baptized by Hut, lived "in want," and that Eukarius Kellermann described himself as a "fugitive" even before the Anabaptists were persecuted in Northern Franconia, then we may conclude that both had judged it safer to leave their home areas after the rebellion. Another Anabaptist from this area was later arrested because he had given lodging to the minister of Wiesenfeld who had been banished after the rebellion.

As of now the background of the eighteen persons baptized by Hut in the Electoral Saxon enclave of Königsberg cannot be examined. But it is significant that Hut and Volk needed to have no fear about introducing themselves as individuals whose return home was impossible because of participation in the uprising. As for the mission in the villages around Königsberg, apart from connections of kinship or occupation, the common experience in the Peasants' War appears to have played its role. At any rate it is conspicuous that in these places generally only a few persons were won to Anabaptism. The connection of some of these to the Peasants' War can be established without difficulty. Lorenz Veit, baptized in Sternberg, had received a passport from the Bildhäuser Peasant Army identifying him as trustworthy. Heinz Schare, won for Anabaptism in Burglauer, had a brother who was one of the two captains of the Bildhäuser Peasants and who was impaled after the war.

An examination of the persons baptized by Hut in the villages around Staffelstein is still lacking. However, it is noteworthy that the villages in which he was active had participated in plundering the chapel on the Staffelstein and the monastery at Langheim. Things are clearer in the case of the Anabaptists in the Regnitz valley around Erlangen. As mentioned earlier, Heinrich Pfeiffer had preached in the area during the fall of 1524. Here Hut, too, must have had contacts from before the time of the Peasants' War. He baptized the brothers Hans, Marx and Michael Meier in Alterlangen. Their actual home was the country town of Herzogenaurach in the territory of Bamberg. In the summer of 1524 they had led the group of peasants from Herzogenaurach to Büchenbach and there plundered the church, the parsonage, the residence of the bailiff and the manor of the cathedral provost. As a result of their involvement they were unable to return home. Apparently friendships dating back to the rebellion were kept intact by the Meiers. At any rate it is striking that two of the Anabaptists from Herzogenaurach, the wheelwright Peter N. and the brickmaker Konz N., had stood out during the Peasants' War. Thus the possibility cannot be ruled out that, during the later mission of the Meier brothers in the area of Ansbach and in the Tauber valley around Creglingen as well, connections were re-established that had begun during the rebellion.

But the Meier brothers were not the only rebels won in this area. Georg Harscher, a peasant baptized in Eltersdorf, was probably a relative of Fritz Harscher from nearby Reutles. Fritz Harscher had led a peasant gathering at Gründlach in 1524 and was later punished by the Nuremberg Council for participation in the rebellion of 1525. Georg had not been baptized by Hut himself but by one of his disciples. Likewise the small circle which received the sign during the spring of 1527 at Uttenreuth could have been connected through common experiences in the Peasants' War. Fritz Strigel is perhaps the "tall Fritz" mentioned after the war in a letter of apology by the community. He would have been related to Hans Strigel whose participation in the rebellion is certain. Also Hans Gruber, the peasant proprietor of the Eggenhof, had after the Peasants' War to submit a letter of apology on behalf of himself and his two sons to the Bishop of Bamberg. All three were baptized by Hut, and one of the sons, Jörg Gruber, has to be reckoned as one of the more important missionaries of Hut's current of Anabaptism. Hans Beck, baptized by Georg Volk in nearby Rosenbach, had also distinguished himself during the Peasants' War. Thus the connection between the Peasants' War and Anabaptism is tangible everywhere.

Even the later missionary activity in Franconia by Hut's disciples appears to have deliberately begun with former rebels. Thus Georg Nespitzer from Stadtlauringen, who had probably fled to Passau after the Peasants' War, baptized an innkeeper in Gründlach. The innkeeper had been fined by the Nuremberg Council in 1525 because he had been with the rebellious peasants for three days. Phillip Tuchscherer was baptized in Windsheim; he came originally from Rothenburg. Karlstadt had hidden in his house there, and it had been the meeting place for those who decisively influenced the rebellion in Rothenburg. Tuchscherer probably brought about the baptism of the tailor Hartmann in Rothenburg. Hartmann was forced to leave Rothenburg in 1525 because of participation in meetings led by Karlstadt. These are but a few indications suggesting how necessary and productive is the exact prosopographical investigation of individual Anabaptists, when discussing the relationship between Peasants' War and Anabaptism.

Given the above, there can be no doubt but that Hut's type of Anabaptism sought and found its followers in Franconia primarily among former rebels. To be sure, one cannot assume from this that these persons were always members of those "robbing and murdering hordes of peasants" depicted in Luther's smearing generalization. On the other hand it must be clear that those whose names were listed in the chronicles and documents of the Peasants' War were not mere fellow travellers but prominent participants in the uprising. Under these circumstances the number of Anabaptists whose participation in the Peasants' War in Franconia can be demonstrated is surprisingly high. This is all the more true because leading persons in the uprising also held leading positions in Anabaptism. It is difficult to accept that these men were above all attracted by Hut's message of a three and a half year period of suffering. The announcement of the Judgment and punishment of the godless clergy and lords and the prospects of an egalitarian kingdom of Christ must have been of greater attraction.

. . . .

In conclusion we can formulate our results as follows: since the summer of 1526 an apocalyptical theology came to Franconia with Hut's type of Anabaptism. It had little in common with the aims of the local peasant movement. Nevertheless, it could expect a following among the more radical spirits. As Müntzer's theology had previously done, this type of Anabaptism counted on the imminent and final destruction of the godless spiritual and secular lords by the events of war, and on the establishment thereafter of an egalitarian communist kingdom of Christ. The Anabaptists wanted to participate in the annihilation of the godless. Müntzer's person was thus valued positively. The insurrection of the peasants was not rejected as such, but merely its aims and timing. The propagators of this message were deliberate and successful in establishing relations to former insurrectionists. Their success remained, however, numerically small because the authorities moved immediately and severely against the Anabaptists. Nevertheless, we ought not to underestimate the significance of the relatively short episode of Hut's Anabaptism with its connection of Peasants' War and Anabaptism. For long before Münster, and very unjustly so, it burdened the whole Anabaptist movement wih the odium of insurrection.

Bibliography

I. Prior Publication of Contents of This Volume

Bender, Harold S. "The Anabaptist Vision," *Church History* XIII (1944), pp. 3–24; also *Mennonite Quarterly Review* XVIII (1944), pp. 67–88; also in Guy E. Hershberger (ed.), *The Recovery of the Anabaptist Vision* (Scottdale, Penna: Herald, 1957), pp. 29–54.

Friedmann, Robert, "The Doctrine of the Two Worlds," in Guy E. Hershberger (ed.), *The Recovery of the Anabaptist Vision* (Scottdale, Penna.: Herald, 1957), pp. 105–118.

Zschäbitz, Gerhard, "Die Stellung der Täuferbewegung im Spannungsbogen der deutschen frühbürgerlichen Revolution," in Gerhard Brendler (ed.), *Die frühbürgerliche Revolution in Deutschland* (Berlin: Akademie-Verlag, 1961), pp. 152–162.

Clasen, Claus-Peter, *Anabaptism. A Social History, 1525–1618. Switzerland, Austria, Moravia and South and Central Germany* (Ithaca & London: Cornell University Press, 1972).

Bainton, Roland H., "The Left Wing of the Reformation," *The Journal of Religion* XXI (1941), pp. 124–134; also in Roland H. Bainton, *Studies on the Reformation* (Boston: Beacon, 1963), pp. 119–129.

Hillerbrand, Hans J., "Anabaptism and the Reformation: Another Look," *Church History* XXIX (1960), pp. 404–424.

Davis, Kenneth R., *Anabaptism and Asceticism. A Study in Intellectual Origins* (Scottdale, Penna.: Herald, 1974).

Yoder, John Howard, "The Turning Point in the Zwinglian Reformation," *Mennonite Quarterly Review* XXXII (1958), pp. 128–140.

Walton, Robert C., "Was There a Turning Point of the Zwinglian Reformation?," *Mennonite Quarterly Review* XLII (1968), pp. 45–56.

Haas, Martin, "Der Weg der Täufer in die Absonderung. Zur Interdependenz von Theologie und sozialem Verhalten," in Hans-Jürgen Goertz (ed.), *Umstrittenes Täufertum 1525–1975. Neue Forschungen* (Göttingen: Vandenhoeck & Ruprecht, 1975), pp. 50–78.

Vos, Karel, "Revolutionnaire Hervorming," *De Gids* LXXXIV–4 (1920), pp. 433–450.

Kühler, W.J., "Het Anabaptisme in Nederland," *De Gids* LXXXV–3 (1921), pp. 249–278.

Nipperdey, Thomas, "Theologie und Revolution bei Thomas Müntzer," *Archiv für Reformationsgeschichte* LIV (1963), pp. 145–179; also in Thomas Nipperdey, *Reformation, Revolution, Utopie. Studien zum 16. Jahrhundert* (Göttingen: Vandenhoeck & Ruprecht, 1975), pp. 38–76.

Goertz, Hans-Jürgen, "Der Mystiker mit dem Hammer. Die theologische Begründung der Revolution bei Thomas Müntzer," *Kerygma und Dogma* XX (1974), pp. 23–53; also in Abraham Friesen & Hans-Jürgen Goertz (eds.), *Thomas Müntzer* [*Wege der Forschung*, CDXCI] (Darmstadt: Wissenschaftliche Buchgesellschaft, 1978), pp. 403–444; also in Eng. trans. by Elizabeth Bender, "The Mystic with the Hammer: Thomas Müntzer's Theological Basis for Revolution," *Mennonite Quarterly Review* L (1976), pp. 83–113.

Steinmetz, Max, "Thomas Müntzer in der Forschung der Gegenwart," *Zeitschrift für Geschichtswissenschaft* XXXIII (1975), pp. 666–685.

Bender, Harold S., "Die Zwickauer Propheten, Thomas Müntzer und die Täufer," *Theologische Zeitschrift* VIII (1952), pp. 262–278; also in Eng. trans., "The Zwickau Prophets, Thomas Müntzer and the Anabaptists," *Mennonite Quarterly Review* XXVII (1953), pp. 3–16.

Grete Mecenseffy, "Die Herkunft des oberösterreichischen Täufertums," *Archiv für Reformationsgeschichte* XLVII (1956), pp. 252–258.

Gottfried Seebass, "Bauernkrieg und Täufertum in Franken," *Zeitschrift für Kirchengeschichte* LXXXV (1974), pp. 284–300.

II. Major Related Publications of Authors in This Volume

Bender, Harold S., *Conrad Grebel, 1498–1526. The Founder of the Swiss Brethren* (Goshen, Ind.: Mennonite Historical Society, 1950).

Friedmann, Robert, *Mennonite Piety through the Centuries. Its Genius and its Literature* (Goshen, Ind.: Mennonite Historical Society, 1949).

———, *Hutterite Studies* (Goshen, Ind.: Mennonite Historical Society, 1961).

———, *The Theology of Anabaptism* (Scottdale, Penna.: Herald, 1973).

Zschäbitz, Gerhard, *Zur mitteldeutschen Wiedertäuferbewegung nach dem grossen Bauernkrieg* (Berlin: Rütten & Loening, 1958).

Clasen, Claus-Peter, *Die Wiedertäufer im Herzogtum Württemberg und in benachbarten Herrschaften. Ausbreitung, Geisteswelt, und Soziologie* (Stuttgart: Kohlhammer, 1965).

———, *The Anabaptists in South and Central Germany, Switzerland and Austria. Their Names, Occupations, Places of Residence and Dates of Conversion: 1525–1618* (Ann Arbor, Mich.: University Microfilms, 1978).

Bainton, Roland H., *David Joris. Wiedertäufer und Kämpfer für Toleranz im 16. Jahrhundert* [*Archiv für Reformationsgeschichte, Texte und Untersuchungen*, VI] (Leipzig, 1937).

———, *The Travail of Religious Liberty* (New York: Harper, 1958).

Hillerbrand, Hans. J., "The Origins of Sixteenth Century Anabaptism. Another Look," *Archiv für Reformationsgeschichte* LIII (1962), pp. 152–180.

———, *Die politische Ethik des oberdeutschen Täufertums* (Leyden & Cologne: Brill, 1962).

——— (ed.), *Bibliographie des Täufertums, 1520–1630* (Gütersloh: Gerd Mohn, 1962).

Davis, Kenneth R., "Anabaptism as a Charismatic Movement," *Mennonite Quarterly Review* LIII (1979), pp. 219–234.

Yoder, John Howard, *Täufertum und Reformation im Gespräch* (Zurich: EVZ-Verlag, 1968).

———, "The Evolution of the Zwinglian Reformation," *Mennonite Quarterly Review* XLIII (1969), pp. 95–122.

———, "Der Kristallisationspunkt des Täufertums," *Mennonitische Geschichtsblätter* XXIX (1972), pp. 35–47.

Walton, Robert C., *Zwingli's Theocracy* (Toronto: University of Toronto Press, 1967).

Haas, Martin, "Täufertum und Volkskirche—Faktoren der Trennung," *Zwingliana* XIII (1970–1972), pp. 261–278.

———, "Die Täuferkirchen des 16. Jahrhunderts in der Schweiz und in Münster—ein Vergleich," *Zwingliana* XIII (1970–1972), pp. 434–462.

——— (ed.), *Quellen zur Geschichte der Täufer in der Schweiz*, IV: *Drei Täufergespräche* (Zurich: Theol. Verlag, 1974).

Vos, Karel, *Menno Simons, 1496–1561, zijn leven en werken en zijne reformatorische denkbeelden* (Leyden: Brill, 1914).

———, "Kleine bijdragen over de Doopersche beweging in Nederland tot het optreden van Menno Simons," *Doopsgezinde Bijdragen* LIV (1917), pp. 74–202.

Kühler, W.J., *Geschiedenis der Nederlandsche Doopsgezinden in de zestiende eeuw* (Haarlem: Willink, 1932).

———, "Het Nederlandsche Anabaptisme en de revolutionnaire woelingen der zestiende eeuw," *Doopsgezinde Bijdragen* LVI (1919), pp. 124–212.

Nipperdey, Thomas, *Reformation, Revolution, Utopie* (Göttingen: Vandenhoeck & Ruprecht, 1975).

Goertz, Hans-Jürgen, *Innere und äussere Ordnung in der Theologie Thomas Müntzers* (Leyden: Brill, 1967).

——— (ed.), *Umstrittenes Täufertum 1525–1975. Neue Forschungen* (Göttingen: Vandenhoeck & Ruprecht, 1975).

Goertz, Hans-Jürgen (ed.), *Radikale Reformatoren. 21 biographische Skizzen von Thomas Müntzer bis Paracelsus* (Munich: C.H. Beck, 1978).

Steinmetz, Max, *Das Müntzerbild von Martin Luther bis Friedrich Engels* (Berlin: Deutscher Verlag der Wissenschaften, 1971).

Mecenseffy, Grete (ed.), *Quellen zur Geschichte der Täufer*, XI, XIII: *Österreich* Parts I, II (Gütersloh: Gerd Mohn, 1964, 1972).

Seebass, Gottfried, "Müntzers Erbe. Werk, Leben und Theologie des Hans Hut (gestorben 1527)," unpublished Theol. Habilitationsschrift, Erlangen, 1972.

III. Selection of Related Books in English by Other Authors

Armour, Rollin S., *Anabaptist Baptism*. (Scottdale, Penna.: Herald, 1966).

Beachy, Alvin J., *The Concept of Grace in the Radical Reformation*. (Nieuwkoop: De Graaf, 1977).

Bergsten, Torsten, *Balthasar Hubmaier, Anabaptist Theologian and Martyr*. ed. Estep, W.R., Jr. (Valley Forge: Judson Press, 1978).

Blanke, Fritz, *Brothers in Christ*. Transl. N. Nordenhaug. (Scottdale, Penna.: Herald, 1961).

Dyck, Cornelius J. (ed.), *An Introduction to Mennonite History: A Popular History of the Anabaptists and the Mennonites*. (Scottdale, Penna.: Herald, 1967).

Friesen, Abraham, *Reformation and Utopia: The Marxist Interpretation of the Reformation and Its Antecedents*. (Wiesbaden: F. Steiner, 1974).

Gritsch, Eric W., *Reformer without a Church: The Life and Thought of Thomas Muentzer 1488 (?)-1525*. (Philadelphia: Fortress, 1967).

Horst, Irvin B., *The Radical Brethren: Anabaptism and the English Reformation to 1558*. (Nieuwkoop: De Graaf, 1972).

Keeney, William E., *The Development of Dutch Anabaptist Thought and Practice from 1539-1564*. (Nieuwkoop: De Graaf, 1968).

Klaassen, Walter, *Anabaptism: Neither Catholic nor Protestant*. (Waterloo: Conrad Press, 1973).

Klassen, Peter J., *The Economics of Anabaptism (1525-1560)*. (London: Mouton, 1964).

Klassen, William, *Covenant and Community*. (Grand Rapids: W.B. Eerdman, 1968).

Krahn, Cornelius, *Dutch Anabaptism: Origin, Spread, Life and Thought, 1450-1600*. (The Hague: Martinus Nijhoff, 1968).

Littell, Franklin H., *The Anabaptist View of the Church*. (Boston: Beacon, 1958).

Oyer, John S., *Lutheran Reformers Against Anabaptists*. (The Hague: Martinus Nijhoff, 1964).

Packull, Werner O., *Mysticism and the Early South German-Austrian Anabaptist Movement 1525-1531*. (Scottdale, Penna.: Herald, 1977).

Rupp, Gordon, *Patterns of Reformation*. (London: Epworth, 1969).

Stayer, James M., *Anabaptists and the Sword*. (Lawrence, Kansas: Coronado, 1972).

Steinmetz, David C., *Reformers in the Wings*. (Philadelphia: Fortress, 1971).

Williams, George H., *The Radical Reformation*. (Philadelphia: Westminister, 1962).

Zeman, Jarold K., *The Anabaptists and the Czech Brethren in Moravia. A Study of Origin and Contacts*. (The Hague: Mouton, 1969).